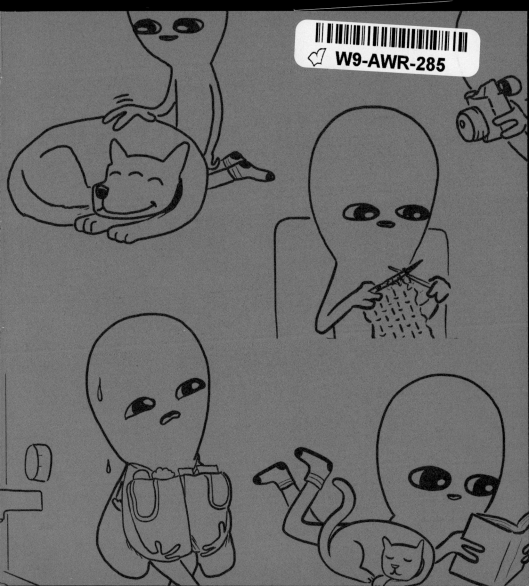

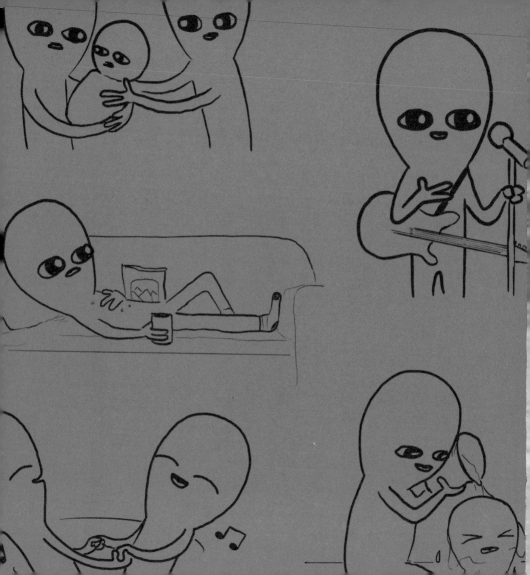

WELCOME BACK TO STRANGE PLANET

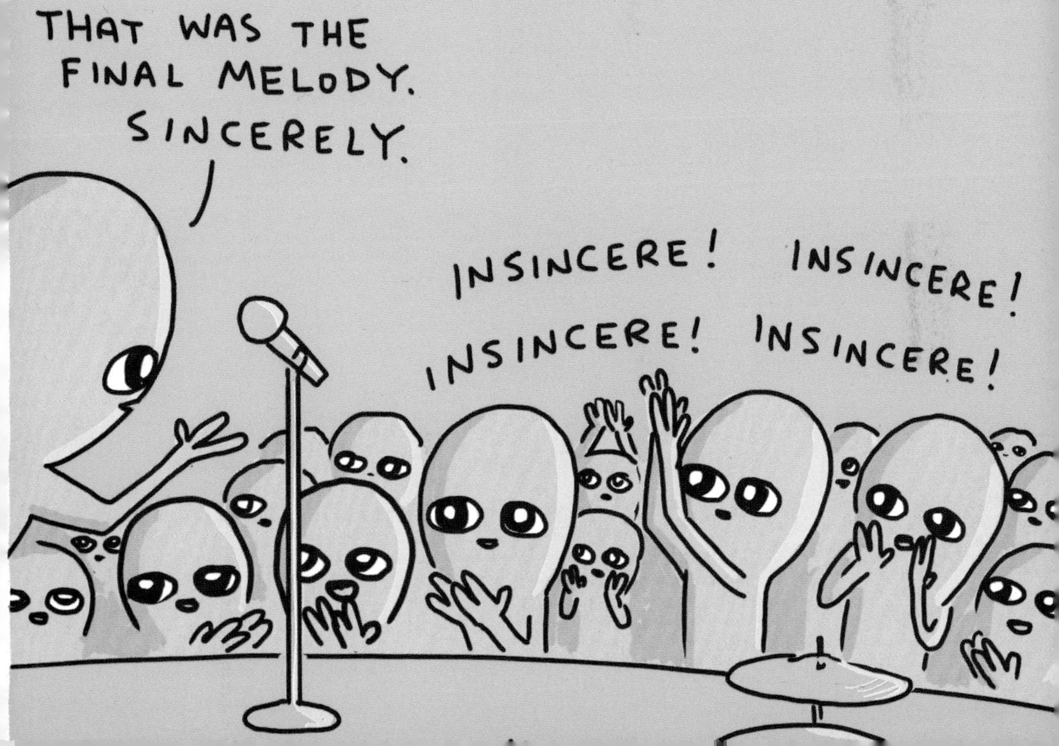

THAT WAS THE FINAL MELODY. SINCERELY.
INSINCERE!
INSINCERE!
INSINCERE!
INSINCERE!

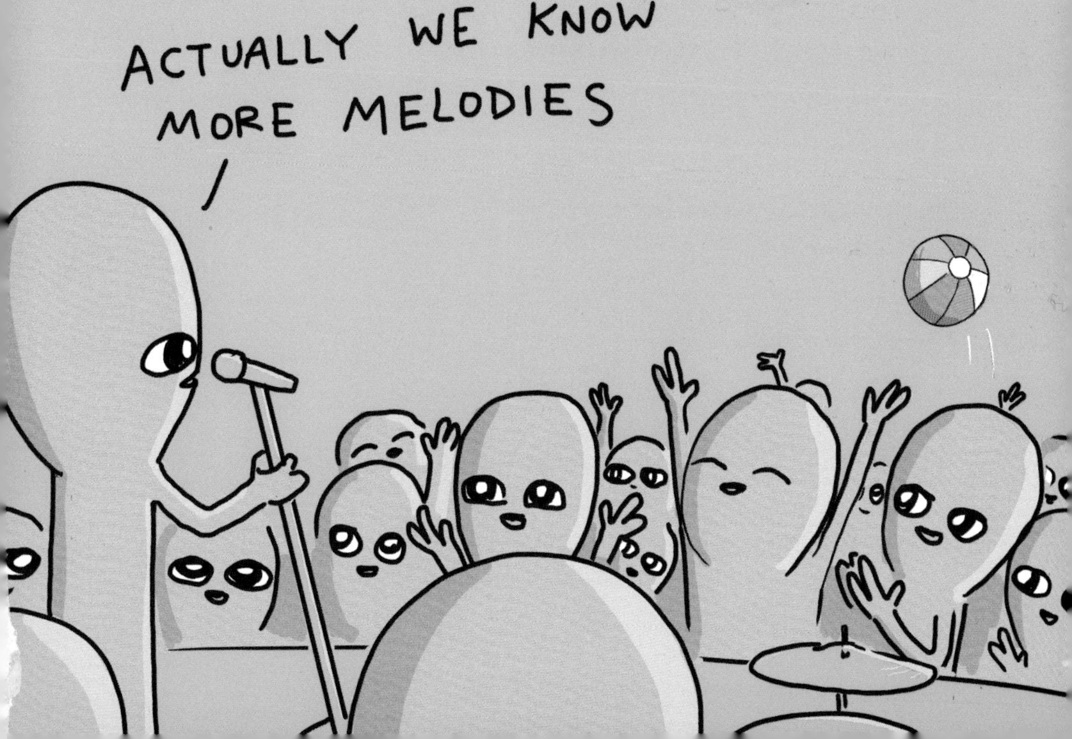
ACTUALLY WE KNOW MORE MELODIES

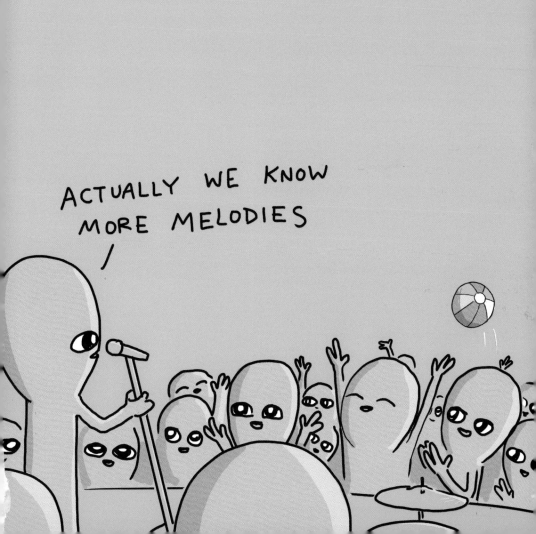

NATHAN W PYLE

STRANGER PLANET

MORROW
GIFT

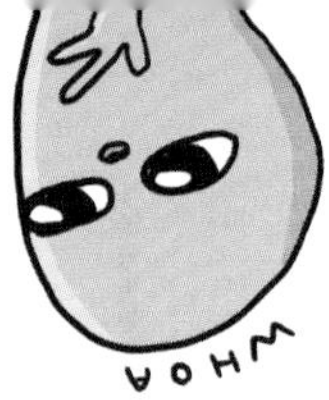
WHOA

 FOR INFORMATION, ADDRESS HARPERCOLLINS PUBLISHERS, 195 BROADWAY, NEW YORK, NY 10007.

HARPERCOLLINS BOOKS MAY BE PURCHASED FOR EDUCATIONAL, BUSINESS, OR SALES PROMOTIONAL USE. FOR INFORMATION, PLEASE EMAIL THE SPECIAL MARKETS DEPARTMENT AT SPSALES@HARPERCOLLINS.COM.

FIRST EDITION

LIBRARY OF CONGRESS CATALOGING-IN-PUBLICATION DATA HAS BEEN APPLIED FOR.

ISBN 978-0-06-302260-7

20 21 22 23 24 LSC 10 9 8 7 6 5 4 3 2 1

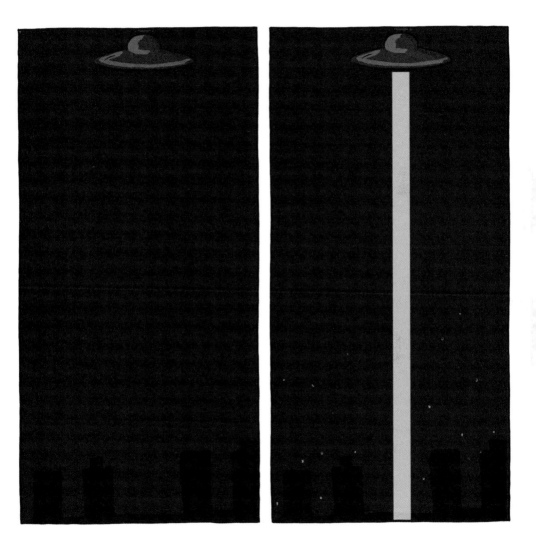

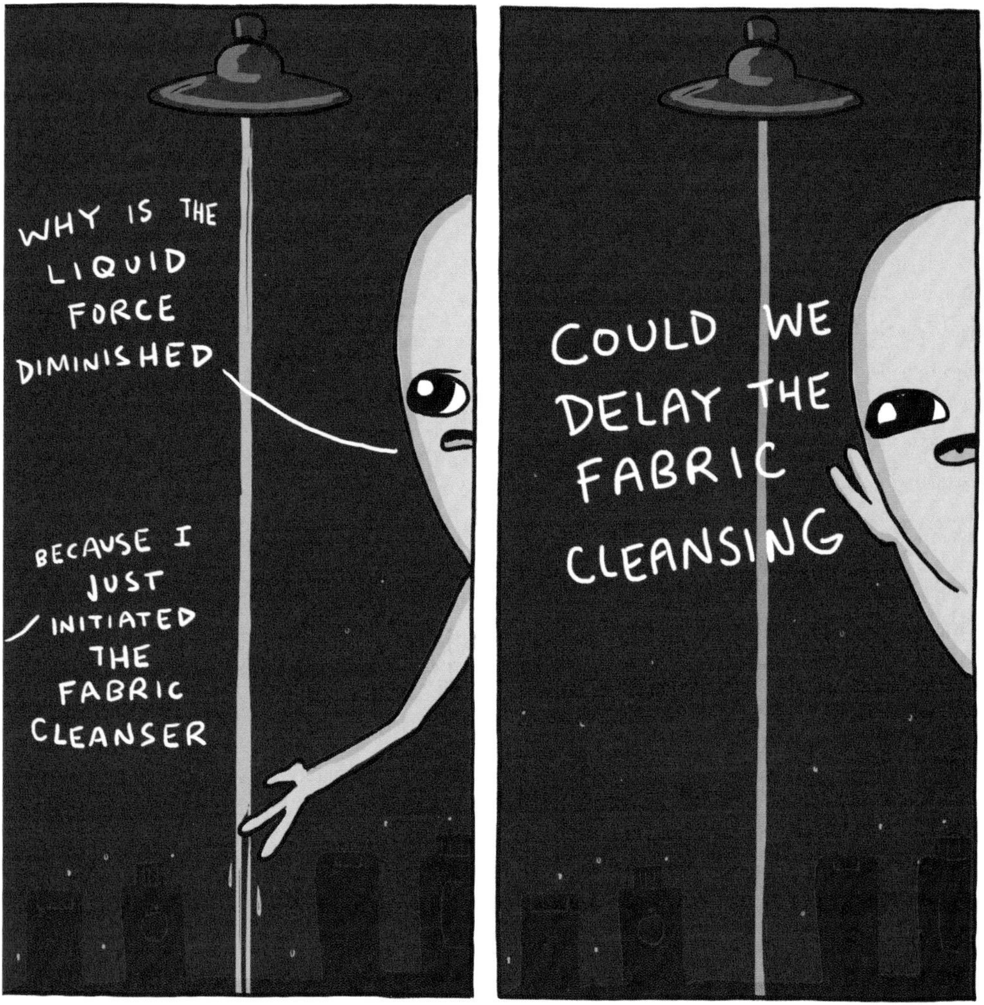
WHY IS THE LIQUID FORCE DIMINISHED
BECAUSE I JUST INITIATED THE FABRIC CLEANSER
COULD WE DELAY THE FABRIC CLEANSING

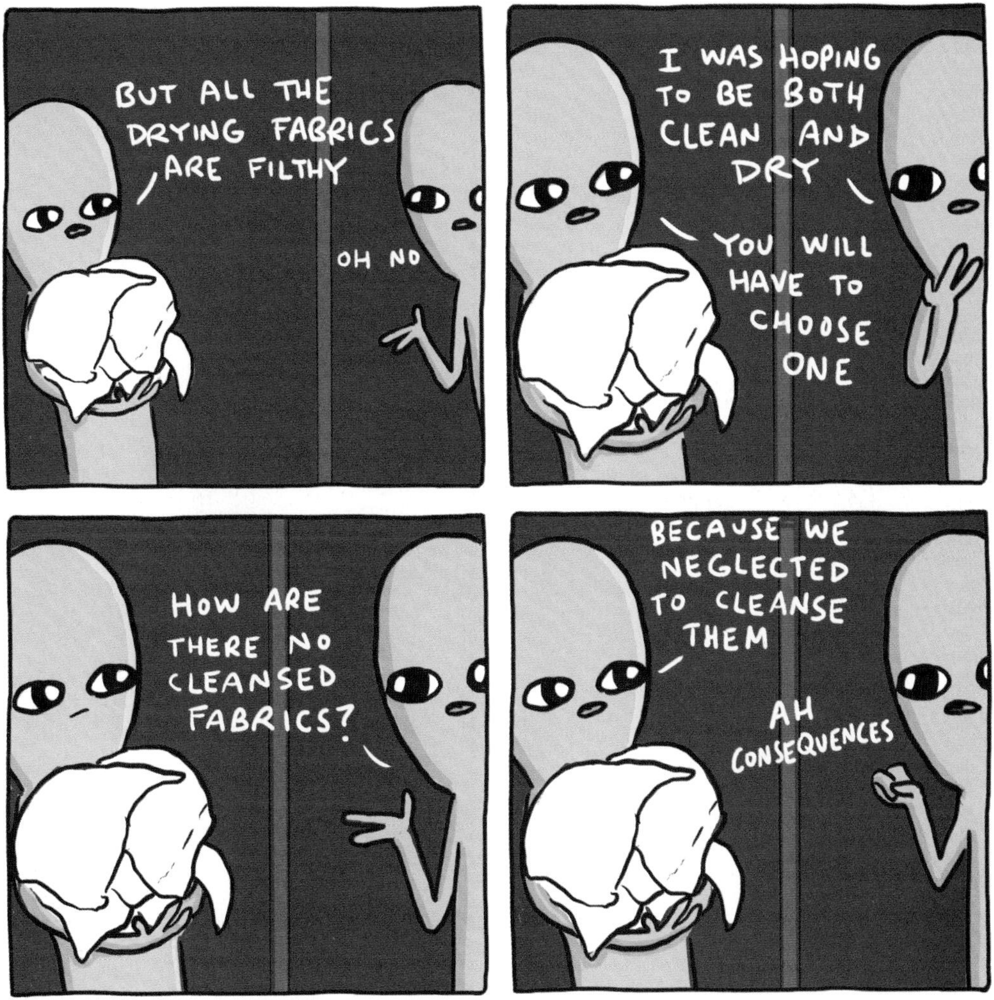
BUT ALL THE DRYING FABRICS ARE FILTHY
OH NO
I WAS HOPING TO BE BOTH CLEAN AND DRY
YOU WILL HAVE TO CHOOSE ONE
HOW ARE THERE NO CLEANSED FABRICS?
BECAUSE WE NEGLECTED TO CLEANSE THEM
AH CONSEQUENCES

TRADITIONS

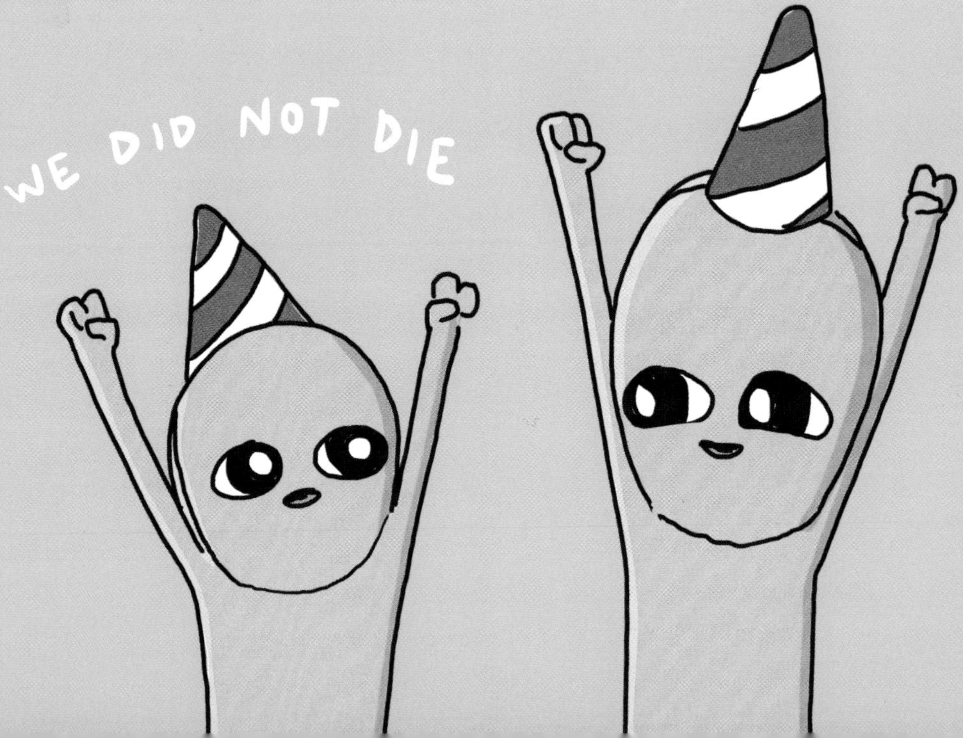
WE DID NOT DIE

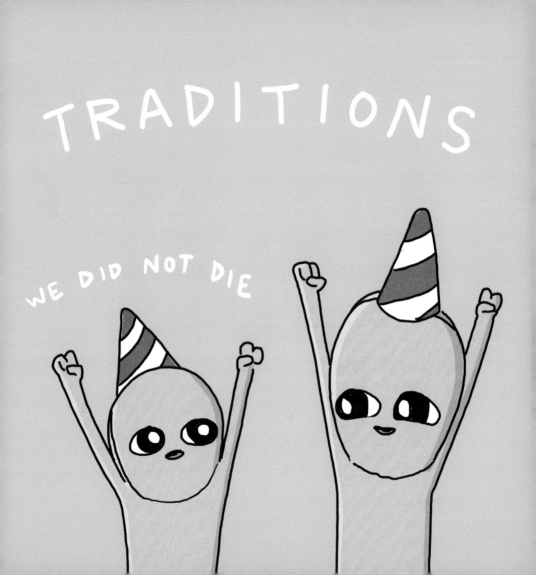

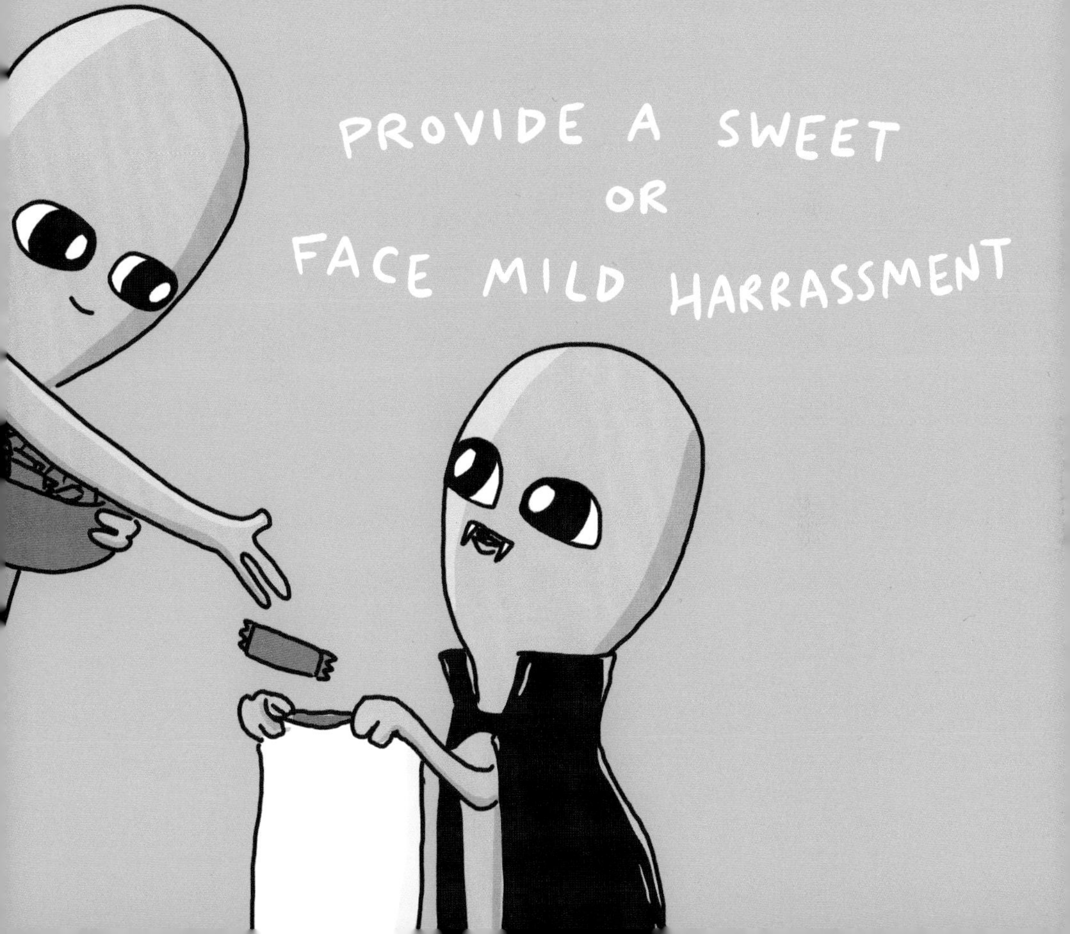
PROVIDE A SWEET
OR
FACE MILD HARRASSMENT

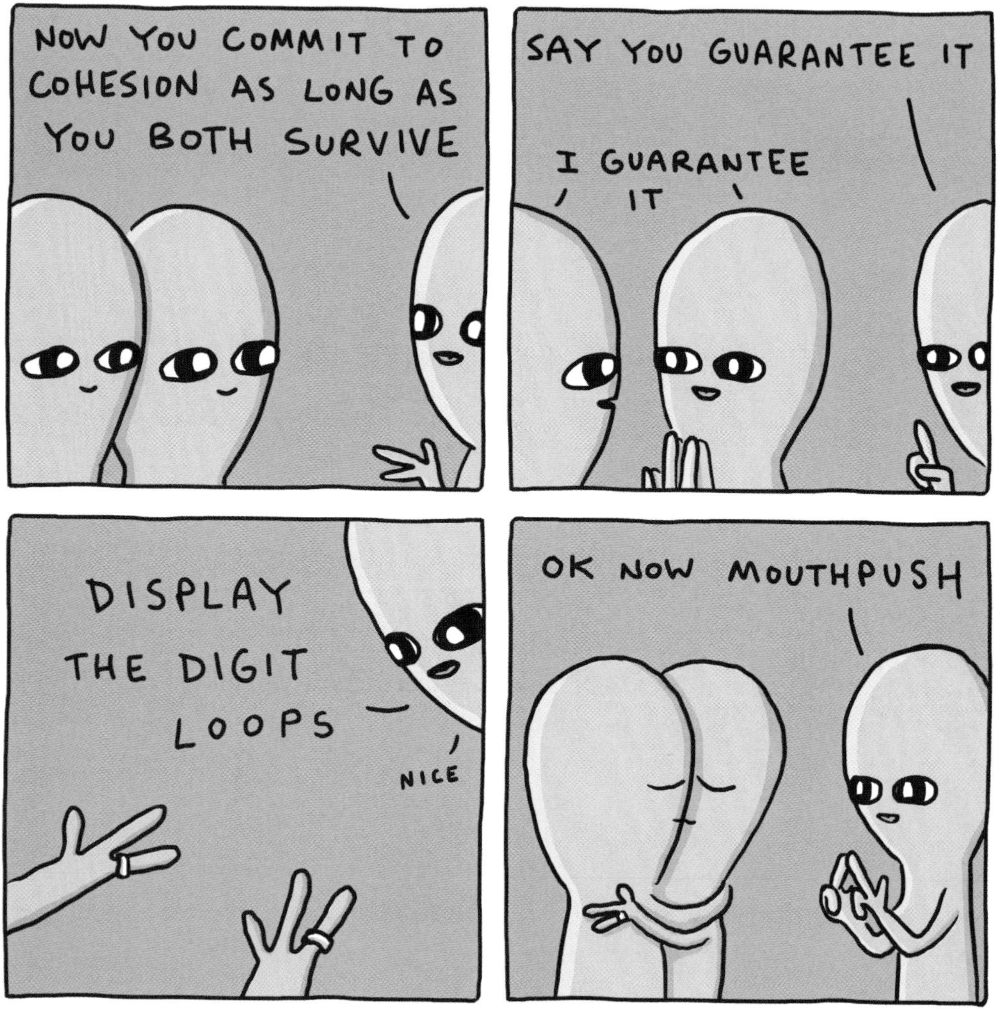
NOW YOU COMMIT TO COHESION AS LONG AS YOU BOTH SURVIVE
SAY YOU GUARANTEE IT
I GUARANTEE IT
DISPLAY THE DIGIT LOOPS
NICE
OK NOW MOUTHPUSH

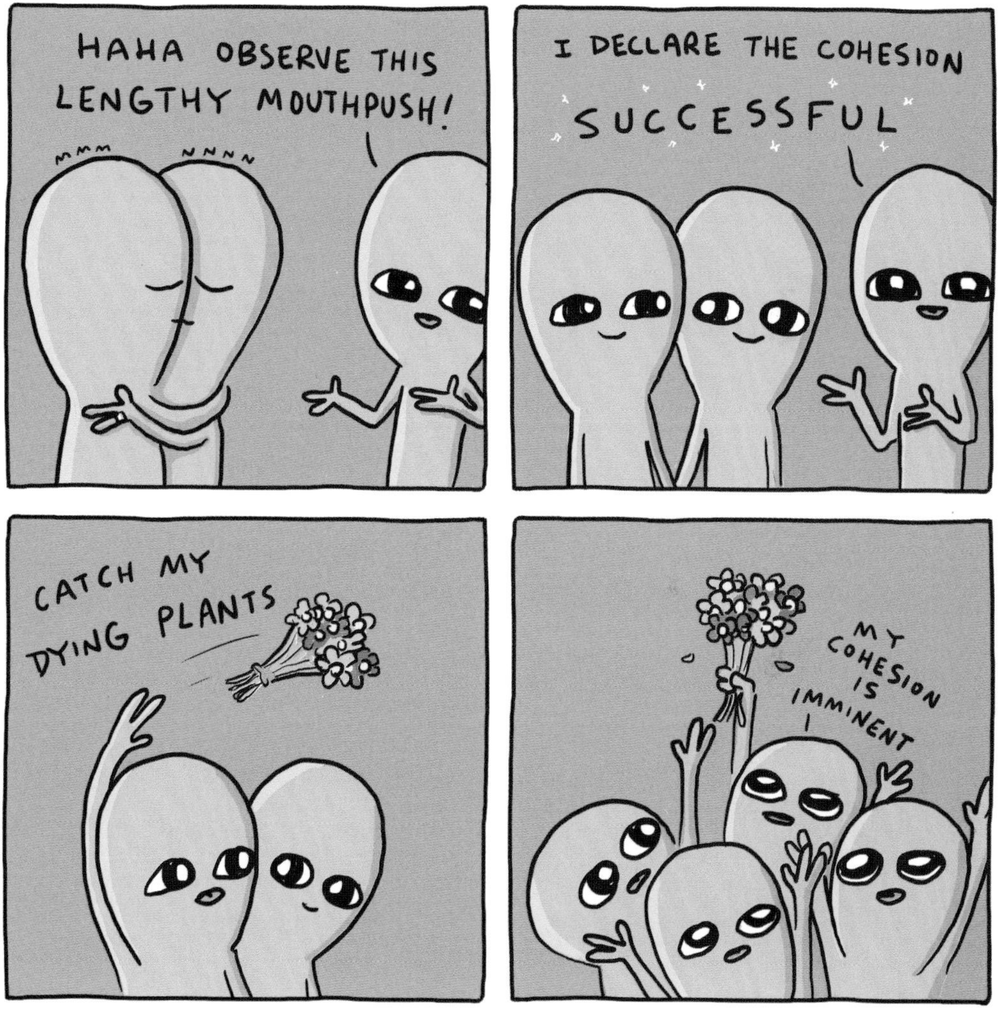

HAHA OBSERVE THIS LENGTHY MOUTHPUSH!
MMM
NNNN
I DECLARE THE COHESION SUCCESSFUL
CATCH MY DYING PLANTS
MY COHESION IS IMMINENT

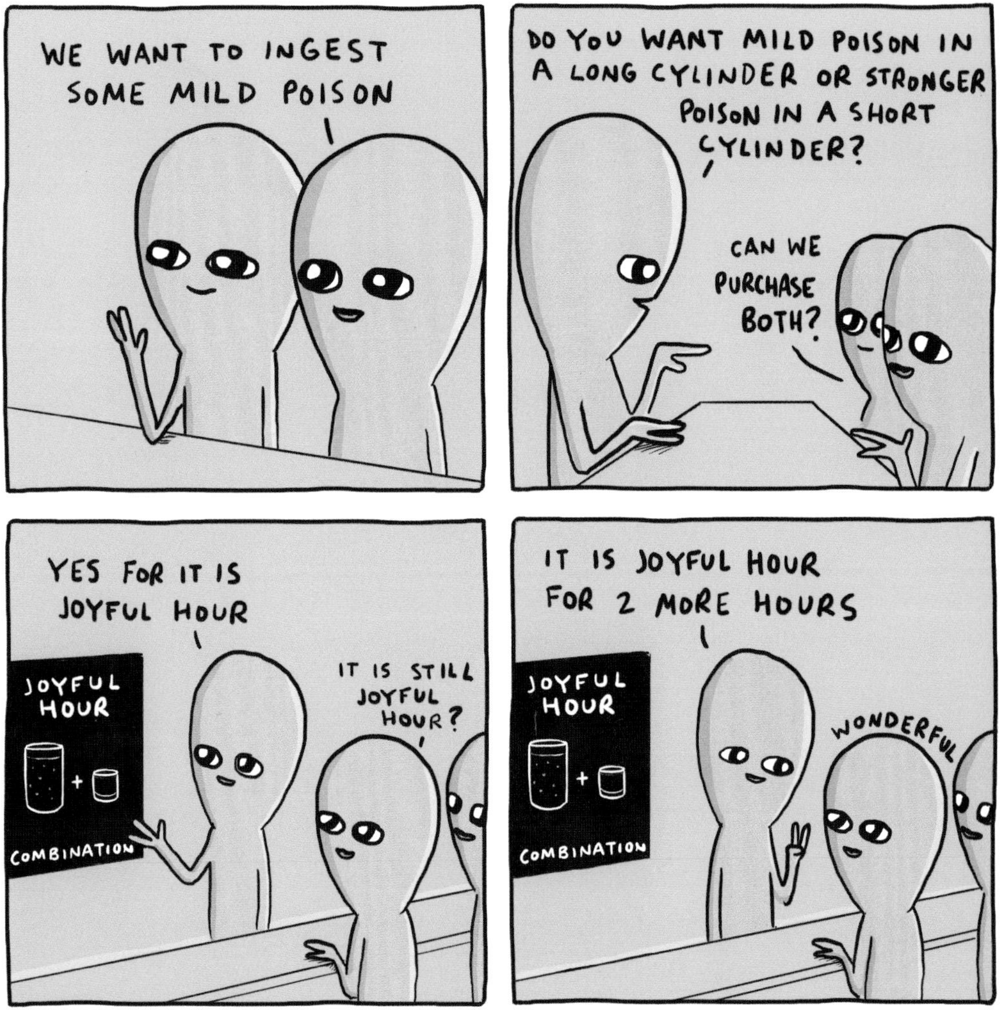
WE WANT TO INGEST SOME MILD POISON
DO YOU WANT MILD POISON IN A LONG CYLINDER OR STRONGER POISON IN A SHORT CYLINDER?
CAN WE PURCHASE BOTH?
YES FOR IT IS JOYFUL HOUR
JOYFUL HOUR
COMBINATION
IT IS STILL JOYFUL HOUR?
IT IS JOYFUL HOUR FOR 2 MORE HOURS
JOYFUL HOUR
COMBINATION
WONDERFUL

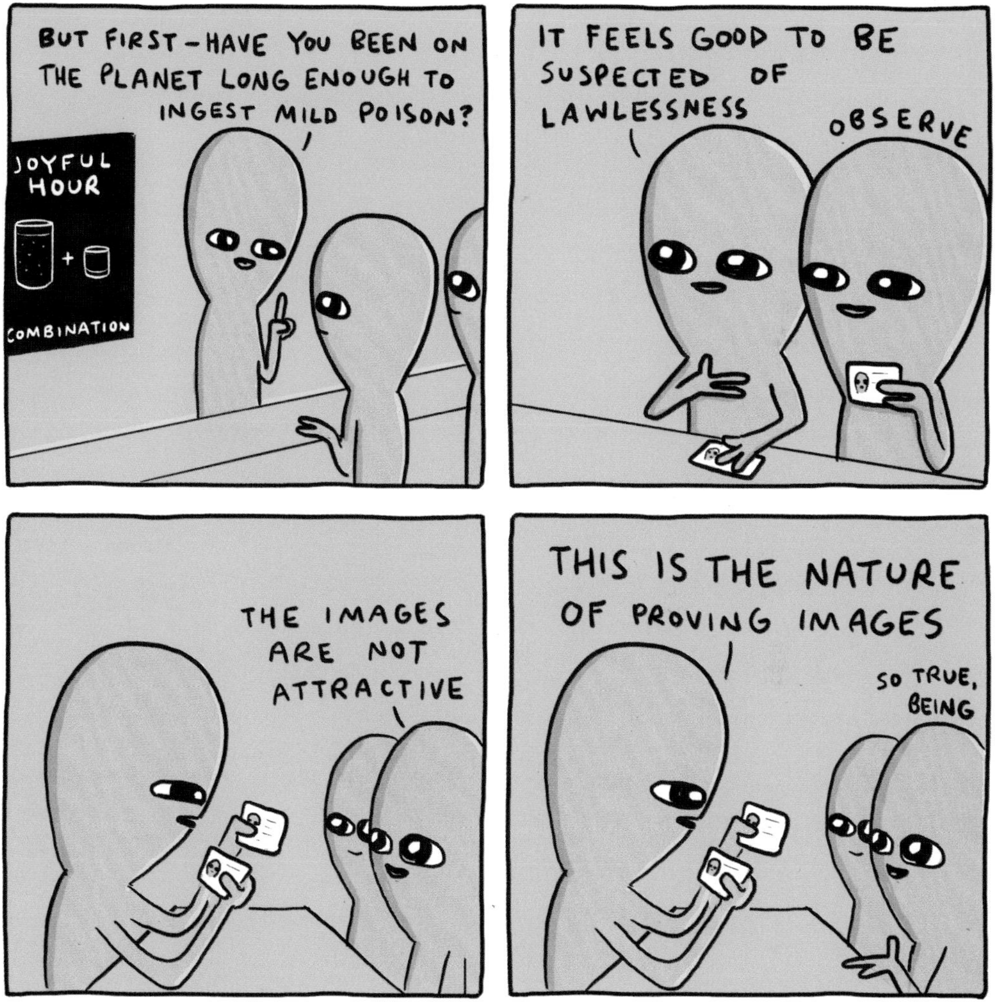
BUT FIRST—HAVE YOU BEEN ON THE PLANET LONG ENOUGH TO INGEST MILD POISON?
JOYFUL HOUR
+
COMBINATION
IT FEELS GOOD TO BE SUSPECTED OF LAWLESSNESS
OBSERVE
THE IMAGES ARE NOT ATTRACTIVE
THIS IS THE NATURE OF PROVING IMAGES
SO TRUE, BEING

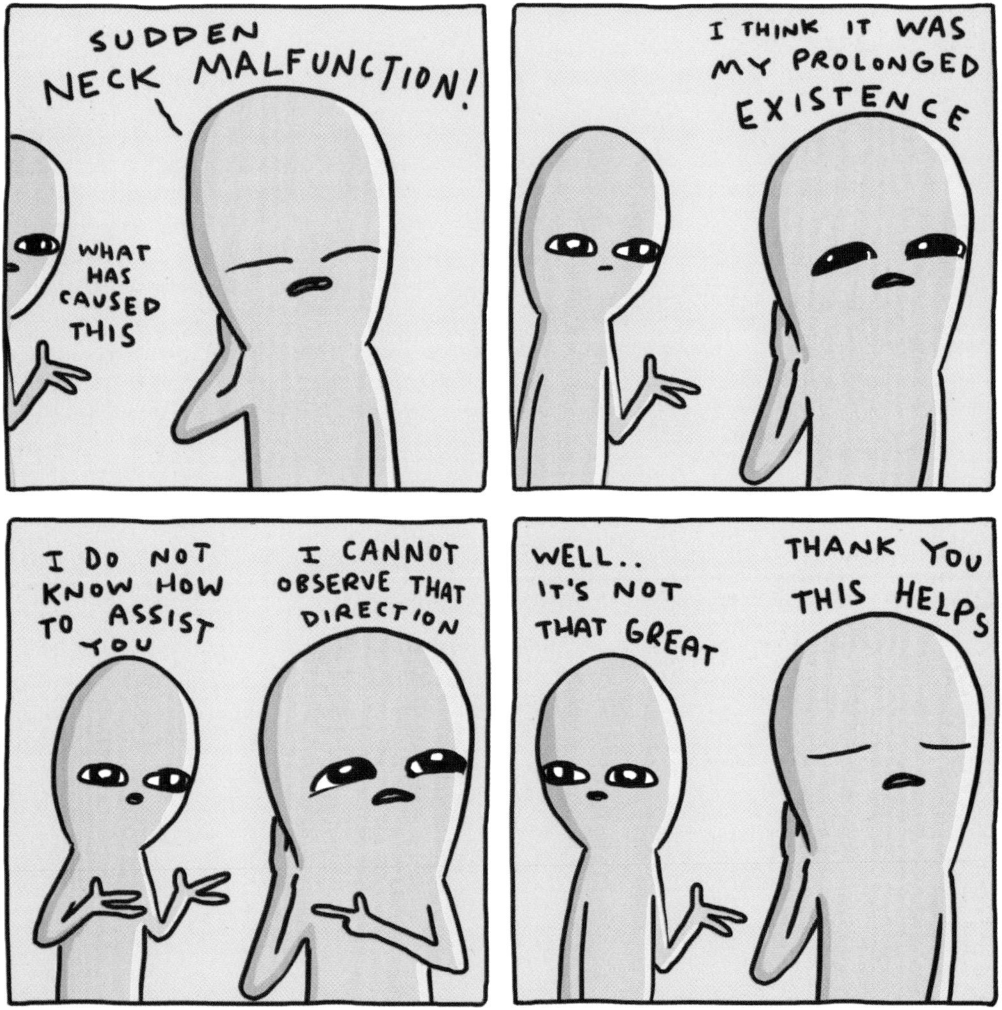
SUDDEN NECK MALFUNCTION!
WHAT HAS CAUSED THIS
I THINK IT WAS MY PROLONGED EXISTENCE
I DO NOT KNOW HOW TO ASSIST YOU
I CANNOT OBSERVE THAT DIRECTION
WELL.. IT'S NOT THAT GREAT
THANK YOU THIS HELPS

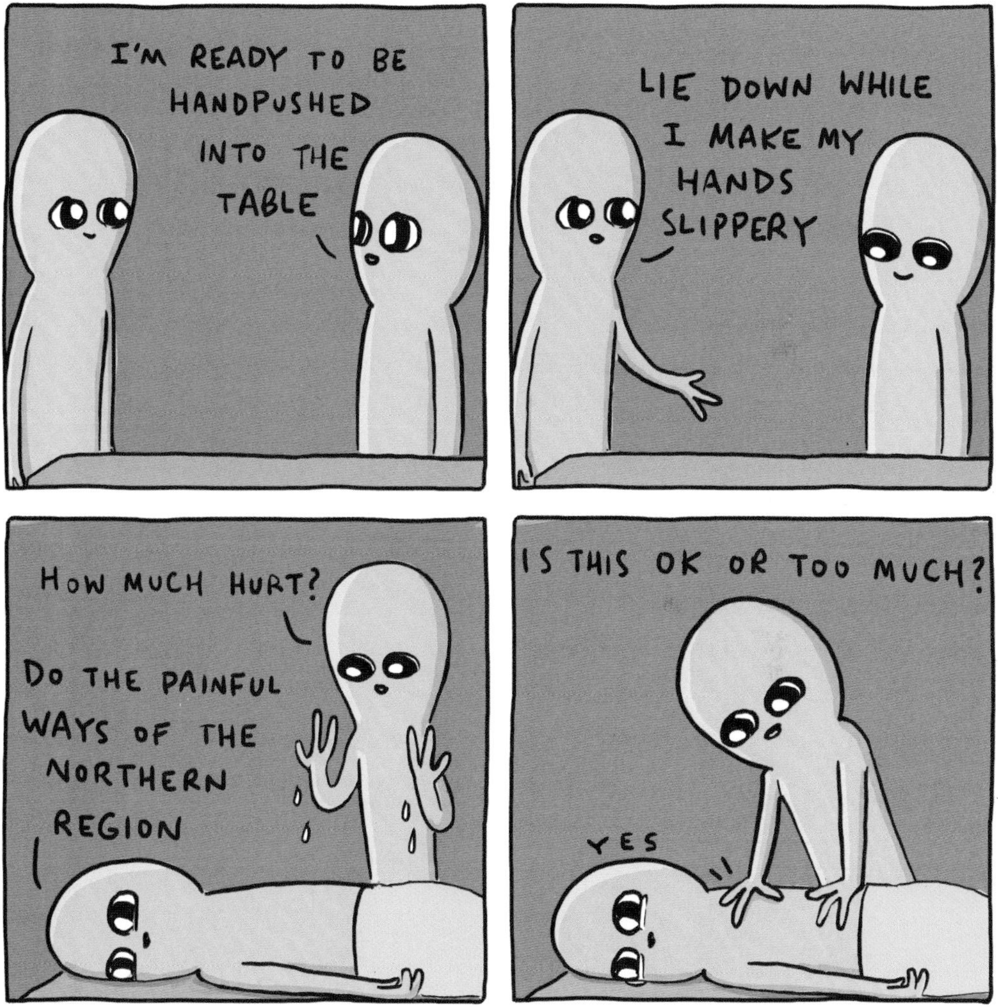
I'M READY TO BE HANDPUSHED INTO THE TABLE
LIE DOWN WHILE I MAKE MY HANDS SLIPPERY
HOW MUCH HURT?
DO THE PAINFUL WAYS OF THE NORTHERN REGION
IS THIS OK OR TOO MUCH?
YES

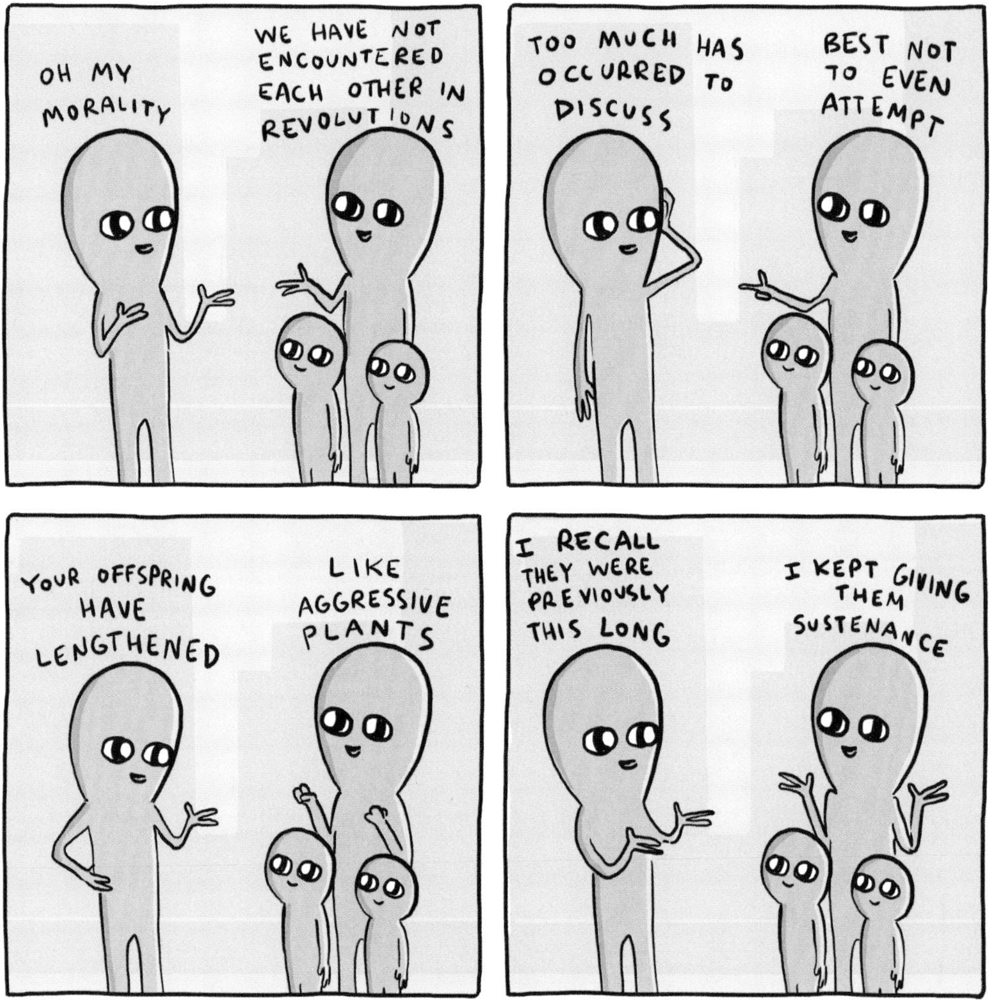
OH MY MORALITY
WE HAVE NOT ENCOUNTERED EACH OTHER IN REVOLUTIONS
TOO MUCH HAS OCCURRED TO DISCUSS
BEST NOT TO EVEN ATTEMPT
YOUR OFFSPRING HAVE LENGTHENED
LIKE AGGRESSIVE PLANTS
I RECALL THEY WERE PREVIOUSLY THIS LONG
I KEPT GIVING THEM SUSTENANCE

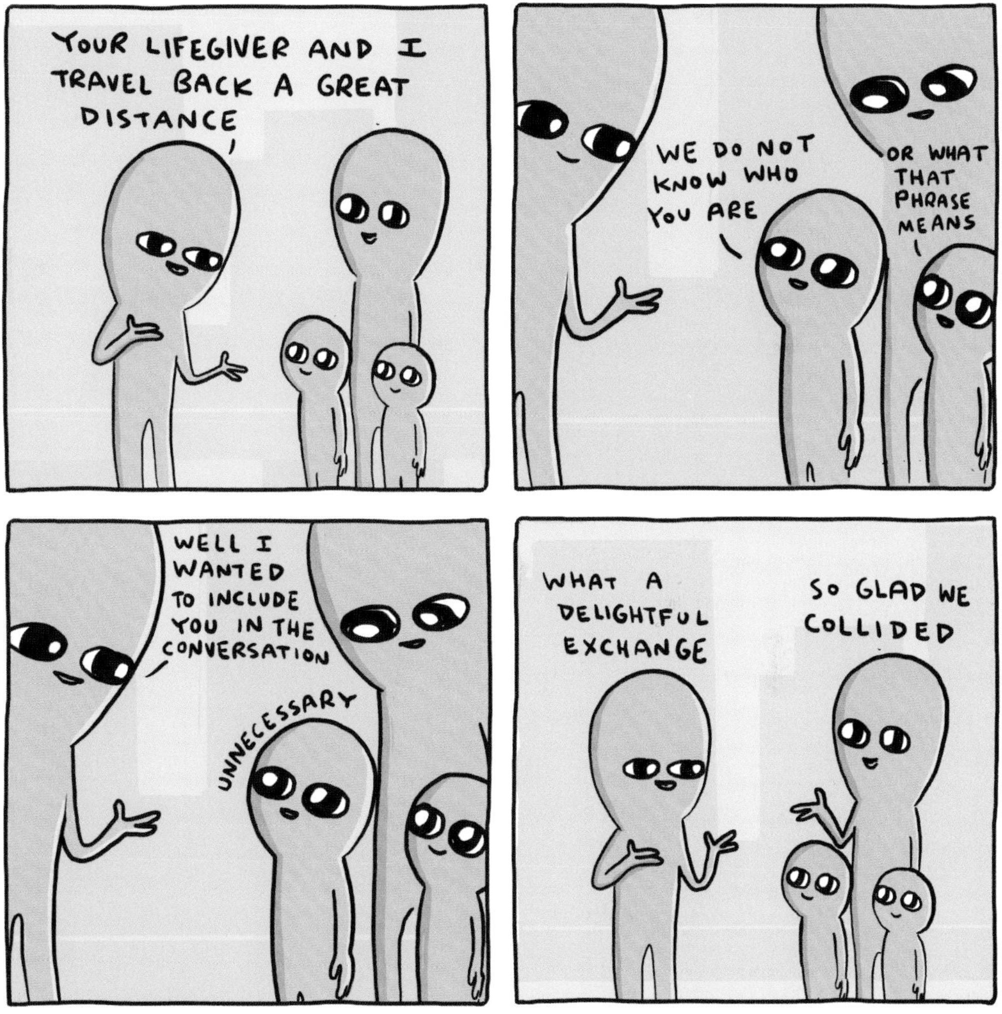
YOUR LIFEGIVER AND I TRAVEL BACK A GREAT DISTANCE
WE DO NOT KNOW WHO YOU ARE
OR WHAT THAT PHRASE MEANS
WELL I WANTED TO INCLUDE YOU IN THE CONVERSATION
UNNECESSARY
WHAT A DELIGHTFUL EXCHANGE
SO GLAD WE COLLIDED

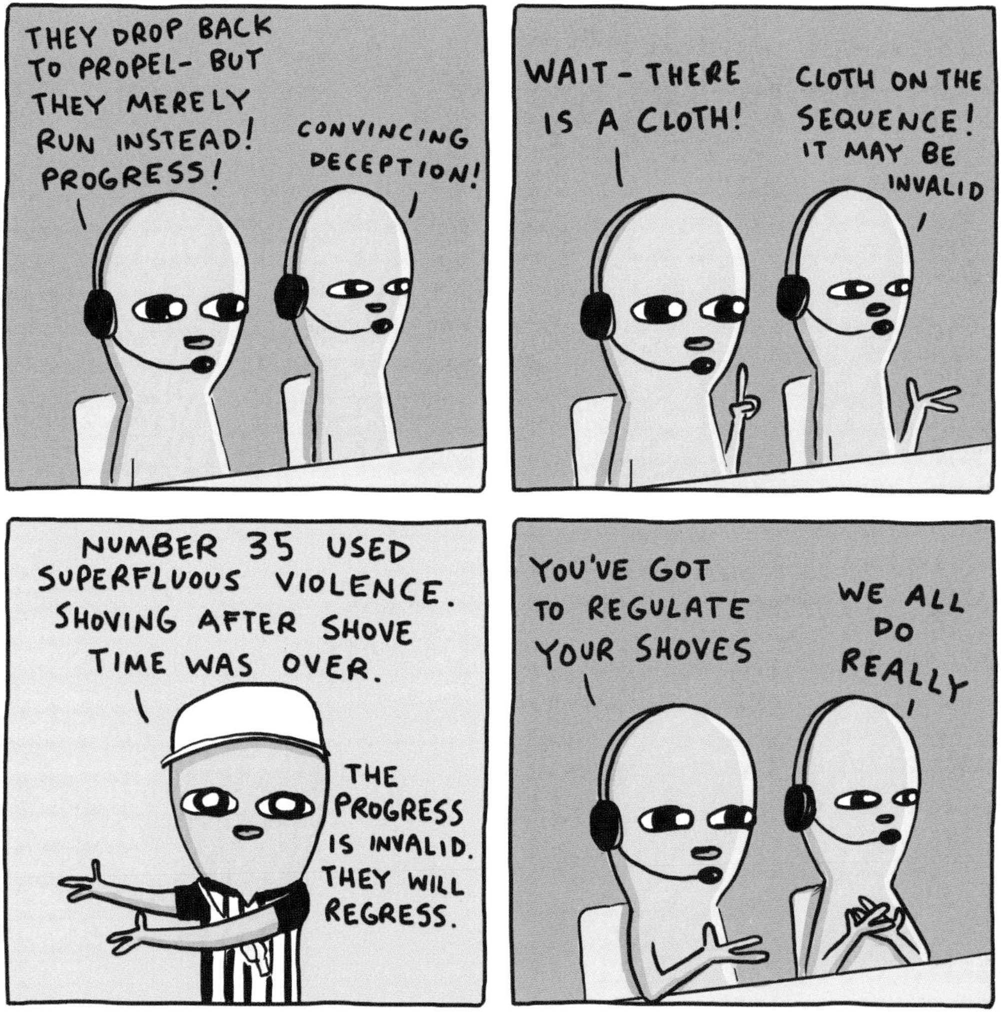
THEY DROP BACK TO PROPEL- BUT THEY MERELY RUN INSTEAD! PROGRESS!
CONVINCING DECEPTION!
WAIT - THERE IS A CLOTH!
CLOTH ON THE SEQUENCE! IT MAY BE INVALID
NUMBER 35 USED SUPERFLUOUS VIOLENCE. SHOVING AFTER SHOVE TIME WAS OVER.
THE PROGRESS IS INVALID. THEY WILL REGRESS.
YOU'VE GOT TO REGULATE YOUR SHOVES
WE ALL DO REALLY

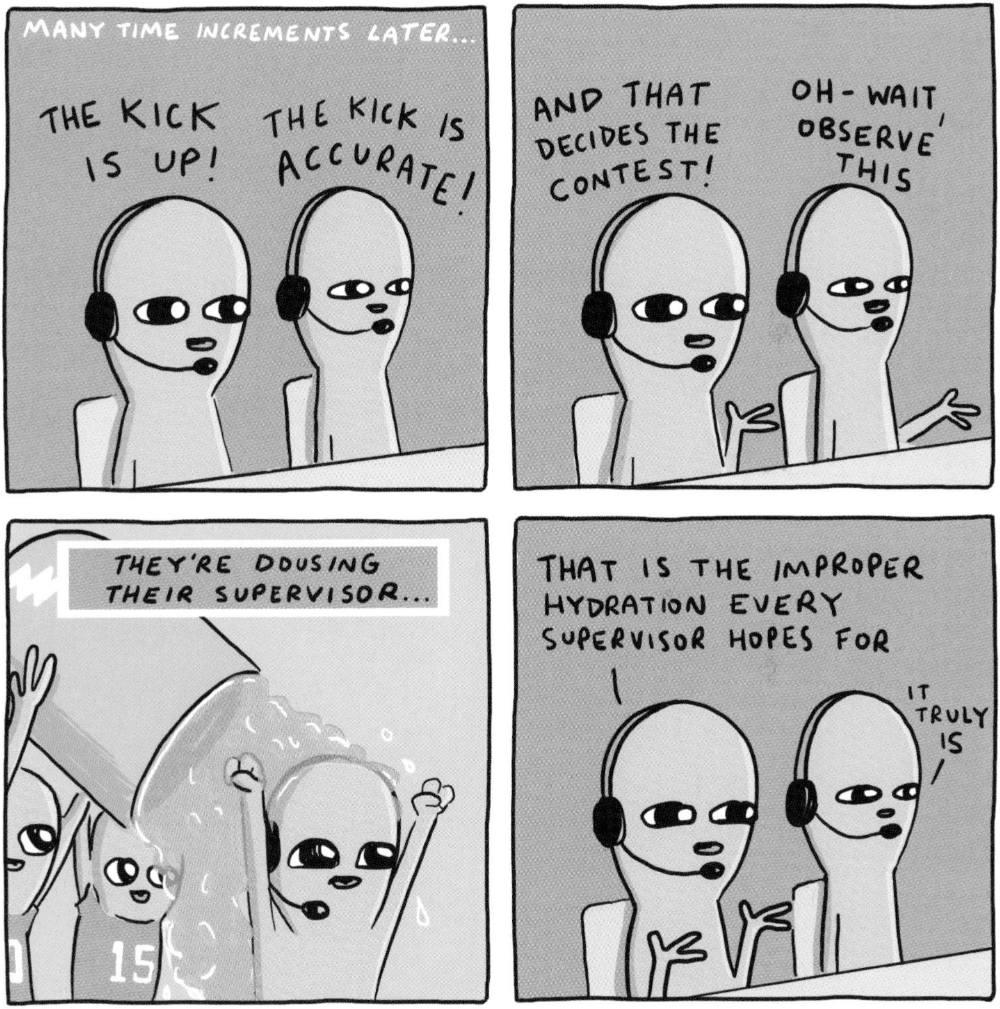
MANY TIME INCREMENTS LATER...
THE KICK IS UP!
THE KICK IS ACCURATE!
AND THAT DECIDES THE CONTEST!
OH- WAIT, OBSERVE THIS
THEY'RE DOUSING THEIR SUPERVISOR...
15
THAT IS THE IMPROPER HYDRATION EVERY SUPERVISOR HOPES FOR
IT TRULY IS

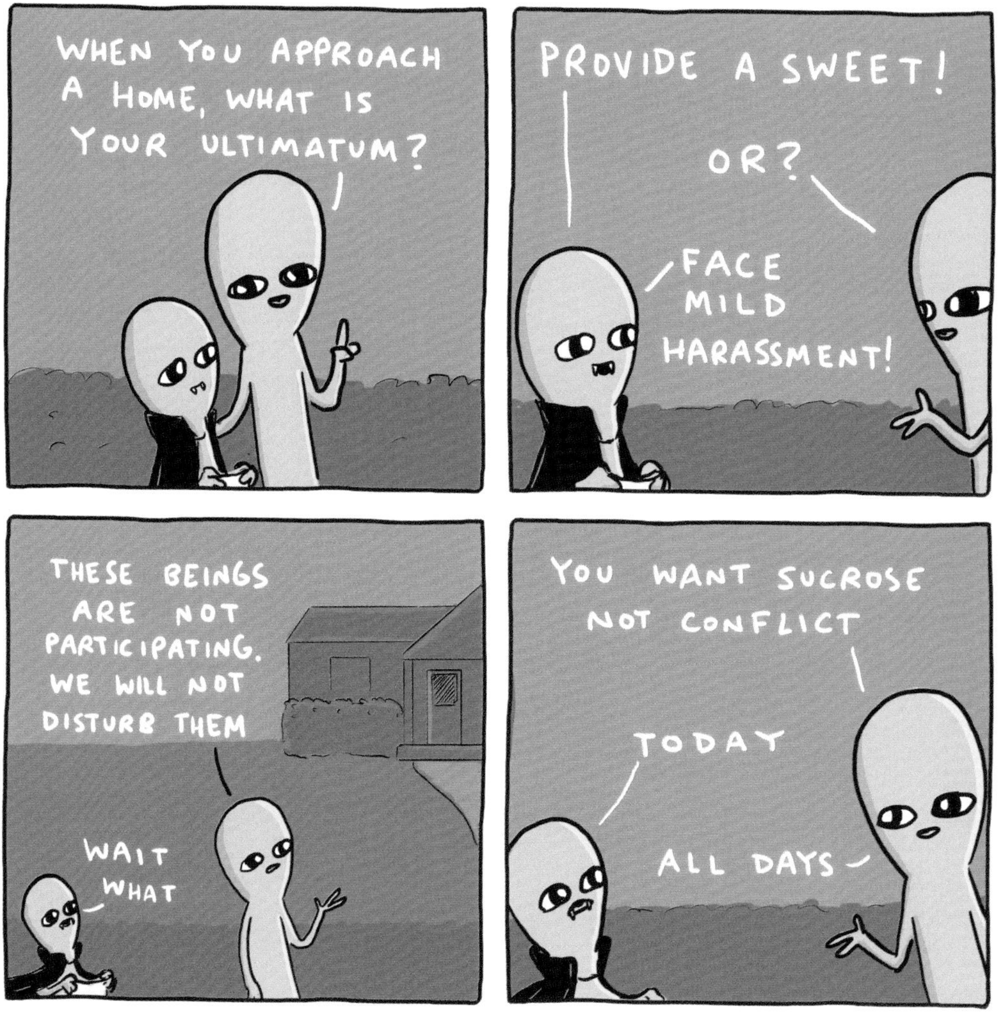
WHEN YOU APPROACH A HOME, WHAT IS YOUR ULTIMATUM?
PROVIDE A SWEET!
OR?
FACE MILD HARASSMENT!
THESE BEINGS ARE NOT PARTICIPATING. WE WILL NOT DISTURB THEM
WAIT WHAT
YOU WANT SUCROSE NOT CONFLICT
TODAY
ALL DAYS

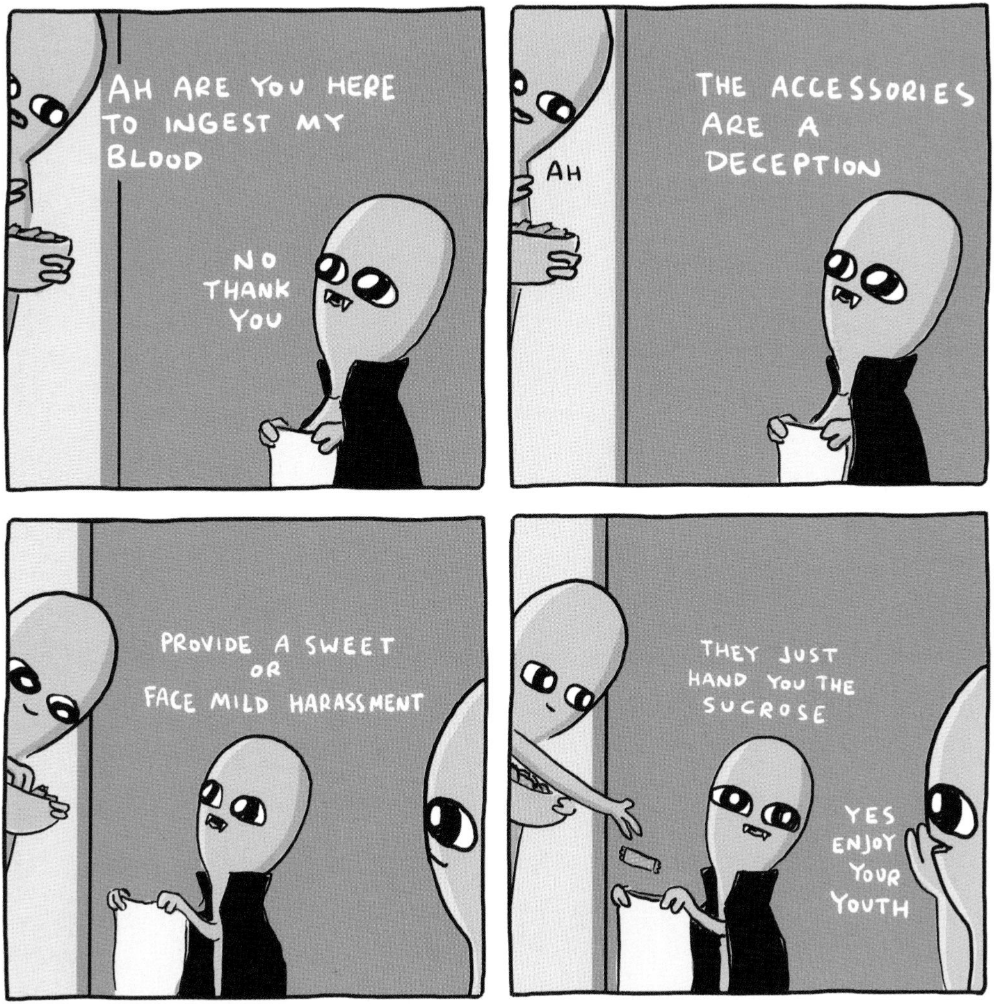
AH ARE YOU HERE TO INGEST MY BLOOD
NO THANK YOU
AH
THE ACCESSORIES ARE A DECEPTION
PROVIDE A SWEET OR FACE MILD HARASSMENT
THEY JUST HAND YOU THE SUCROSE
YES ENJOY YOUR YOUTH

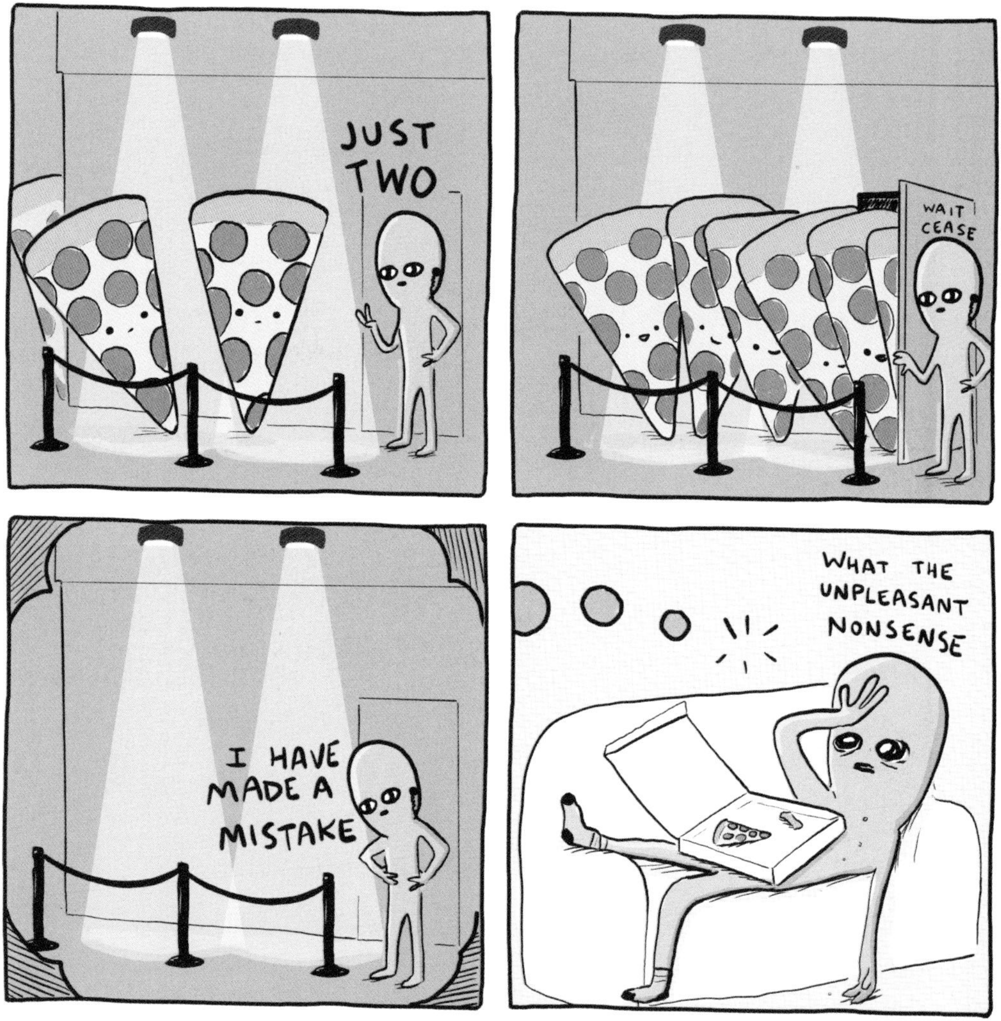
JUST TWO
WAIT CEASE
I HAVE MADE A MISTAKE
WHAT THE UNPLEASANT NONSENSE

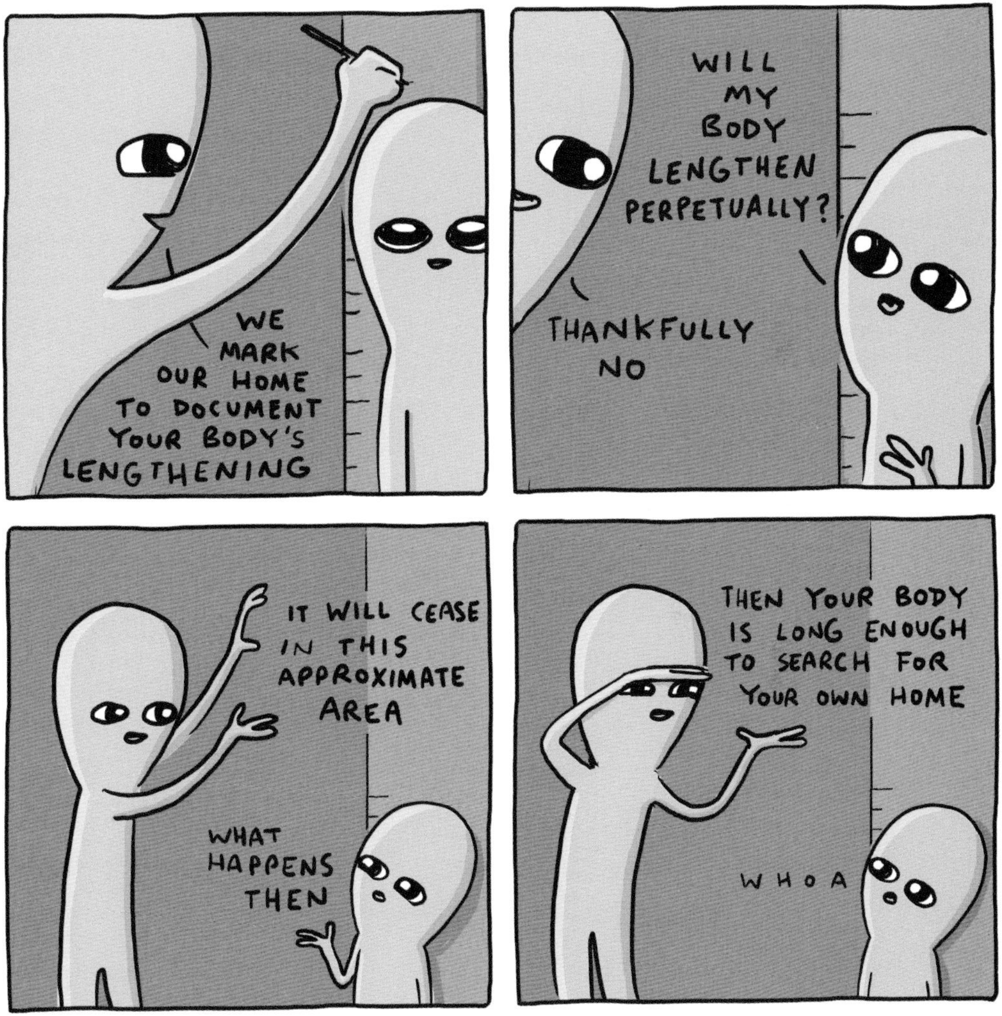
WE MARK OUR HOME TO DOCUMENT YOUR BODY'S LENGTHENING
WILL MY BODY LENGTHEN PERPETUALLY?
THANKFULLY NO
IT WILL CEASE IN THIS APPROXIMATE AREA
WHAT HAPPENS THEN
THEN YOUR BODY IS LONG ENOUGH TO SEARCH FOR YOUR OWN HOME
W H O A

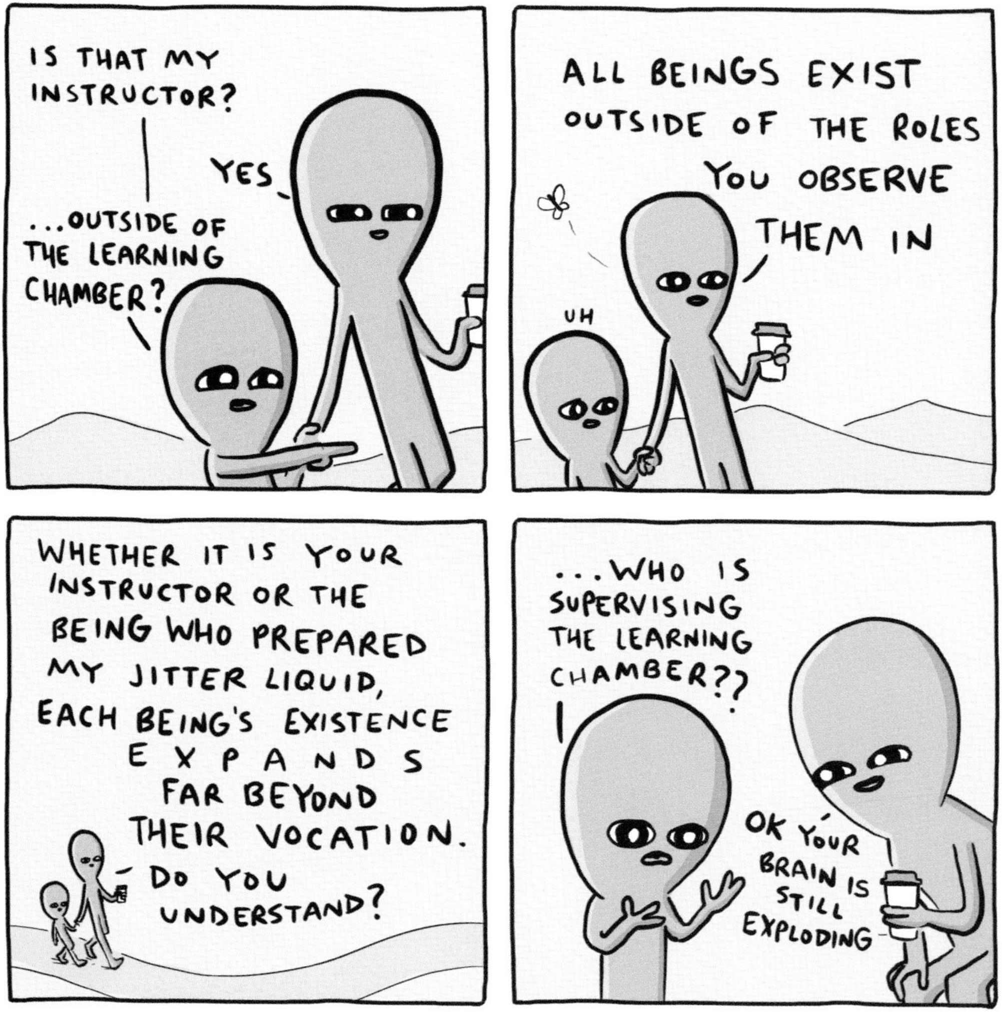
IS THAT MY INSTRUCTOR?
...OUTSIDE OF THE LEARNING CHAMBER?
YES
ALL BEINGS EXIST OUTSIDE OF THE ROLES YOU OBSERVE THEM IN
UH
WHETHER IT IS YOUR INSTRUCTOR OR THE BEING WHO PREPARED MY JITTER LIQUID, EACH BEING'S EXISTENCE E X P A N D S FAR BEYOND THEIR VOCATION.
DO YOU UNDERSTAND?
...WHO IS SUPERVISING THE LEARNING CHAMBER??
OK YOUR BRAIN IS STILL EXPLODING

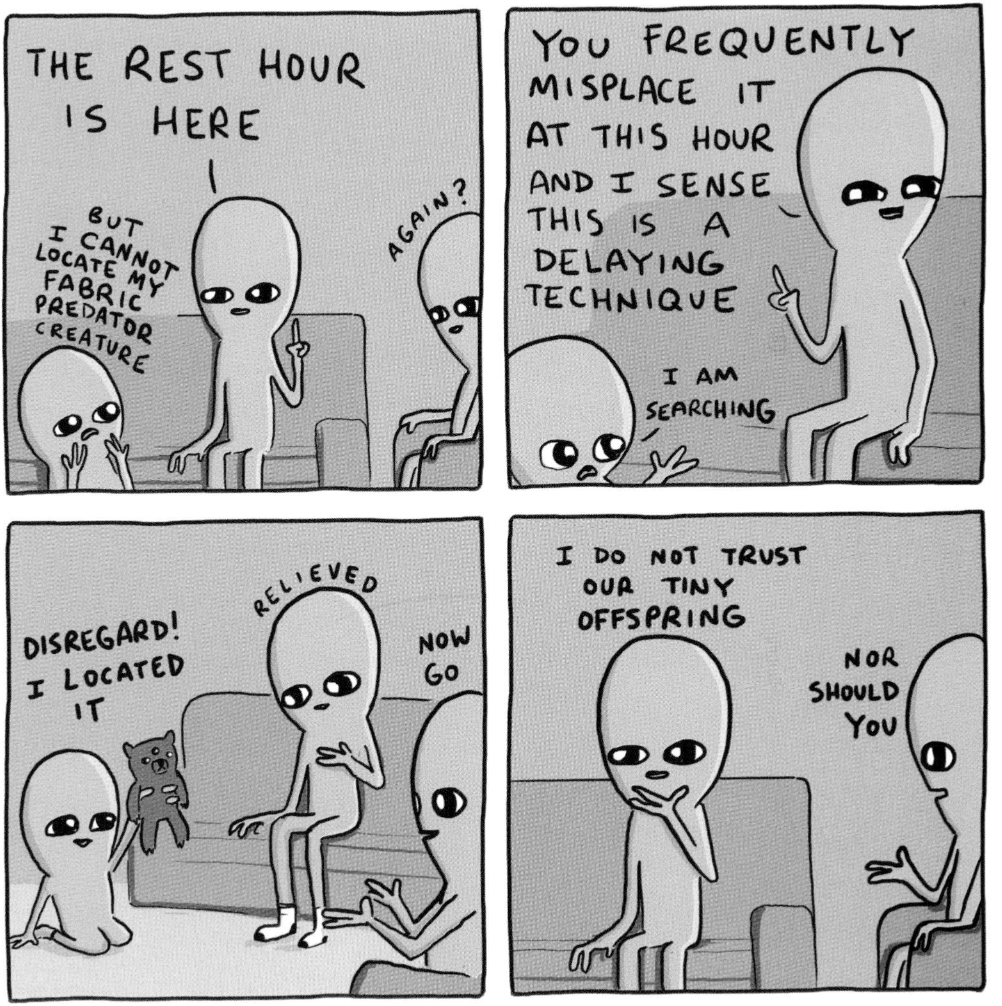
THE REST HOUR IS HERE
BUT I CANNOT LOCATE MY FABRIC PREDATOR CREATURE
AGAIN?
YOU FREQUENTLY MISPLACE IT AT THIS HOUR AND I SENSE THIS IS A DELAYING TECHNIQUE
I AM SEARCHING
DISREGARD! I LOCATED IT
RELIEVED
NOW GO
I DO NOT TRUST OUR TINY OFFSPRING
NOR SHOULD YOU

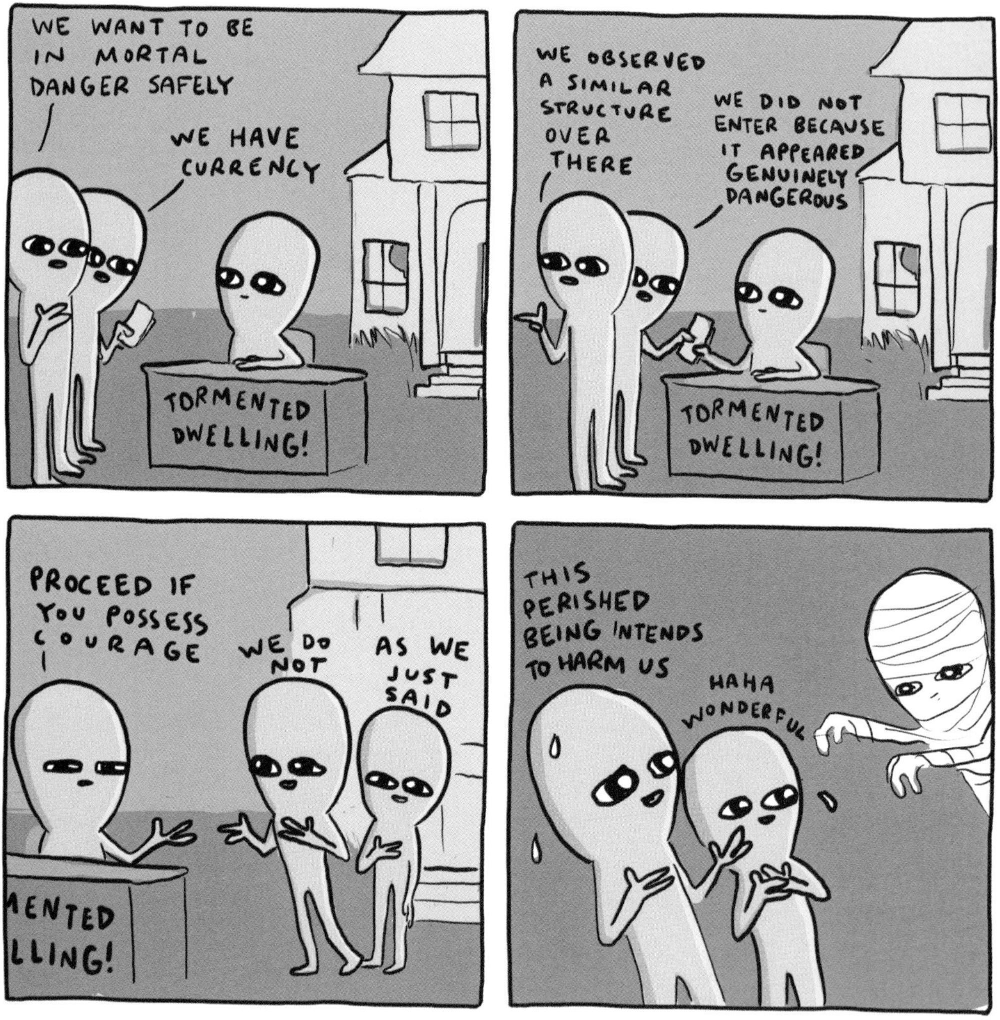
WE WANT TO BE IN MORTAL DANGER SAFELY
WE HAVE CURRENCY
TORMENTED DWELLING!
WE OBSERVED A SIMILAR STRUCTURE OVER THERE
WE DID NOT ENTER BECAUSE IT APPEARED GENUINELY DANGEROUS
TORMENTED DWELLING!
PROCEED IF YOU POSSESS COURAGE
WE DO NOT
AS WE JUST SAID
MENTED
LLING!
THIS PERISHED BEING INTENDS TO HARM US
HAHA WONDERFUL

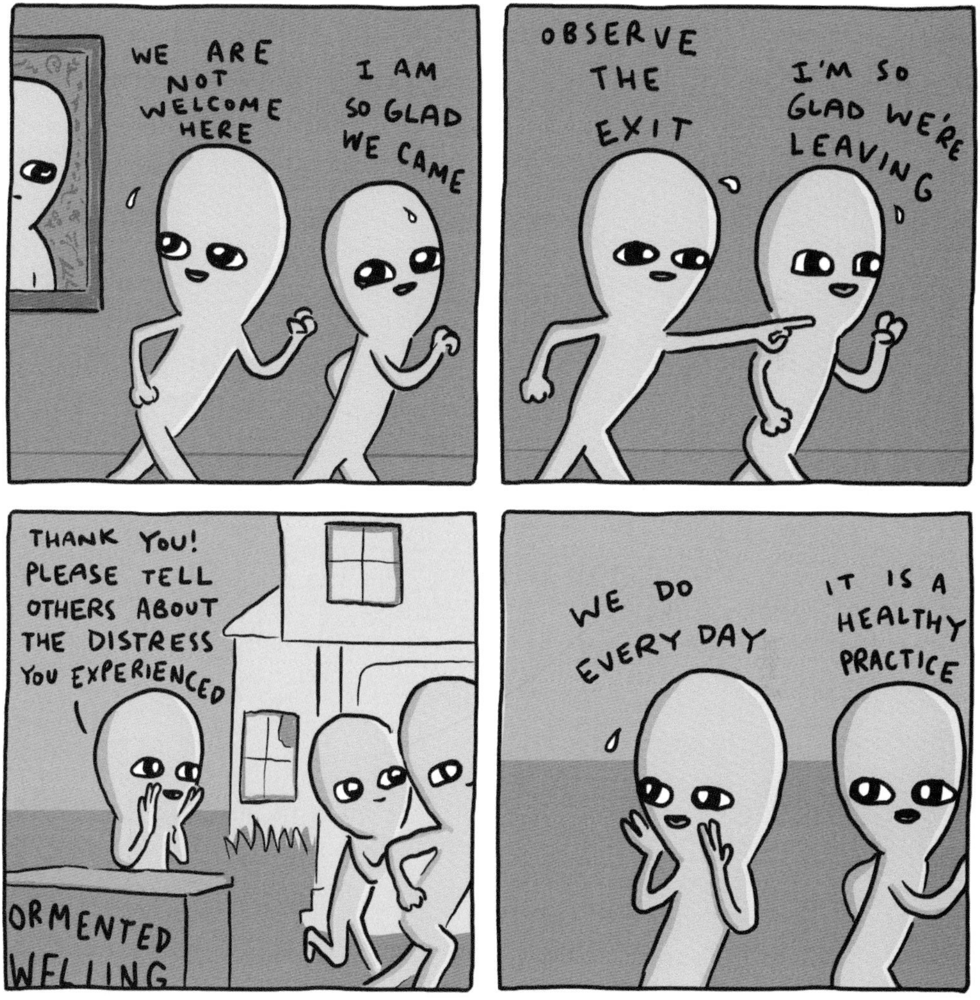
WE ARE NOT WELCOME HERE
I AM SO GLAD WE CAME
OBSERVE THE EXIT
I'M SO GLAD WE'RE LEAVING
THANK YOU! PLEASE TELL OTHERS ABOUT THE DISTRESS YOU EXPERIENCED
ORMENTED
WELLING
WE DO EVERY DAY
IT IS A HEALTHY PRACTICE

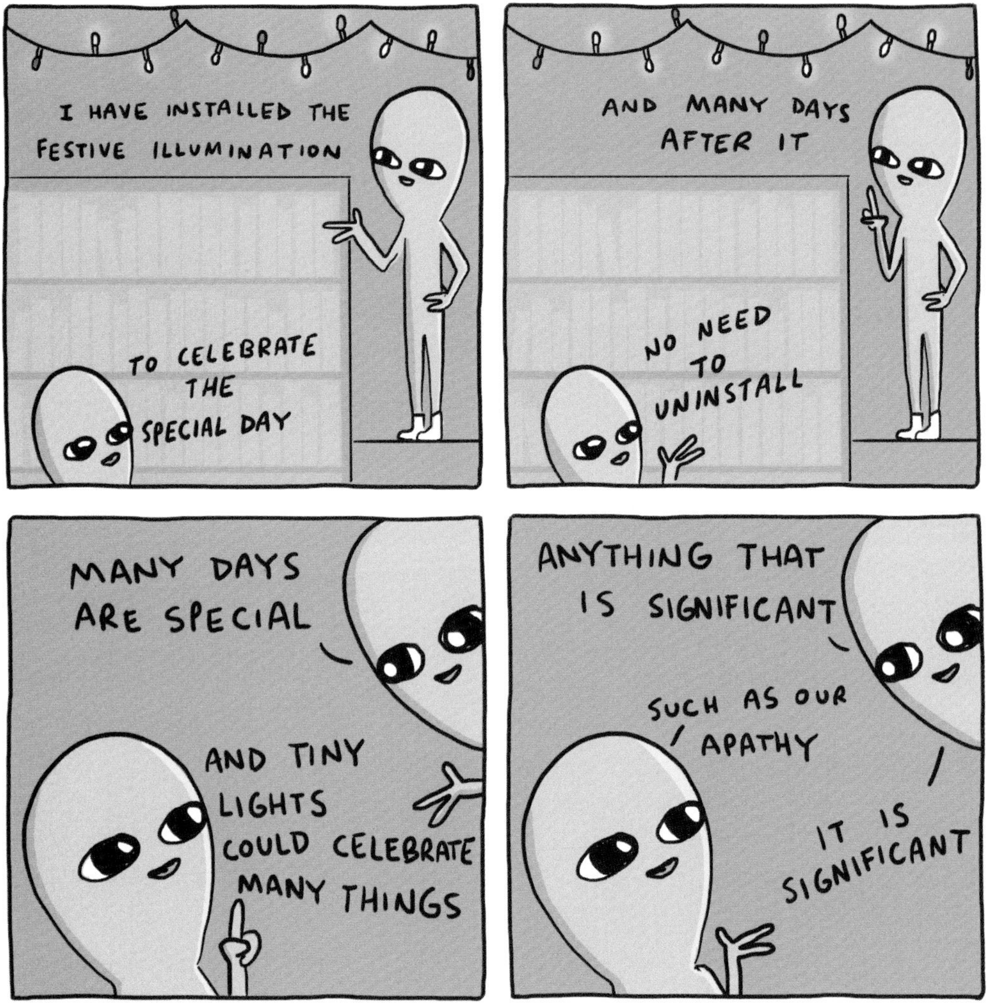
I HAVE INSTALLED THE FESTIVE ILLUMINATION
TO CELEBRATE THE SPECIAL DAY
AND MANY DAYS AFTER IT
NO NEED TO UNINSTALL
MANY DAYS ARE SPECIAL
AND TINY LIGHTS COULD CELEBRATE MANY THINGS
ANYTHING THAT IS SIGNIFICANT
SUCH AS OUR APATHY
IT IS SIGNIFICANT

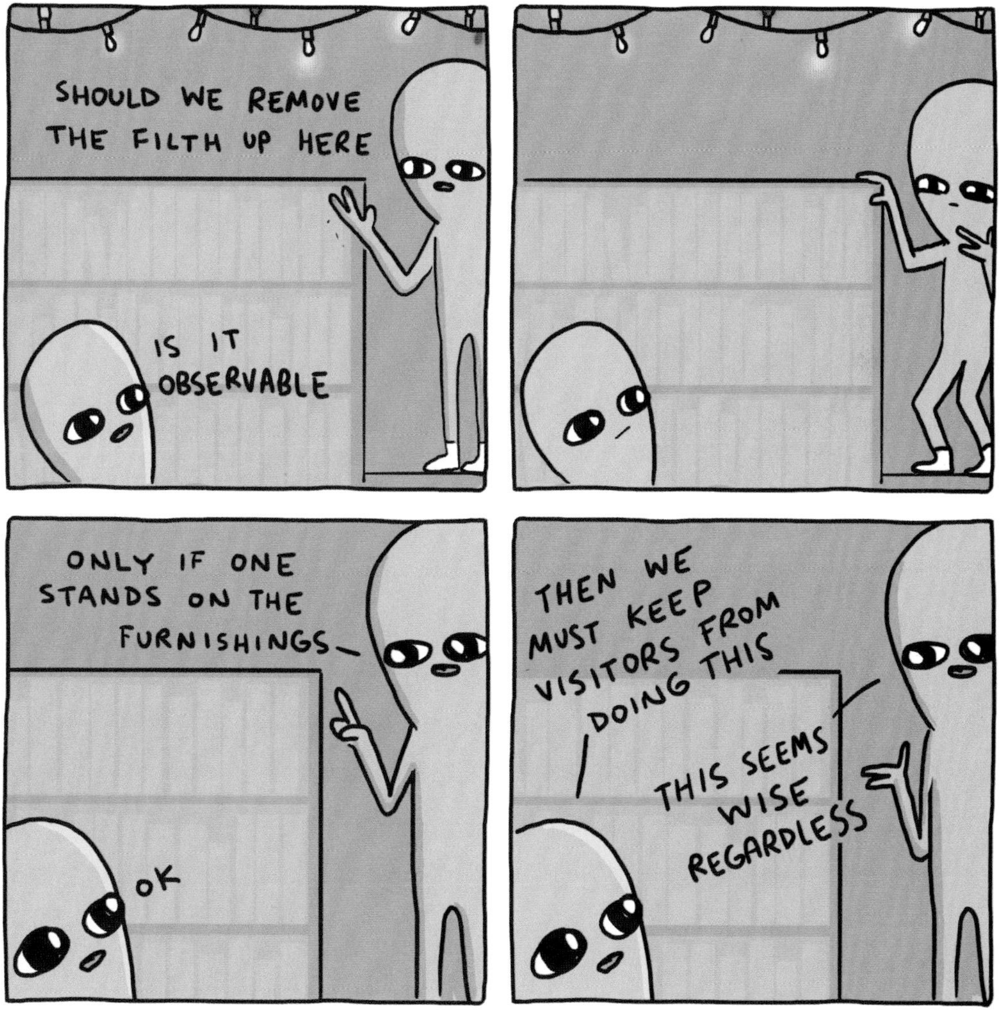
SHOULD WE REMOVE THE FILTH UP HERE
IS IT OBSERVABLE
ONLY IF ONE STANDS ON THE FURNISHINGS
OK
THEN WE MUST KEEP VISITORS FROM DOING THIS
THIS SEEMS WISE REGARDLESS

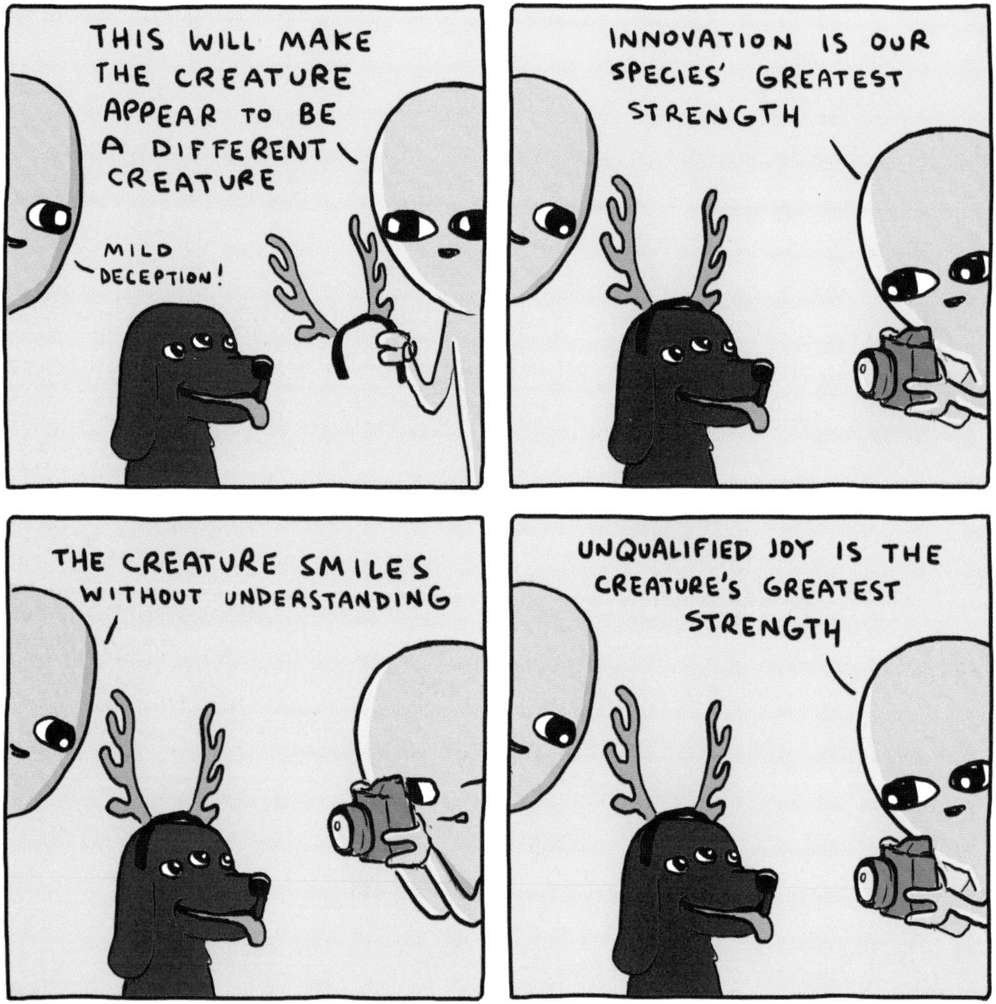
THIS WILL MAKE THE CREATURE APPEAR TO BE A DIFFERENT CREATURE
MILD DECEPTION!
INNOVATION IS OUR SPECIES' GREATEST STRENGTH
THE CREATURE SMILES WITHOUT UNDERSTANDING
UNQUALIFIED JOY IS THE CREATURE'S GREATEST STRENGTH

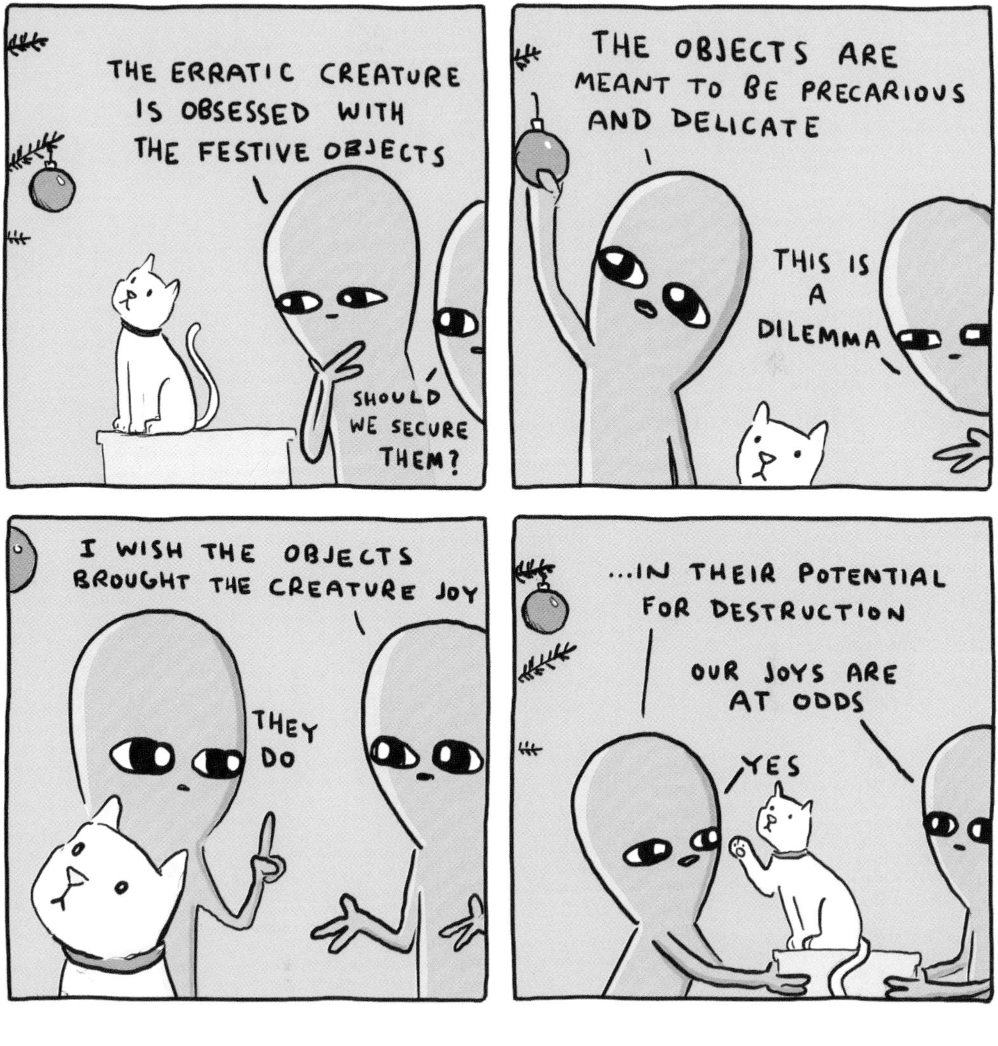
THE ERRATIC CREATURE IS OBSESSED WITH THE FESTIVE OBJECTS
SHOULD WE SECURE THEM?
THE OBJECTS ARE MEANT TO BE PRECARIOUS AND DELICATE
THIS IS A DILEMMA
I WISH THE OBJECTS BROUGHT THE CREATURE JOY
THEY DO
...IN THEIR POTENTIAL FOR DESTRUCTION
OUR JOYS ARE AT ODDS
YES

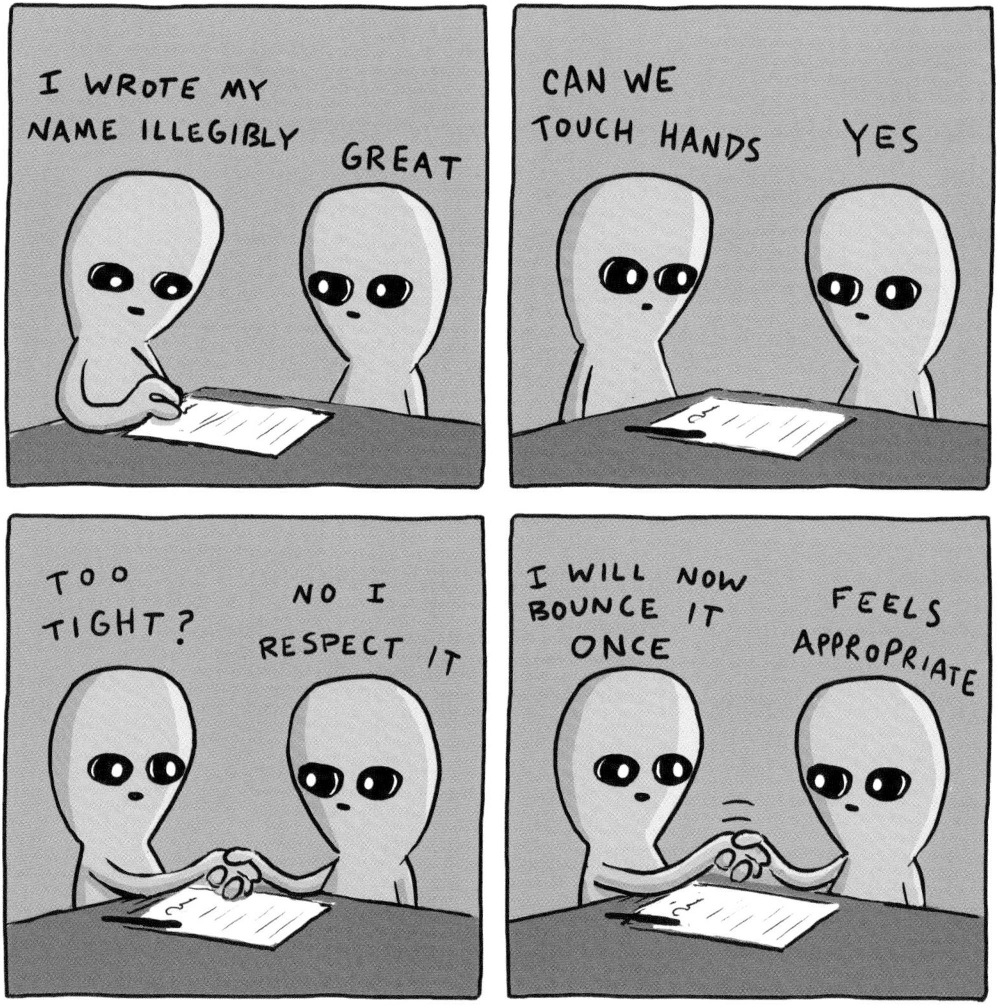
I WROTE MY NAME ILLEGIBLY
GREAT
CAN WE TOUCH HANDS
YES
TOO TIGHT?
NO I RESPECT IT
I WILL NOW BOUNCE IT ONCE
FEELS APPROPRIATE

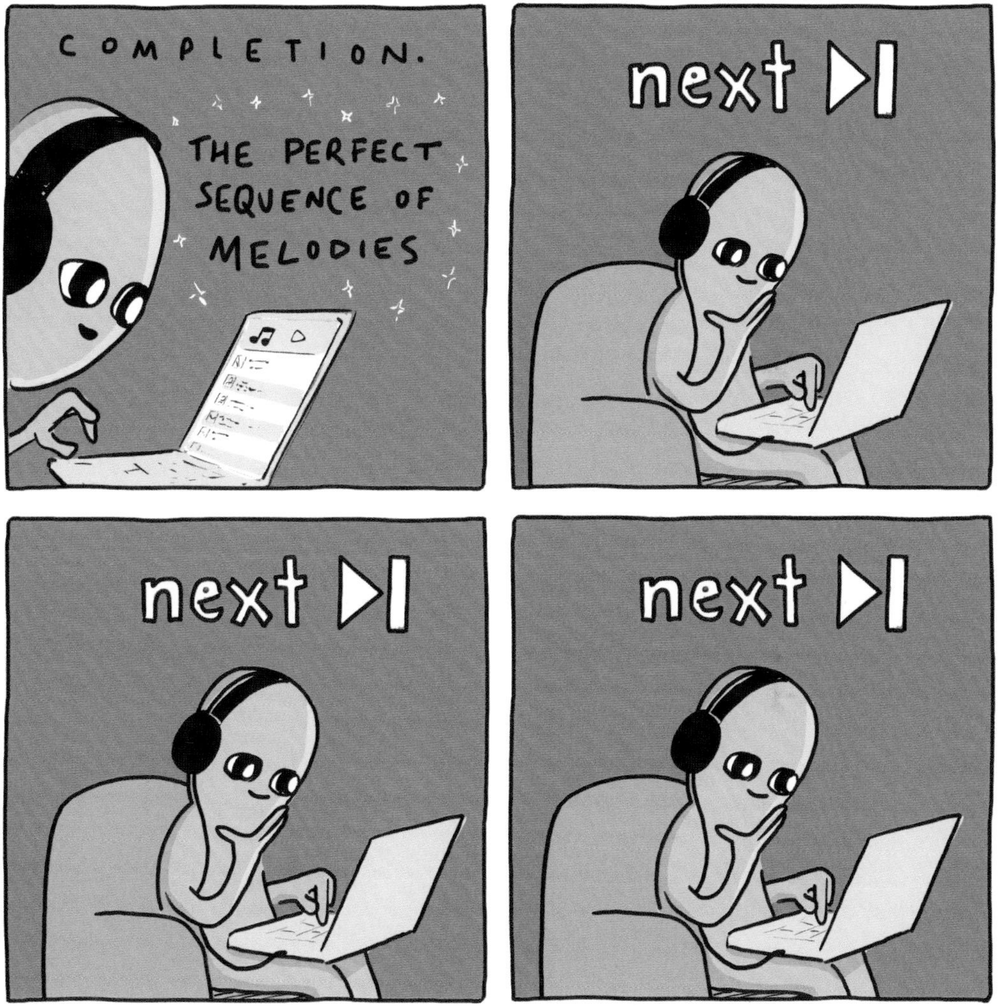
COMPLETION.
THE PERFECT SEQUENCE OF MELODIES
next
next
next

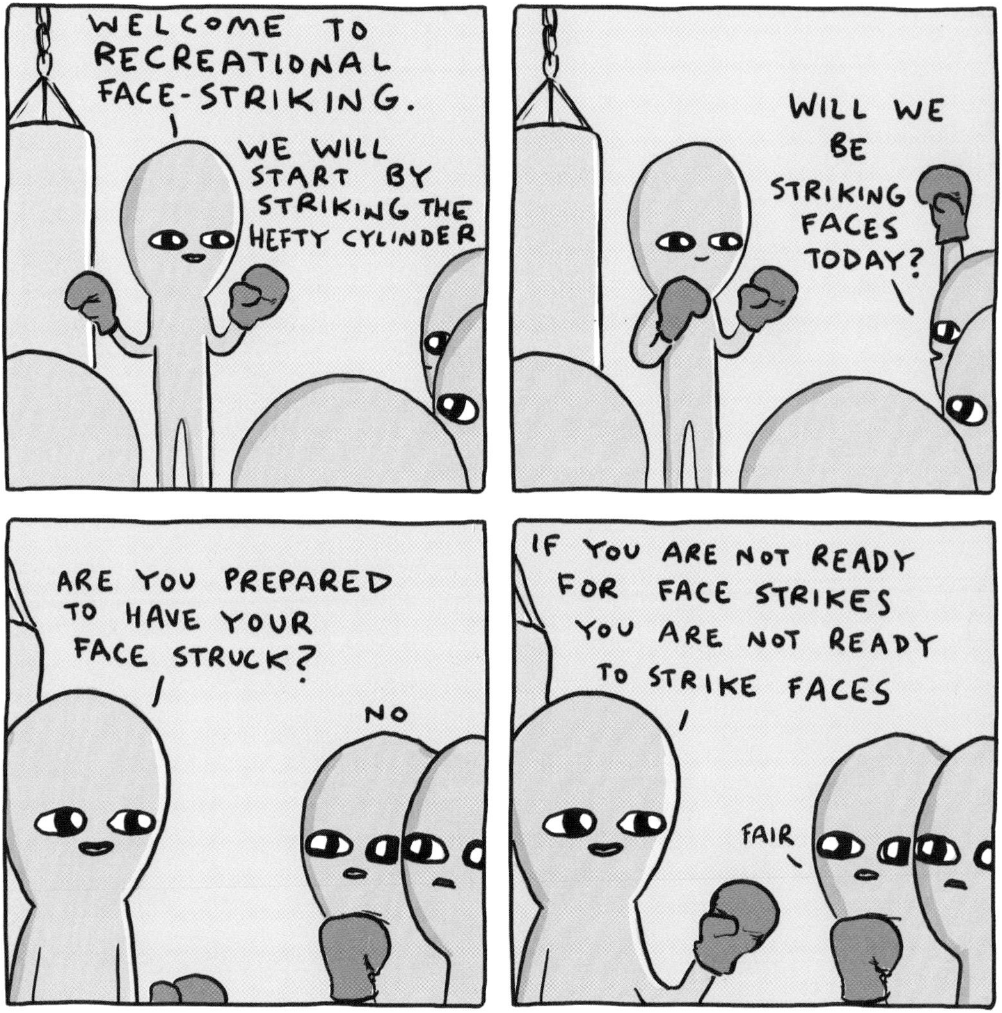
WELCOME TO RECREATIONAL FACE-STRIKING.
WE WILL START BY STRIKING THE HEFTY CYLINDER
WILL WE BE STRIKING FACES TODAY?
ARE YOU PREPARED TO HAVE YOUR FACE STRUCK?
NO
IF YOU ARE NOT READY FOR FACE STRIKES YOU ARE NOT READY TO STRIKE FACES
FAIR

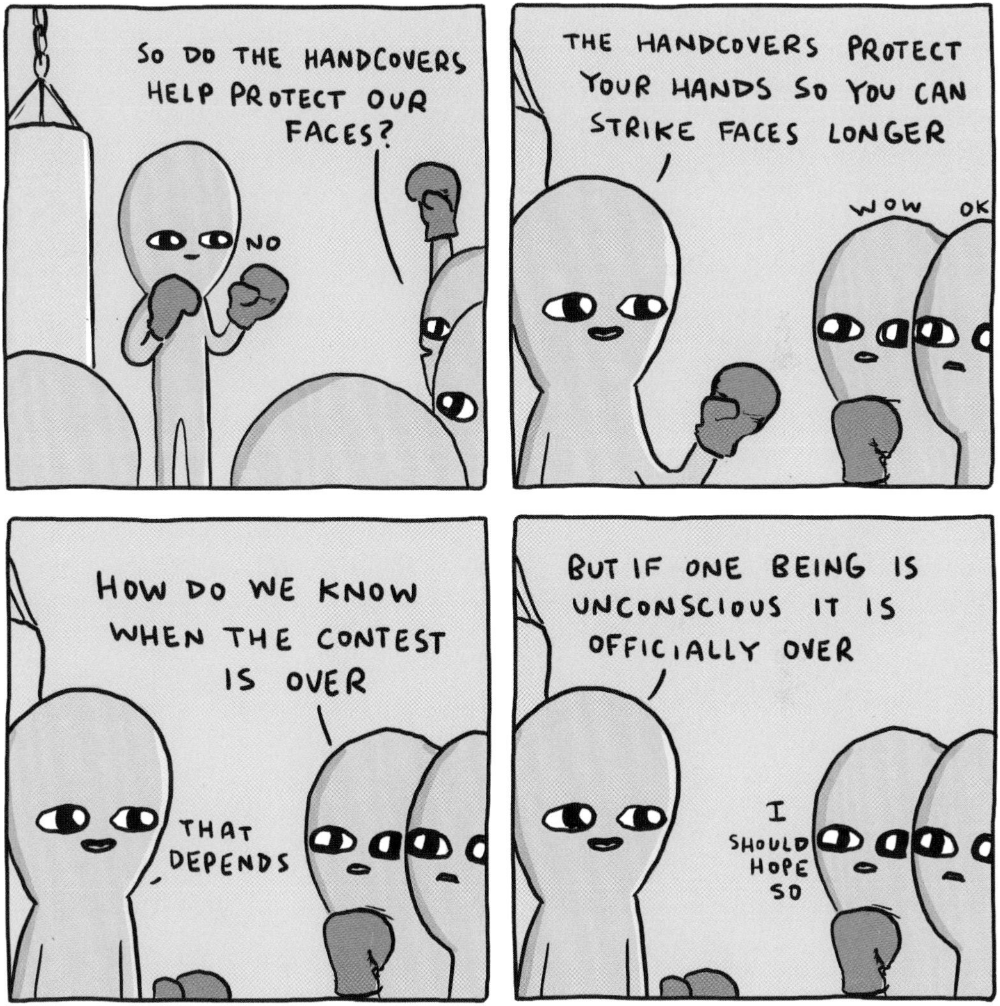
SO DO THE HANDCOVERS HELP PROTECT OUR FACES?
NO
THE HANDCOVERS PROTECT YOUR HANDS SO YOU CAN STRIKE FACES LONGER
WOW
OK
HOW DO WE KNOW WHEN THE CONTEST IS OVER
THAT DEPENDS
BUT IF ONE BEING IS UNCONSCIOUS IT IS OFFICIALLY OVER
I SHOULD HOPE SO

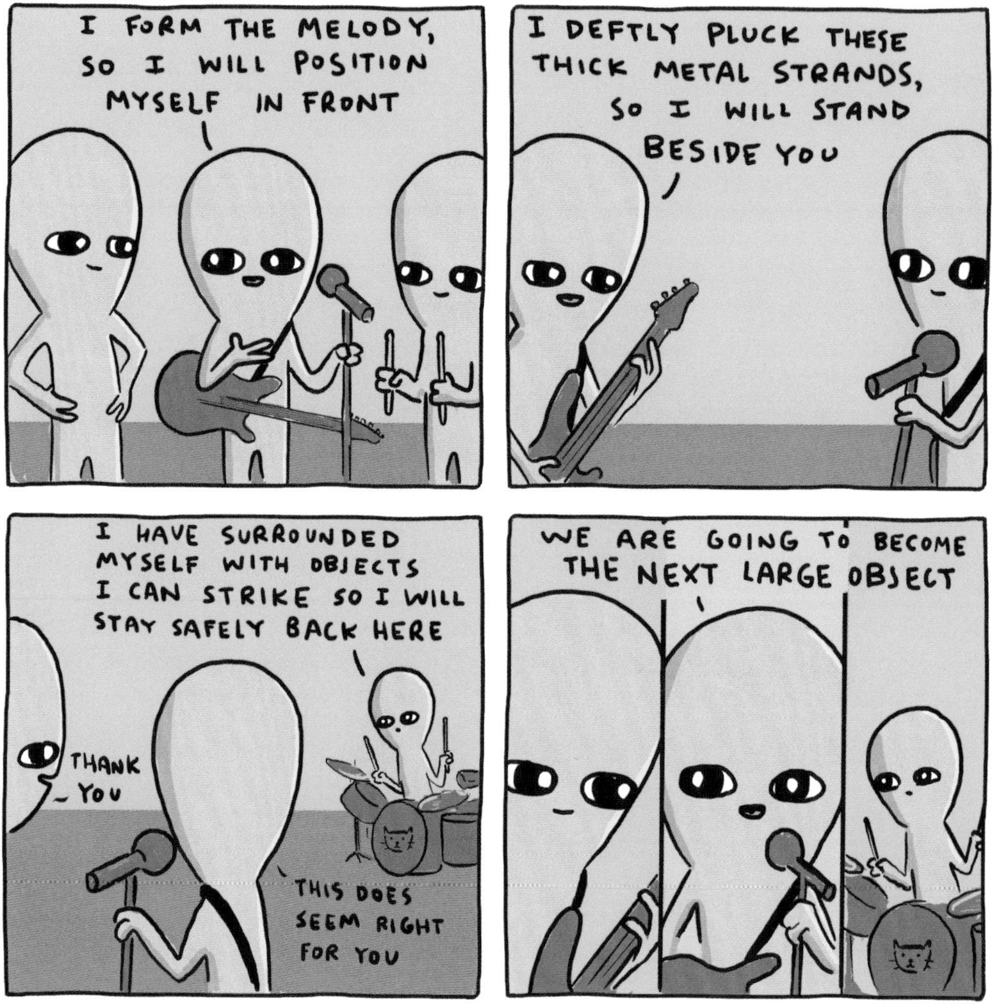
I FORM THE MELODY, SO I WILL POSITION MYSELF IN FRONT
I DEFTLY PLUCK THESE THICK METAL STRANDS, SO I WILL STAND BESIDE YOU
I HAVE SURROUNDED MYSELF WITH OBJECTS I CAN STRIKE SO I WILL STAY SAFELY BACK HERE
THANK YOU
THIS DOES SEEM RIGHT FOR YOU
WE ARE GOING TO BECOME THE NEXT LARGE OBJECT

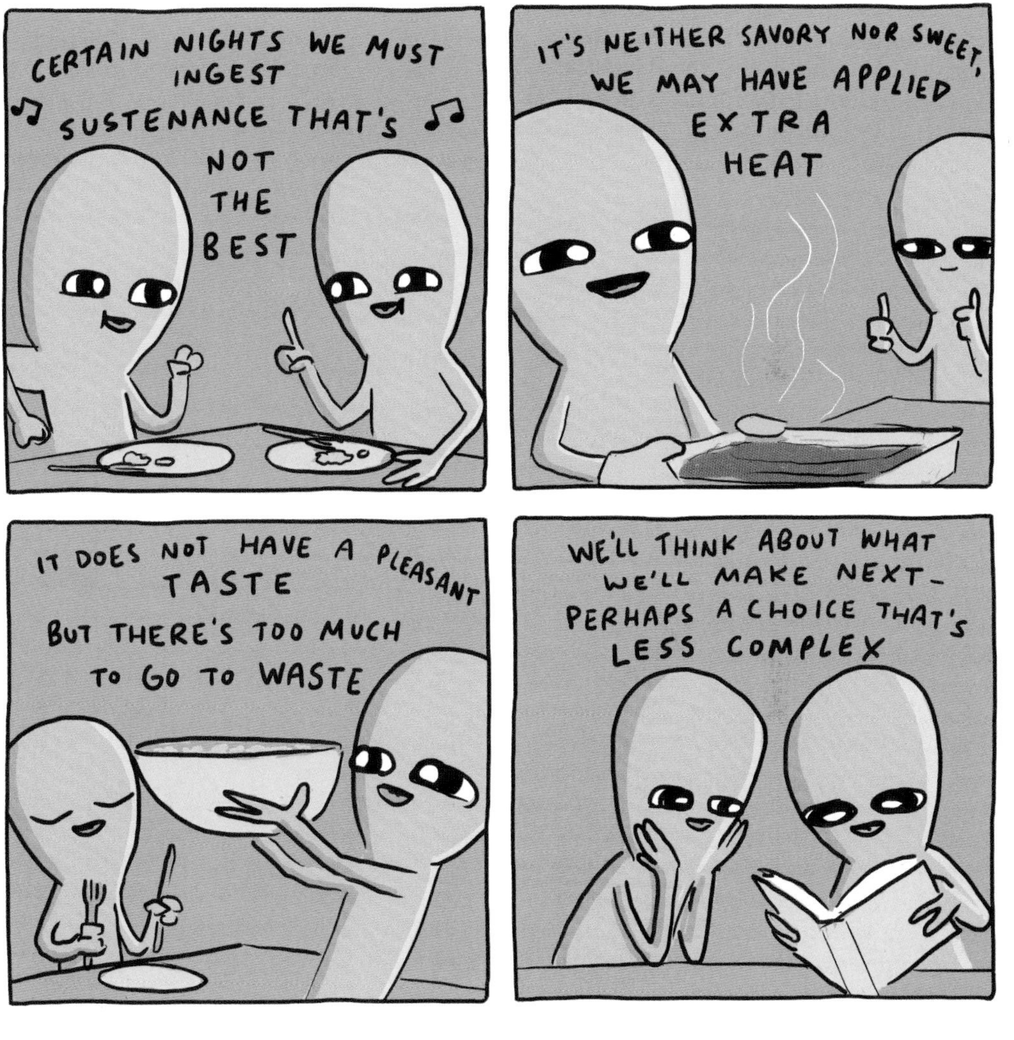
CERTAIN NIGHTS WE MUST INGEST
SUSTENANCE THAT'S NOT THE BEST
IT'S NEITHER SAVORY NOR SWEET,
WE MAY HAVE APPLIED EXTRA HEAT
IT DOES NOT HAVE A PLEASANT TASTE
BUT THERE'S TOO MUCH TO GO TO WASTE
WE'LL THINK ABOUT WHAT WE'LL MAKE NEXT-
PERHAPS A CHOICE THAT'S LESS COMPLEX

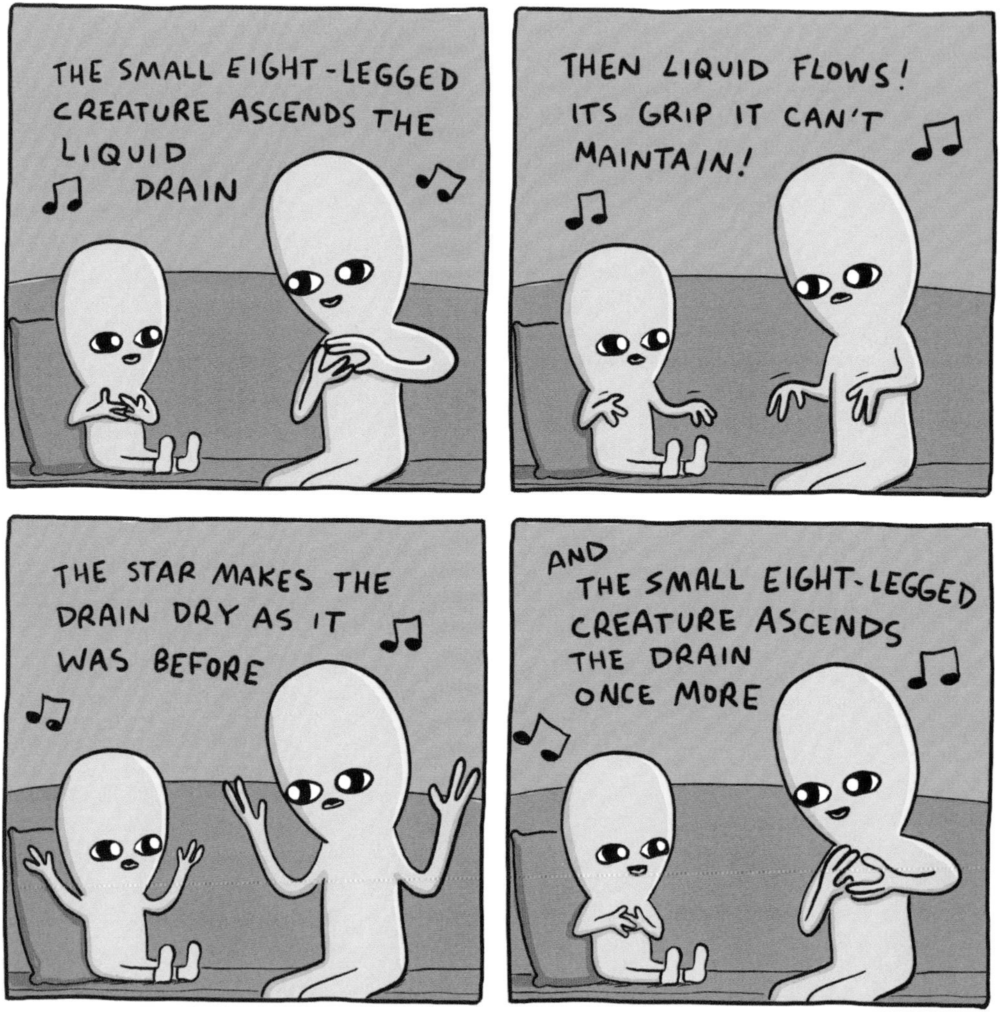

THE SMALL EIGHT-LEGGED CREATURE ASCENDS THE LIQUID DRAIN
THEN LIQUID FLOWS! ITS GRIP IT CAN'T MAINTAIN!
THE STAR MAKES THE DRAIN DRY AS IT WAS BEFORE
AND THE SMALL EIGHT-LEGGED CREATURE ASCENDS THE DRAIN ONCE MORE

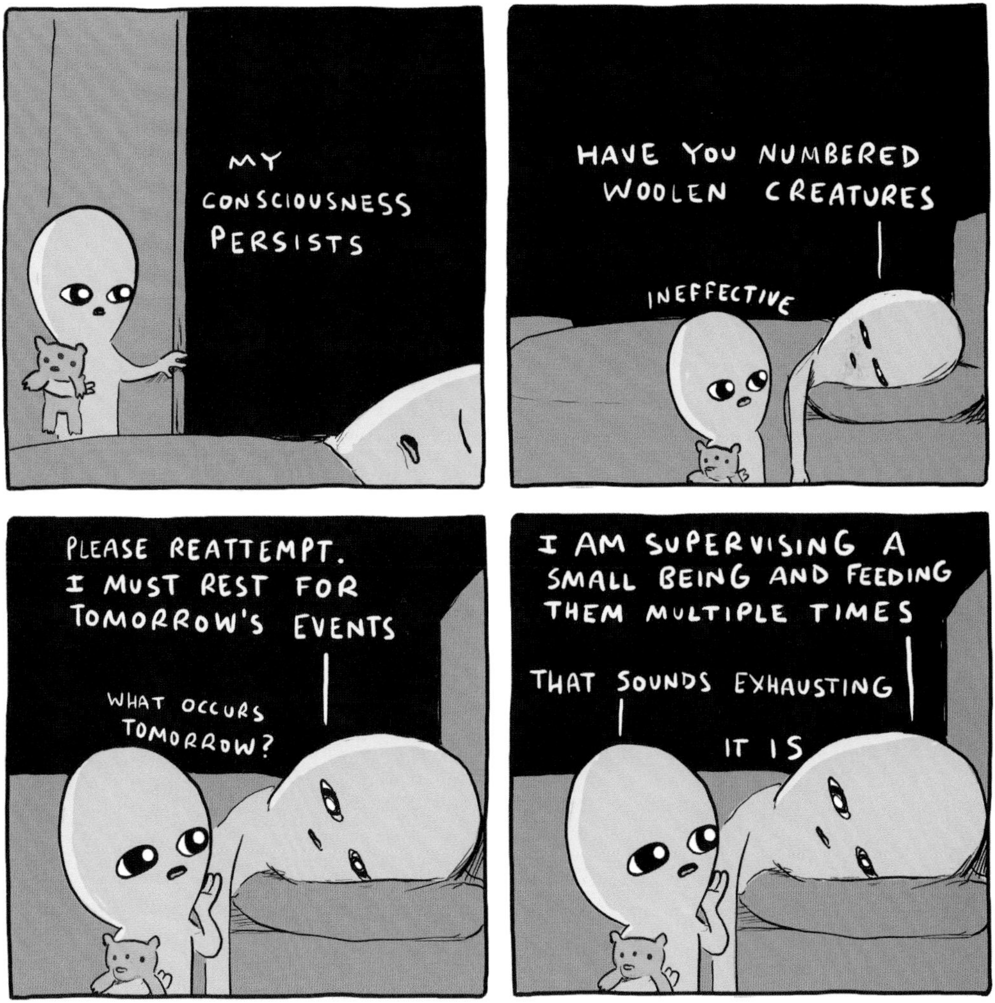
MY CONSCIOUSNESS PERSISTS
HAVE YOU NUMBERED WOOLEN CREATURES
INEFFECTIVE
PLEASE REATTEMPT. I MUST REST FOR TOMORROW'S EVENTS
WHAT OCCURS TOMORROW?
I AM SUPERVISING A SMALL BEING AND FEEDING THEM MULTIPLE TIMES
THAT SOUNDS EXHAUSTING
IT IS

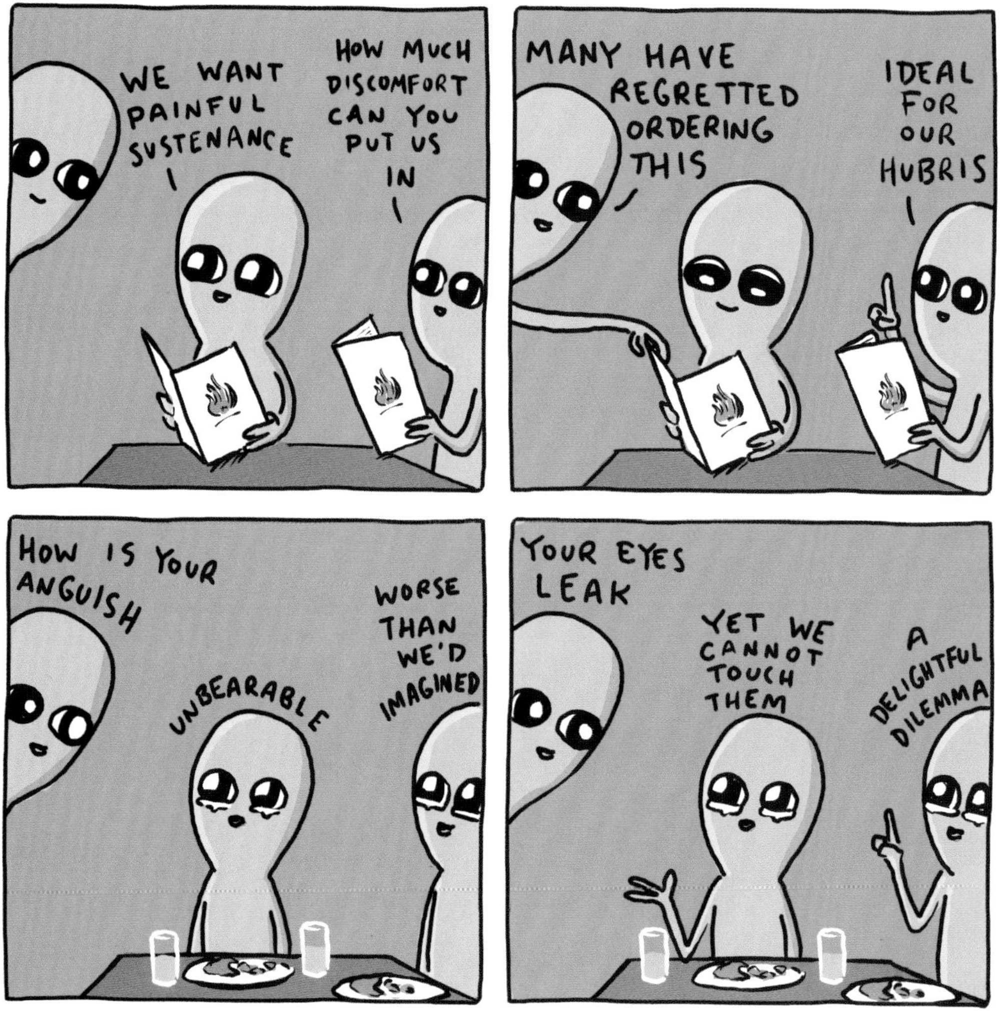
WE WANT PAINFUL SUSTENANCE
HOW MUCH DISCOMFORT CAN YOU PUT US IN
MANY HAVE REGRETTED ORDERING THIS
IDEAL FOR OUR HUBRIS
HOW IS YOUR ANGUISH
UNBEARABLE
WORSE THAN WE'D IMAGINED
YOUR EYES LEAK
YET WE CANNOT TOUCH THEM
A DELIGHTFUL DILEMMA

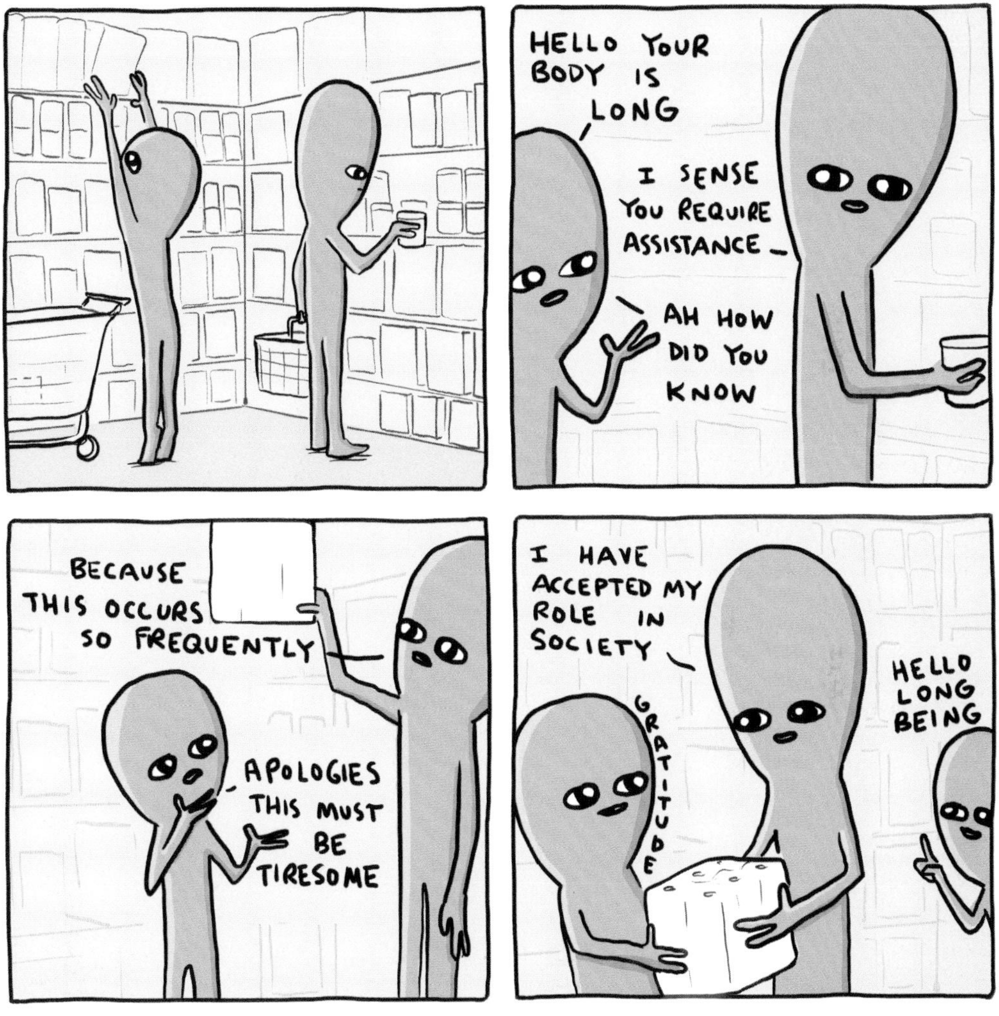
HELLO YOUR BODY IS LONG
I SENSE YOU REQUIRE ASSISTANCE
AH HOW DID YOU KNOW
BECAUSE THIS OCCURS SO FREQUENTLY
APOLOGIES THIS MUST BE TIRESOME
I HAVE ACCEPTED MY ROLE IN SOCIETY
GRATITUDE
HELLO LONG BEING

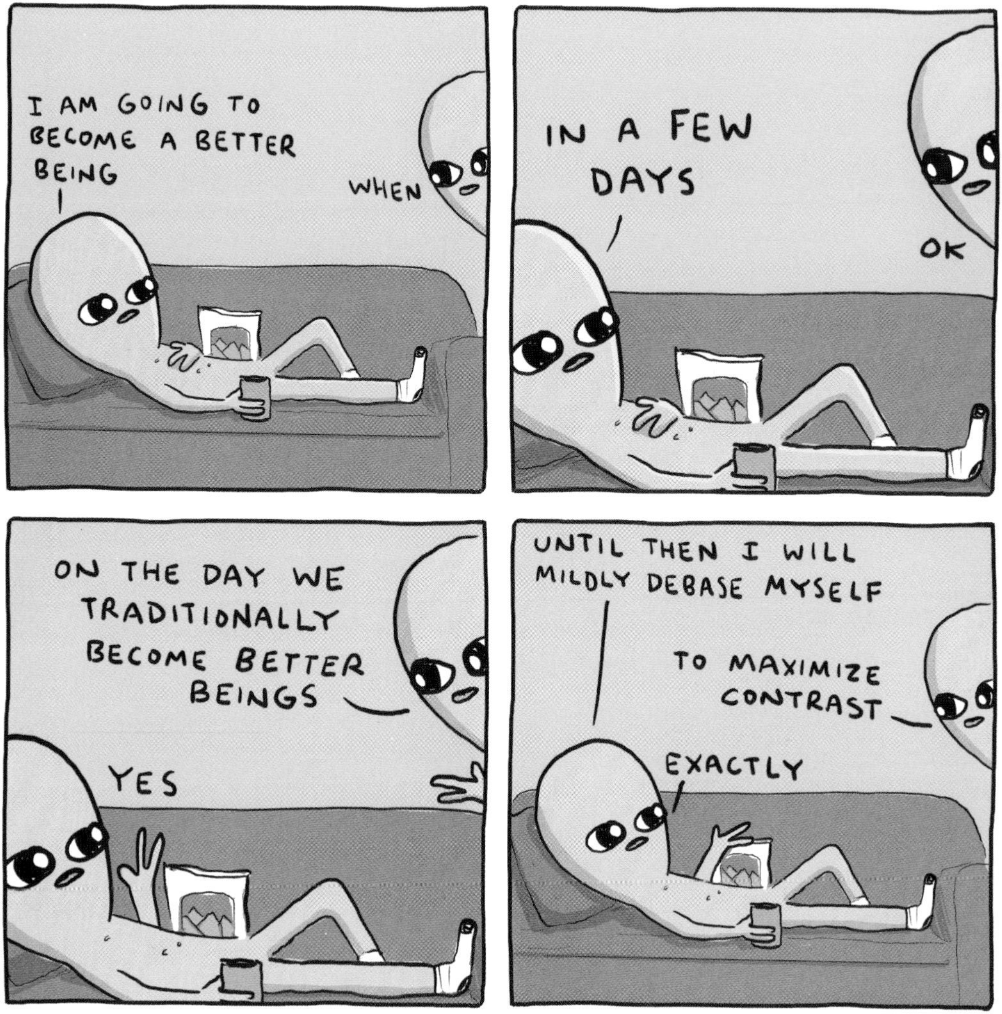
I AM GOING TO BECOME A BETTER BEING
WHEN
IN A FEW DAYS
OK
ON THE DAY WE TRADITIONALLY BECOME BETTER BEINGS
YES
UNTIL THEN I WILL MILDLY DEBASE MYSELF
TO MAXIMIZE CONTRAST
EXACTLY

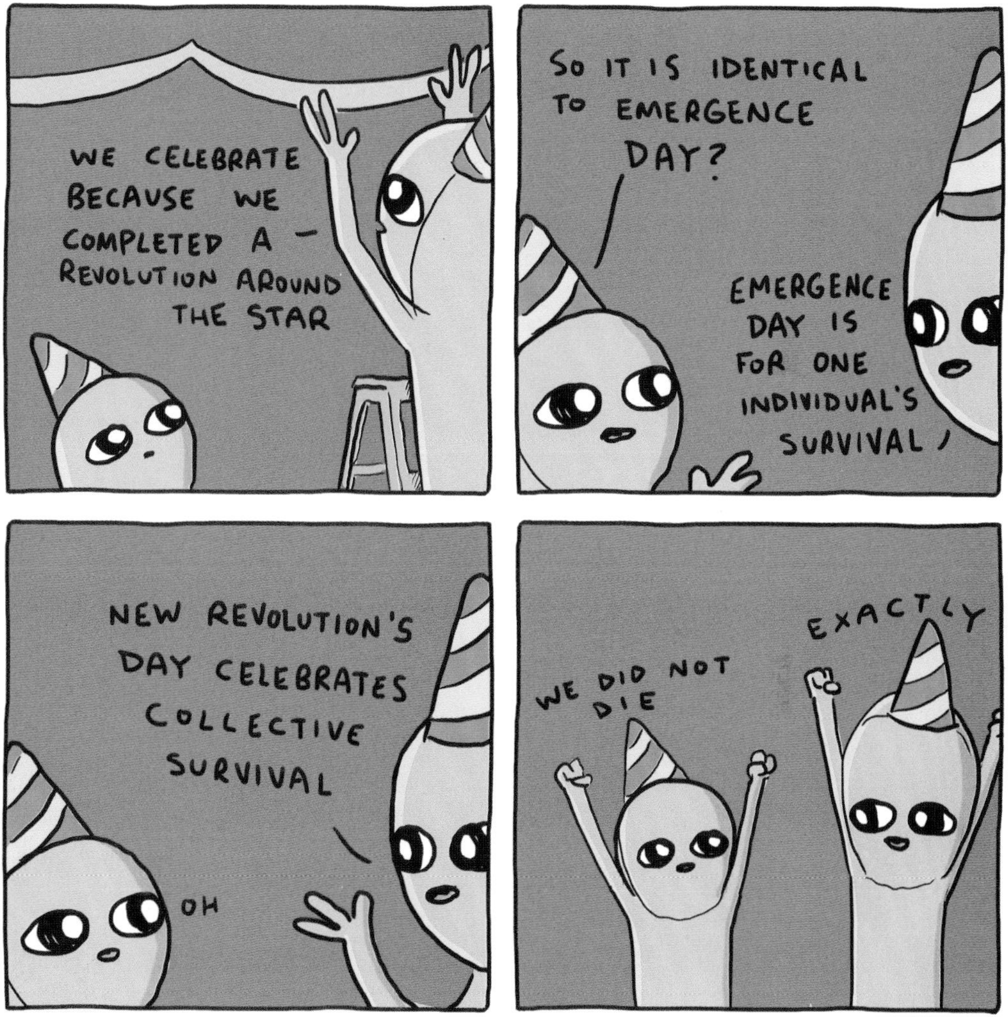
WE CELEBRATE BECAUSE WE COMPLETED A REVOLUTION AROUND THE STAR
SO IT IS IDENTICAL TO EMERGENCE DAY?
EMERGENCE DAY IS FOR ONE INDIVIDUAL'S SURVIVAL
NEW REVOLUTION'S DAY CELEBRATES COLLECTIVE SURVIVAL
OH
WE DID NOT DIE
EXACTLY

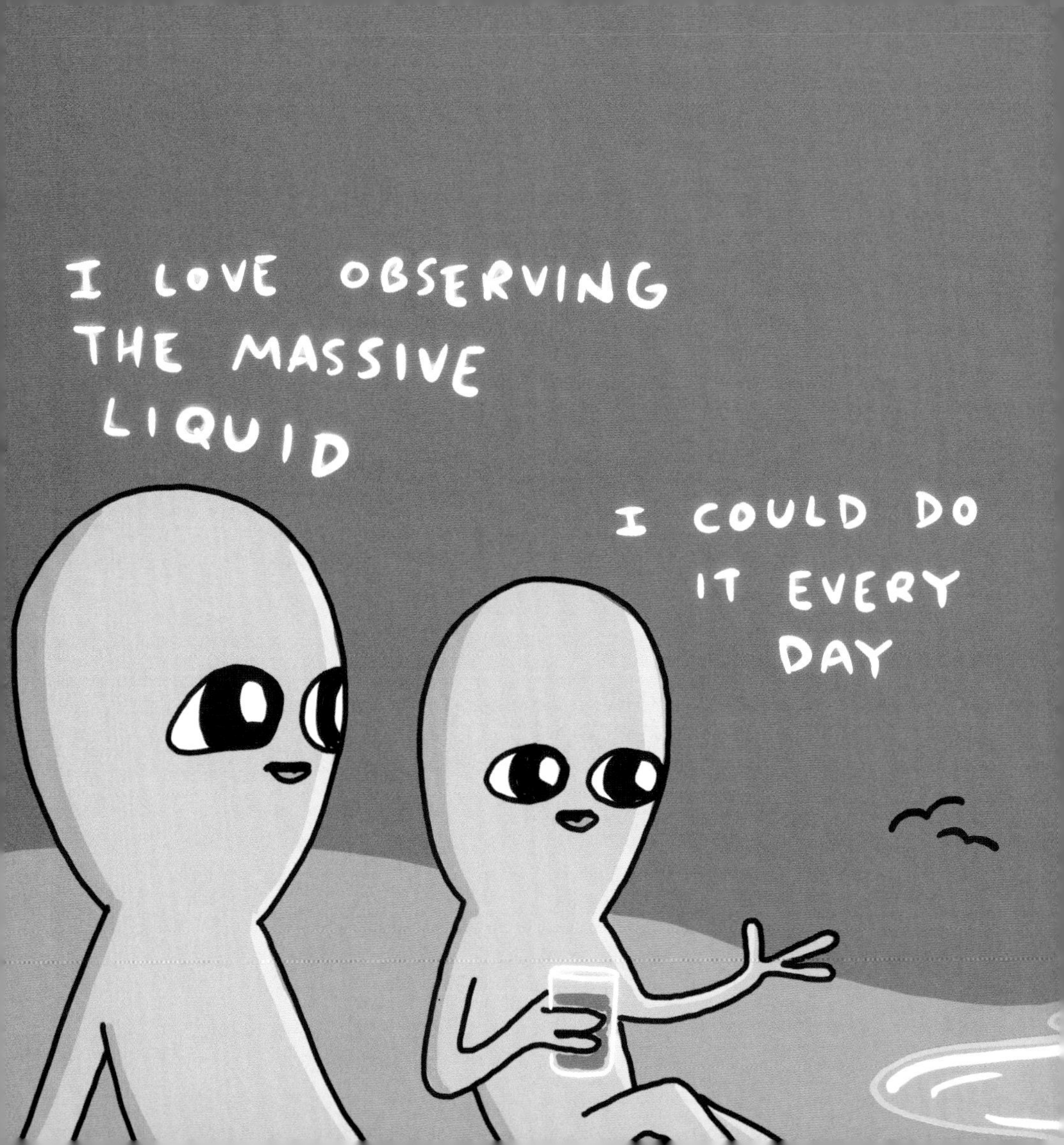
I LOVE OBSERVING THE MASSIVE LIQUID
I COULD DO IT EVERY DAY

NATURE

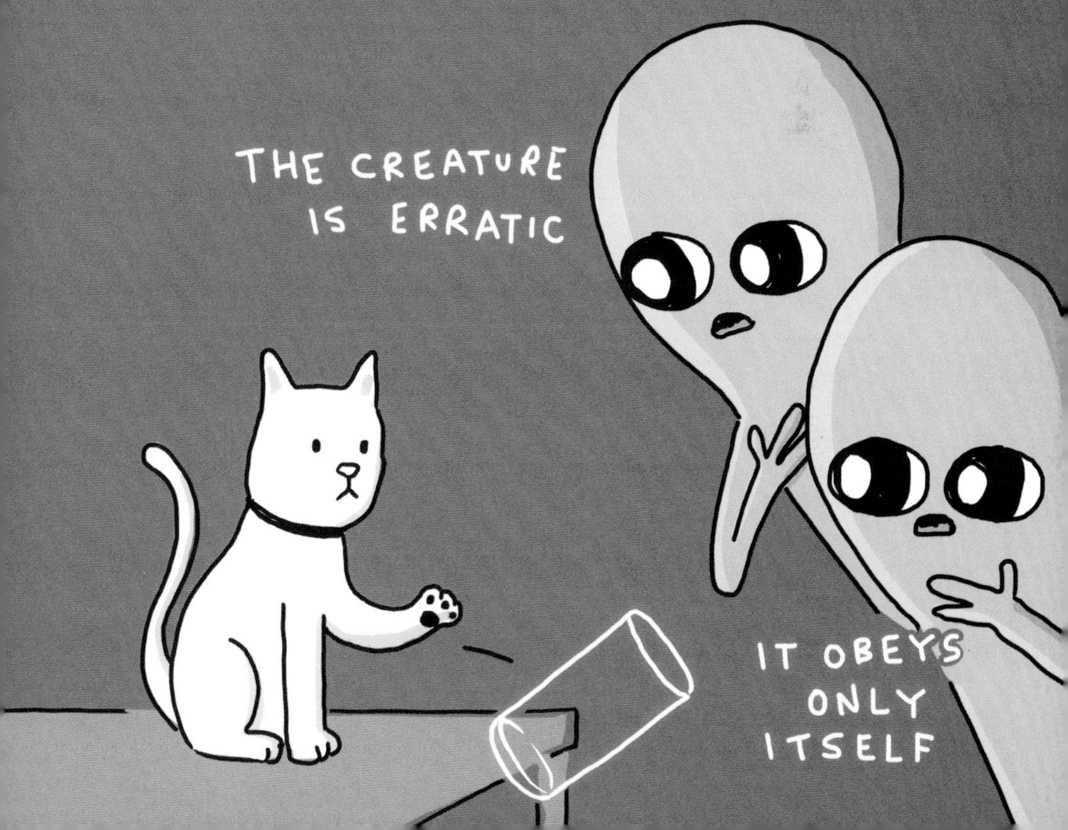

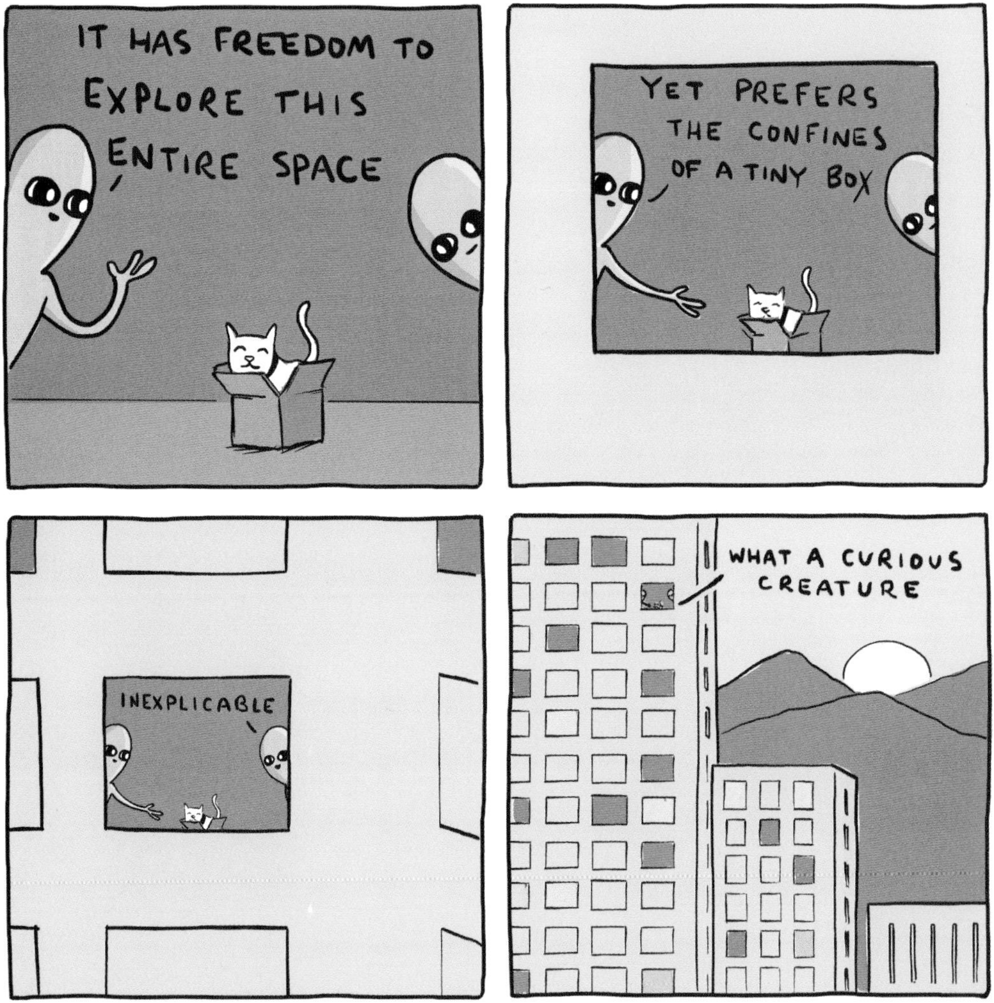
IT HAS FREEDOM TO EXPLORE THIS ENTIRE SPACE
YET PREFERS THE CONFINES OF A TINY BOX
INEXPLICABLE
WHAT A CURIOUS CREATURE

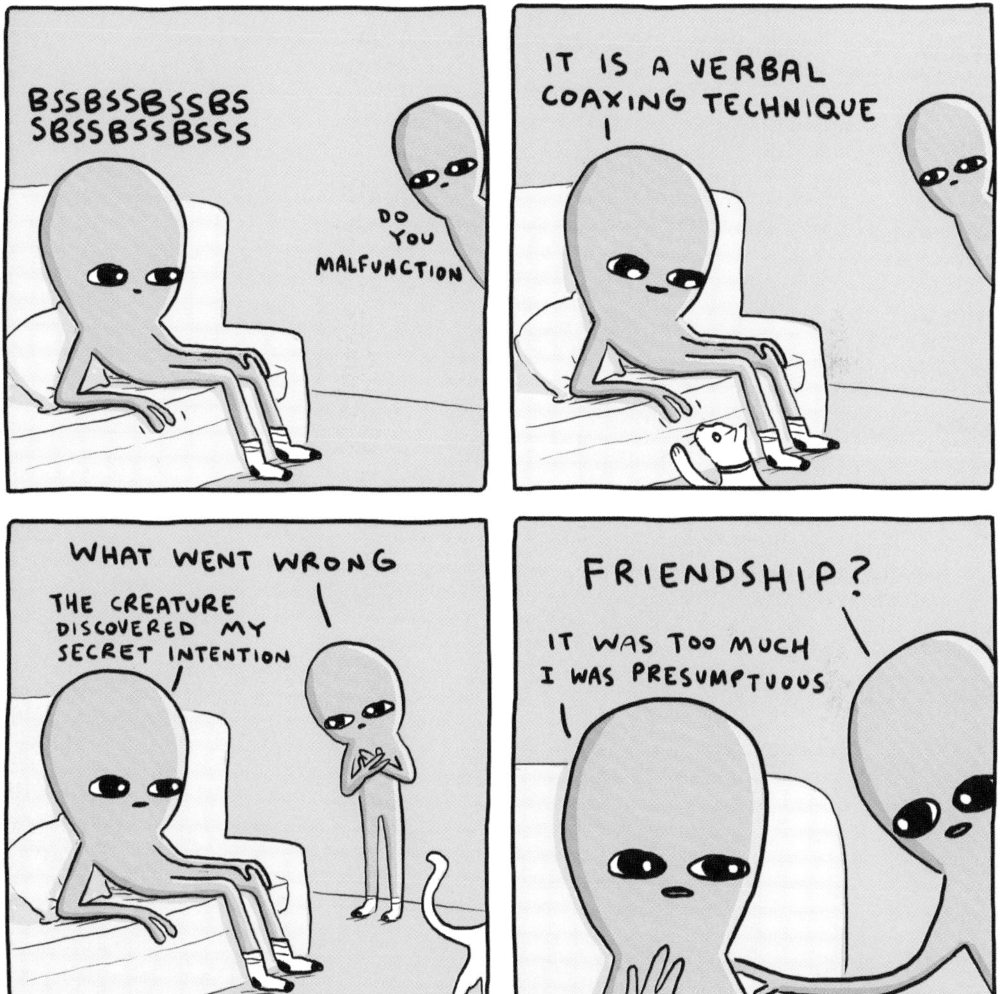
BSSBSSBSSBS SBSSBSSBSSS
DO YOU MALFUNCTION
IT IS A VERBAL COAXING TECHNIQUE
WHAT WENT WRONG
THE CREATURE DISCOVERED MY SECRET INTENTION
FRIENDSHIP?
IT WAS TOO MUCH I WAS PRESUMPTUOUS

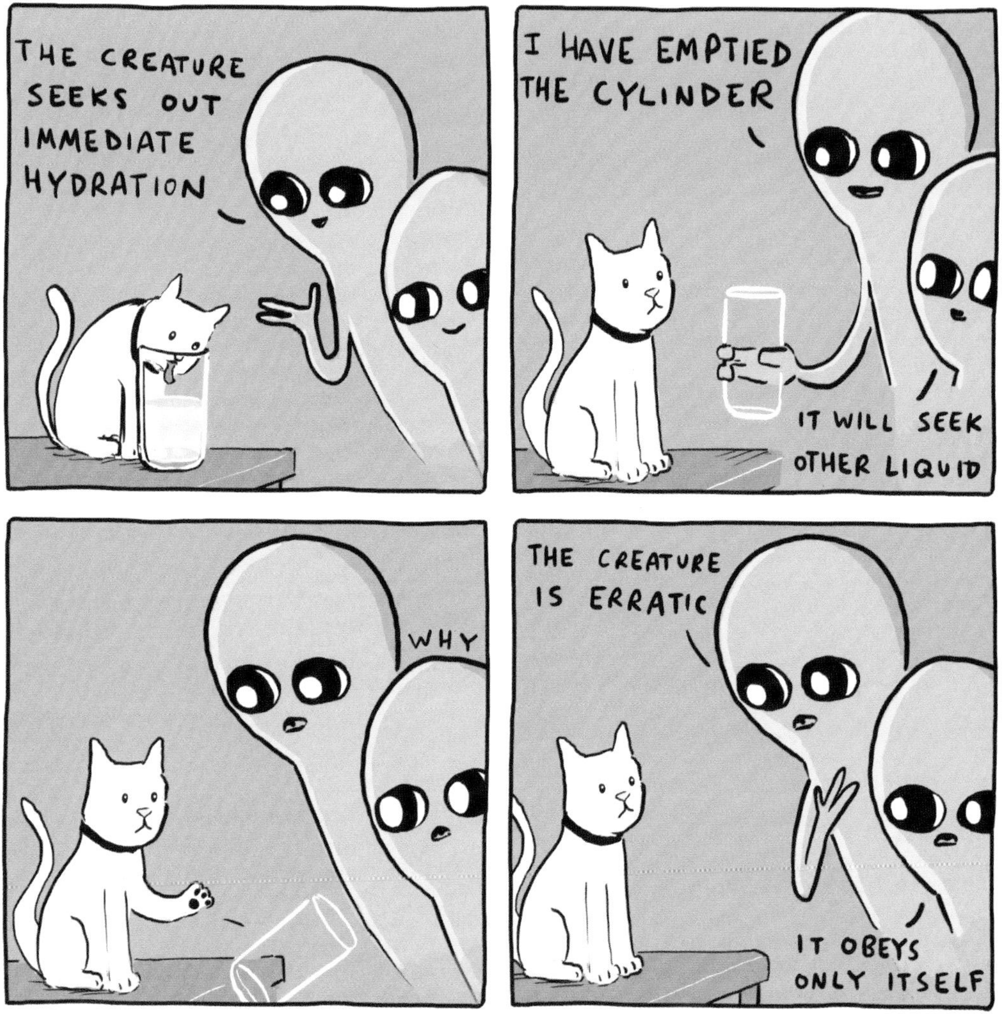
THE CREATURE SEEKS OUT IMMEDIATE HYDRATION
I HAVE EMPTIED THE CYLINDER
IT WILL SEEK OTHER LIQUID
WHY
THE CREATURE IS ERRATIC
IT OBEYS ONLY ITSELF

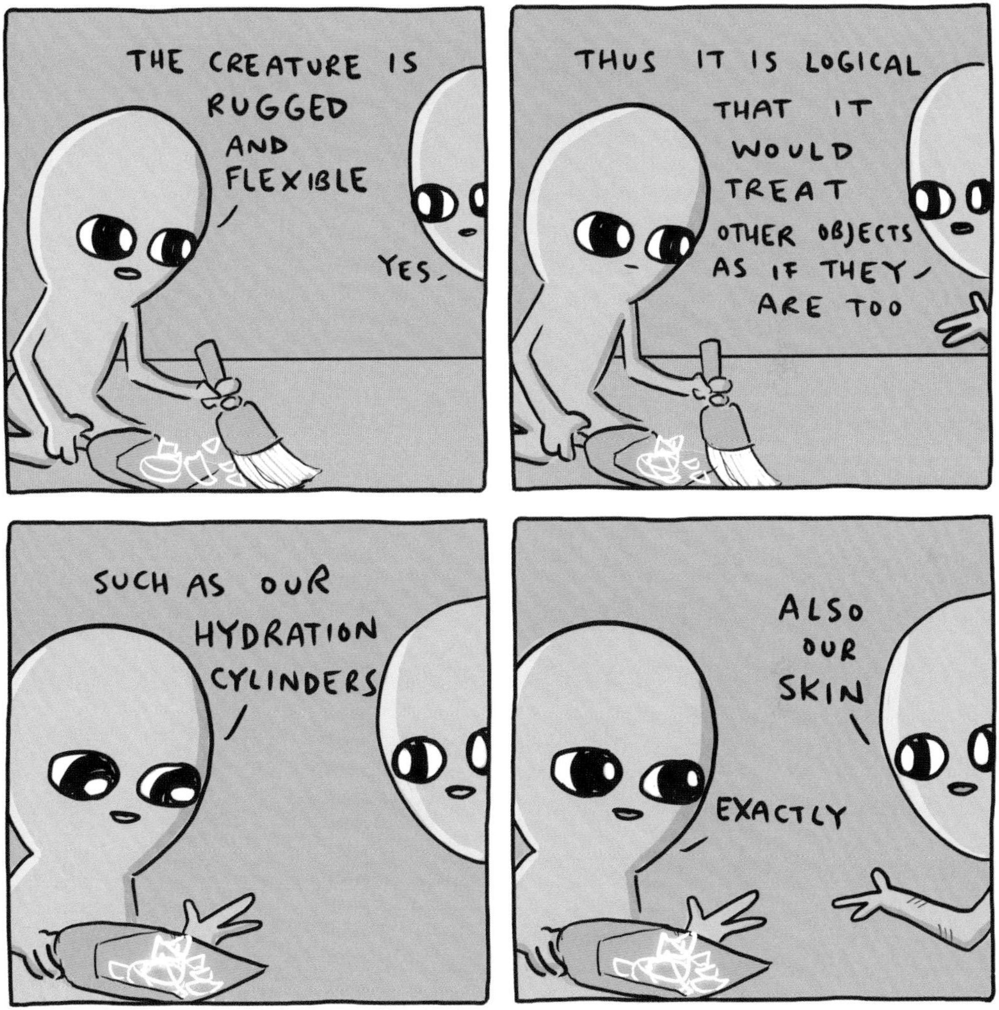
THE CREATURE IS RUGGED AND FLEXIBLE
YES.
THUS IT IS LOGICAL THAT IT WOULD TREAT OTHER OBJECTS AS IF THEY ARE TOO
SUCH AS OUR HYDRATION CYLINDERS
ALSO OUR SKIN
EXACTLY

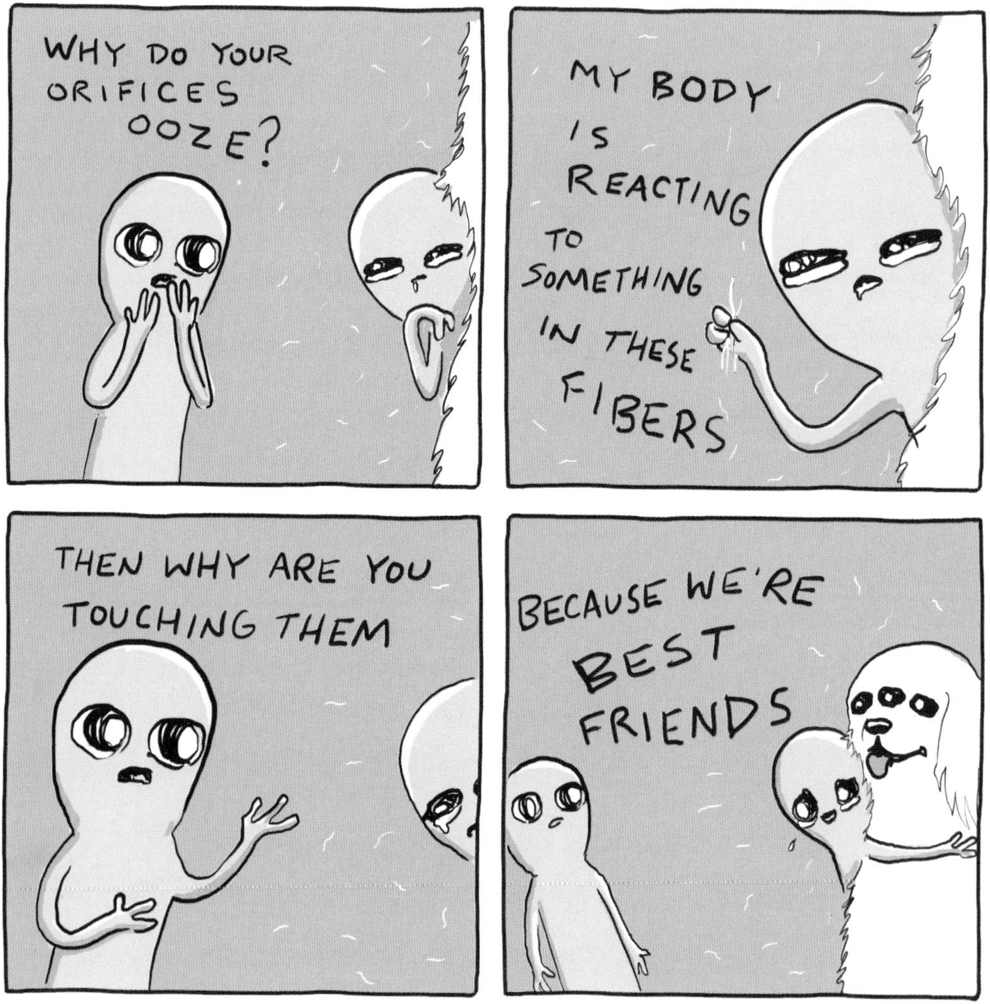
WHY DO YOUR ORIFICES OOZE?
MY BODY IS REACTING TO SOMETHING IN THESE FIBERS
THEN WHY ARE YOU TOUCHING THEM
BECAUSE WE'RE BEST FRIENDS

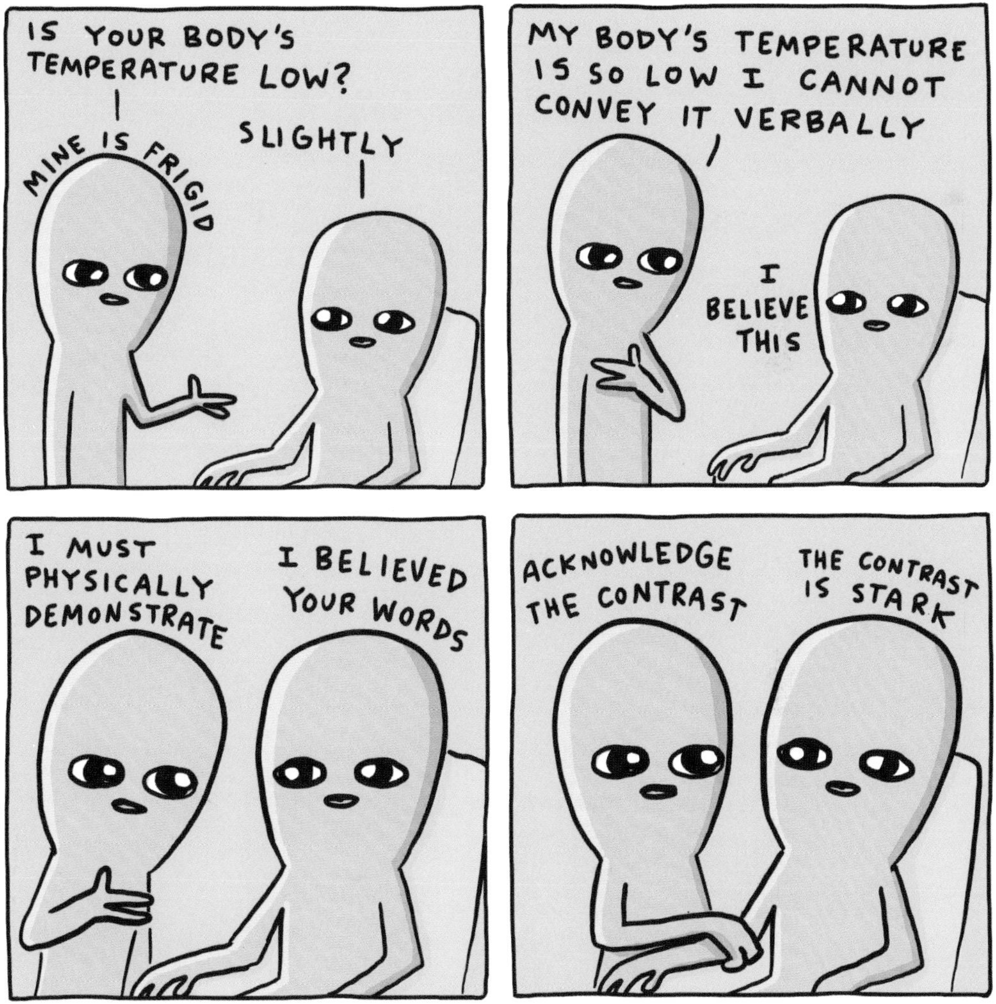
IS YOUR BODY'S TEMPERATURE LOW?
MINE IS FRIGID
SLIGHTLY
MY BODY'S TEMPERATURE IS SO LOW I CANNOT CONVEY IT VERBALLY
I BELIEVE THIS
I MUST PHYSICALLY DEMONSTRATE
I BELIEVED YOUR WORDS
ACKNOWLEDGE THE CONTRAST
THE CONTRAST IS STARK

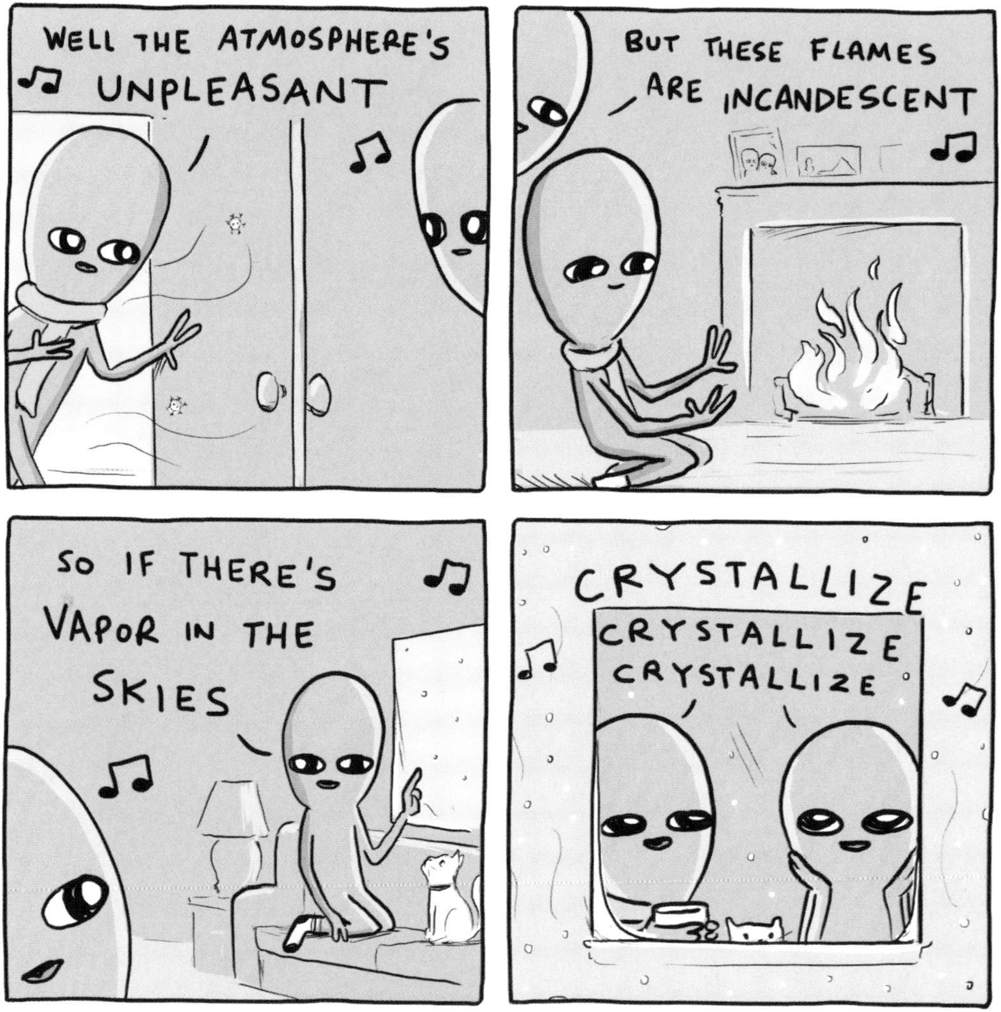
WELL THE ATMOSPHERE'S
UNPLEASANT
BUT THESE FLAMES
ARE INCANDESCENT
SO IF THERE'S
VAPOR IN THE
SKIES
CRYSTALLIZE
CRYSTALLIZE
CRYSTALLIZE

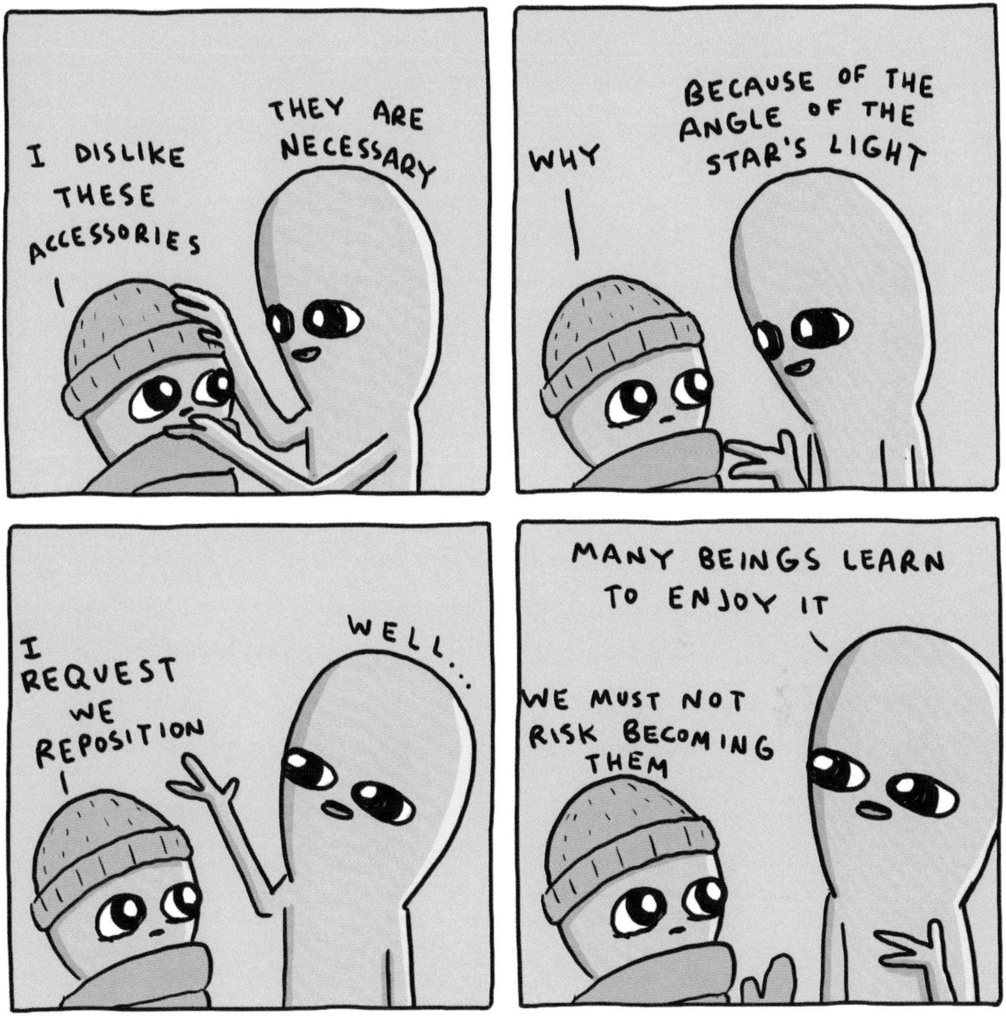
I DISLIKE THESE ACCESSORIES
THEY ARE NECESSARY
WHY
BECAUSE OF THE ANGLE OF THE STAR'S LIGHT
I REQUEST WE REPOSITION
WELL...
MANY BEINGS LEARN TO ENJOY IT
WE MUST NOT RISK BECOMING THEM

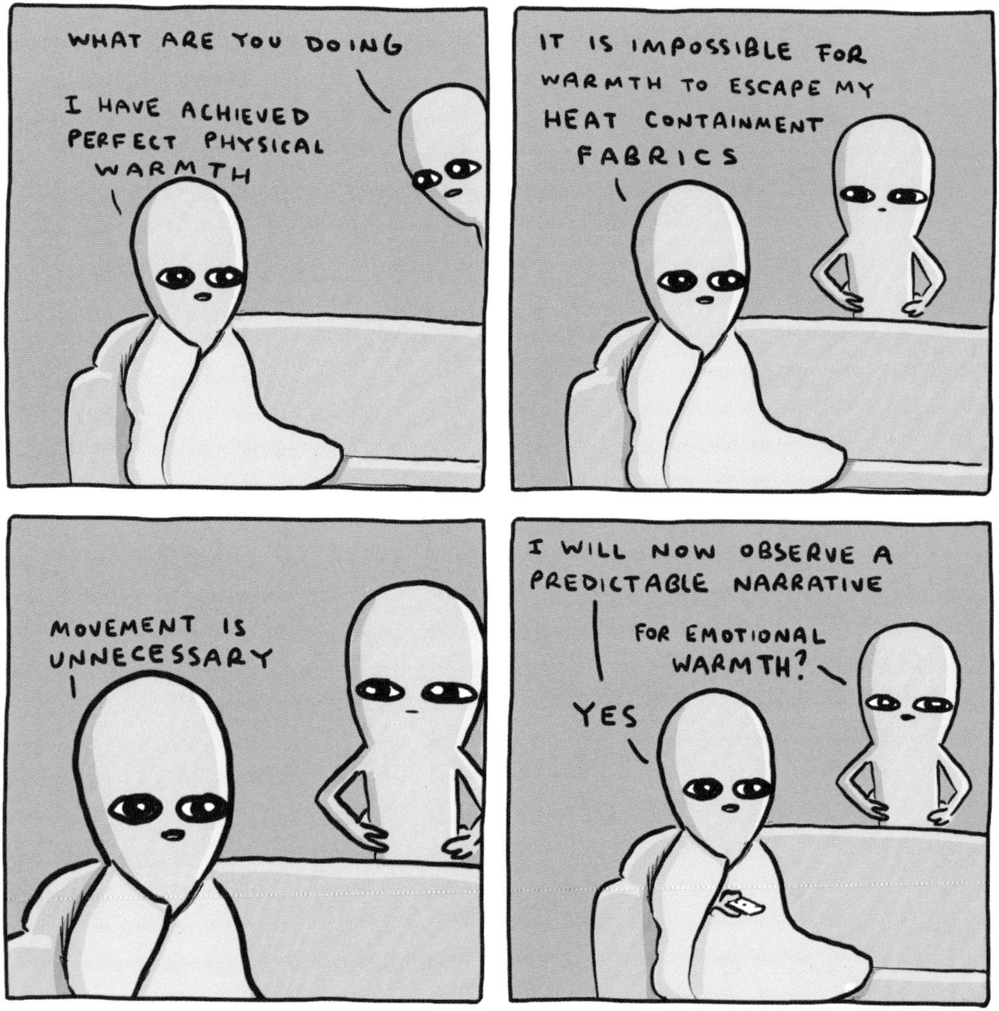
WHAT ARE YOU DOING
I HAVE ACHIEVED PERFECT PHYSICAL WARMTH
IT IS IMPOSSIBLE FOR WARMTH TO ESCAPE MY HEAT CONTAINMENT FABRICS
MOVEMENT IS UNNECESSARY
I WILL NOW OBSERVE A PREDICTABLE NARRATIVE
FOR EMOTIONAL WARMTH?
YES

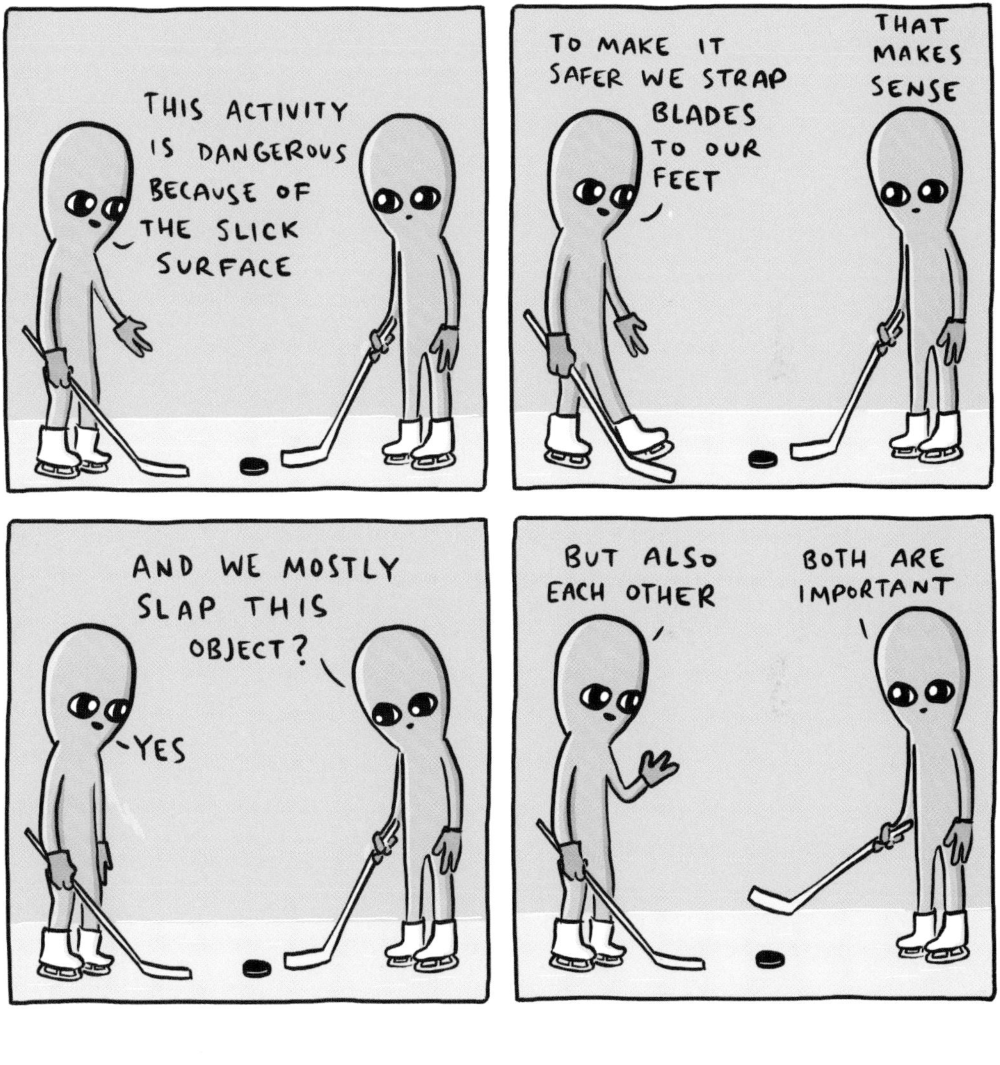
THIS ACTIVITY IS DANGEROUS BECAUSE OF THE SLICK SURFACE
TO MAKE IT SAFER WE STRAP BLADES TO OUR FEET
THAT MAKES SENSE
AND WE MOSTLY SLAP THIS OBJECT?
YES
BUT ALSO EACH OTHER
BOTH ARE IMPORTANT

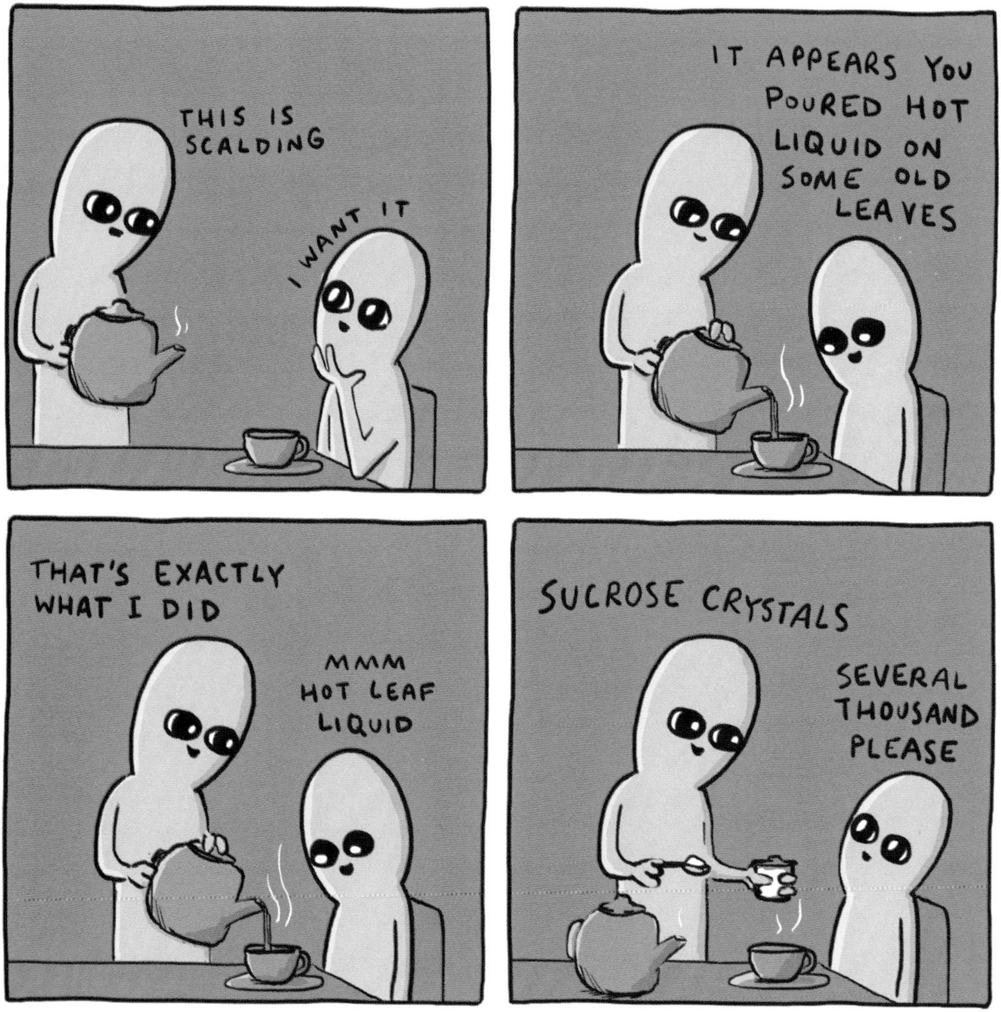
THIS IS SCALDING
I WANT IT
IT APPEARS YOU POURED HOT LIQUID ON SOME OLD LEAVES
THAT'S EXACTLY WHAT I DID
MMM HOT LEAF LIQUID
SUCROSE CRYSTALS
SEVERAL THOUSAND PLEASE

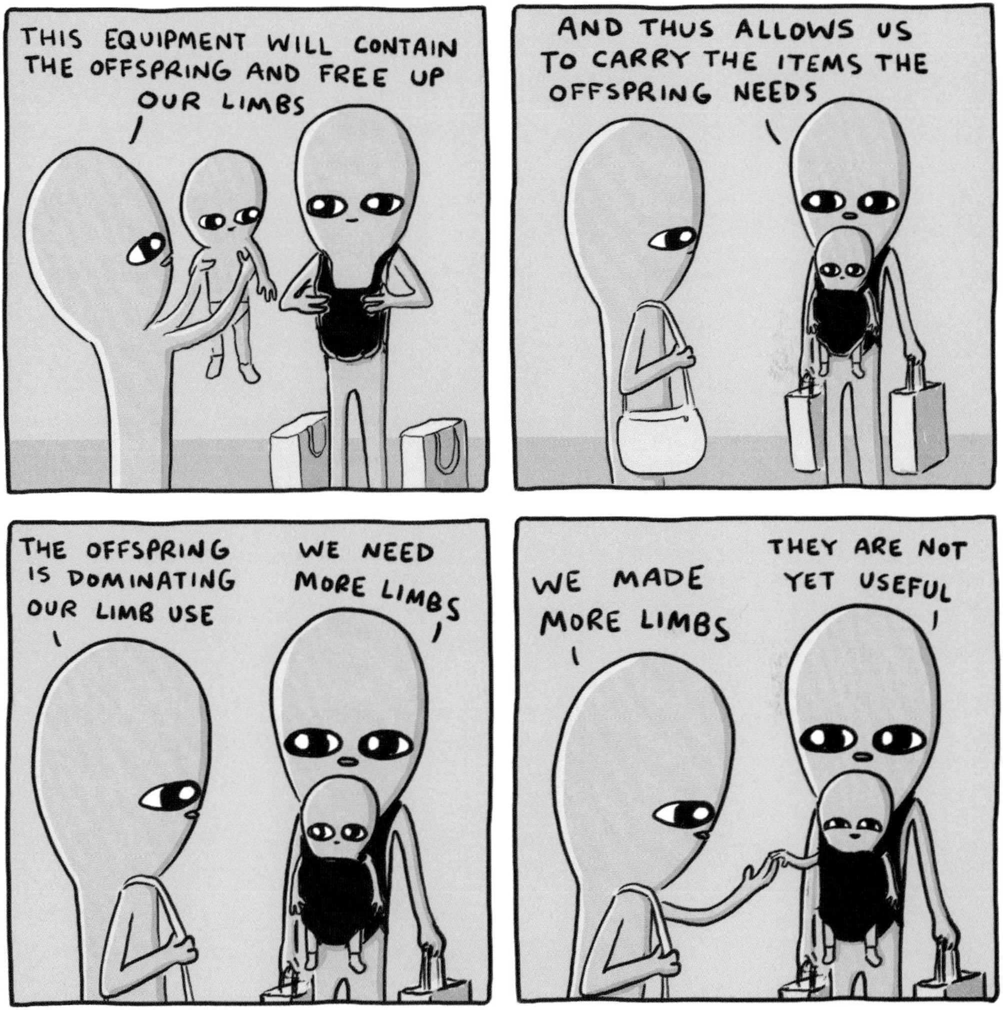
THIS EQUIPMENT WILL CONTAIN THE OFFSPRING AND FREE UP OUR LIMBS
AND THUS ALLOWS US TO CARRY THE ITEMS THE OFFSPRING NEEDS
THE OFFSPRING IS DOMINATING OUR LIMB USE
WE NEED MORE LIMBS
WE MADE MORE LIMBS
THEY ARE NOT YET USEFUL

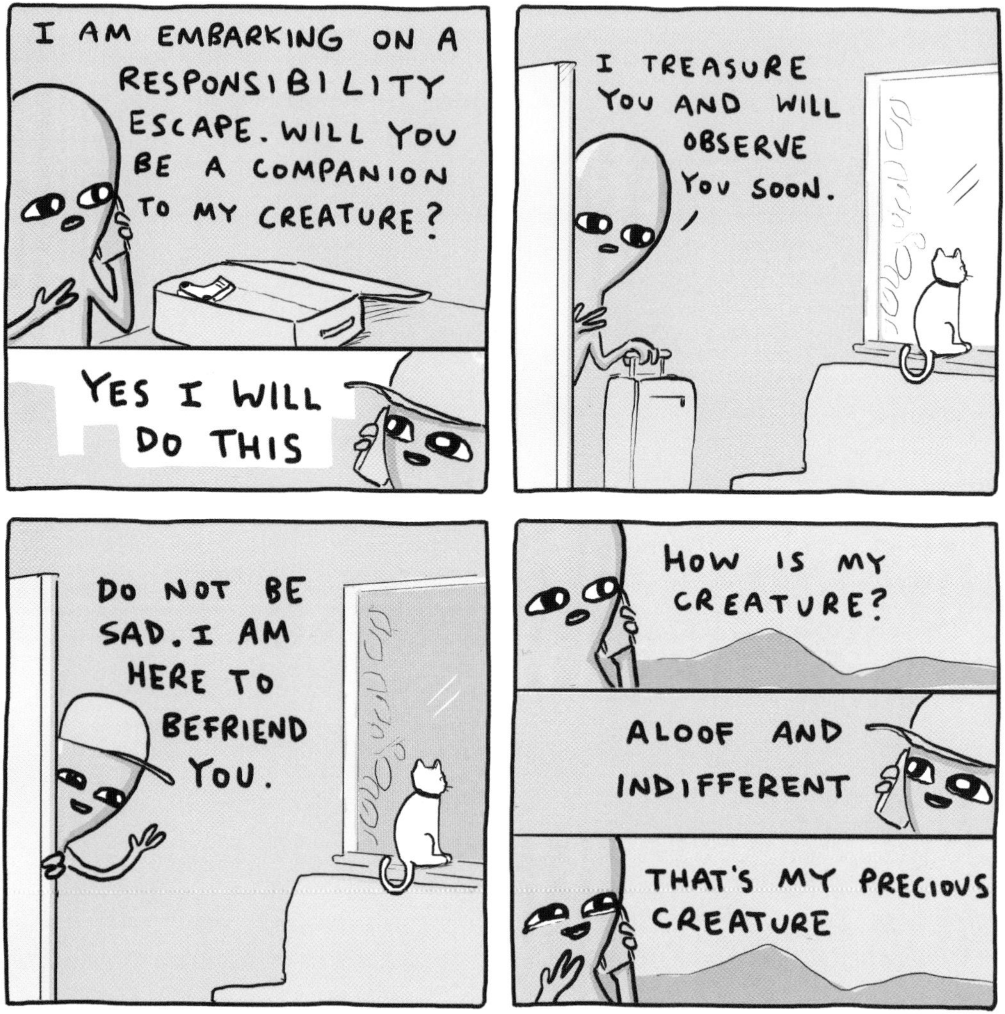
I AM EMBARKING ON A RESPONSIBILITY ESCAPE. WILL YOU BE A COMPANION TO MY CREATURE?
YES I WILL DO THIS
I TREASURE YOU AND WILL OBSERVE YOU SOON.
DO NOT BE SAD. I AM HERE TO BEFRIEND YOU.
HOW IS MY CREATURE?
ALOOF AND INDIFFERENT
THAT'S MY PRECIOUS CREATURE

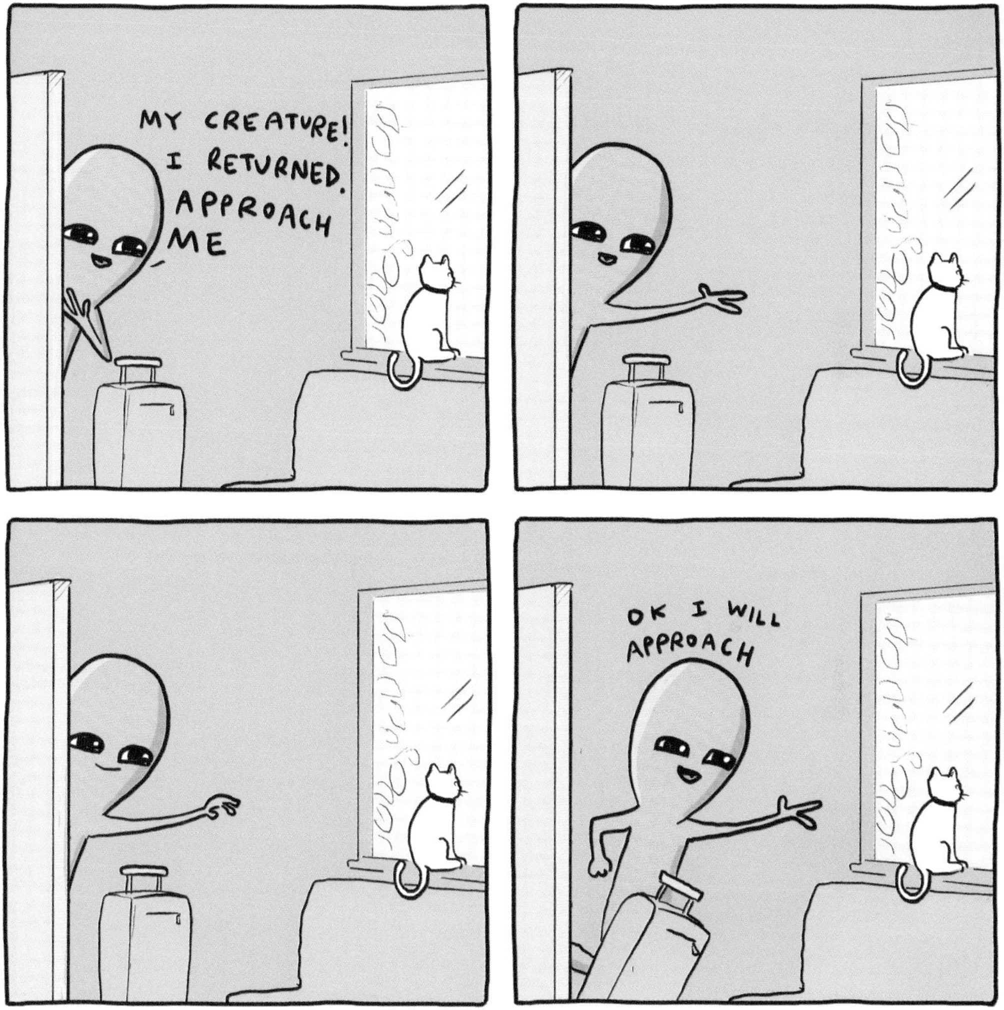
MY CREATURE! I RETURNED. APPROACH ME
OK I WILL APPROACH

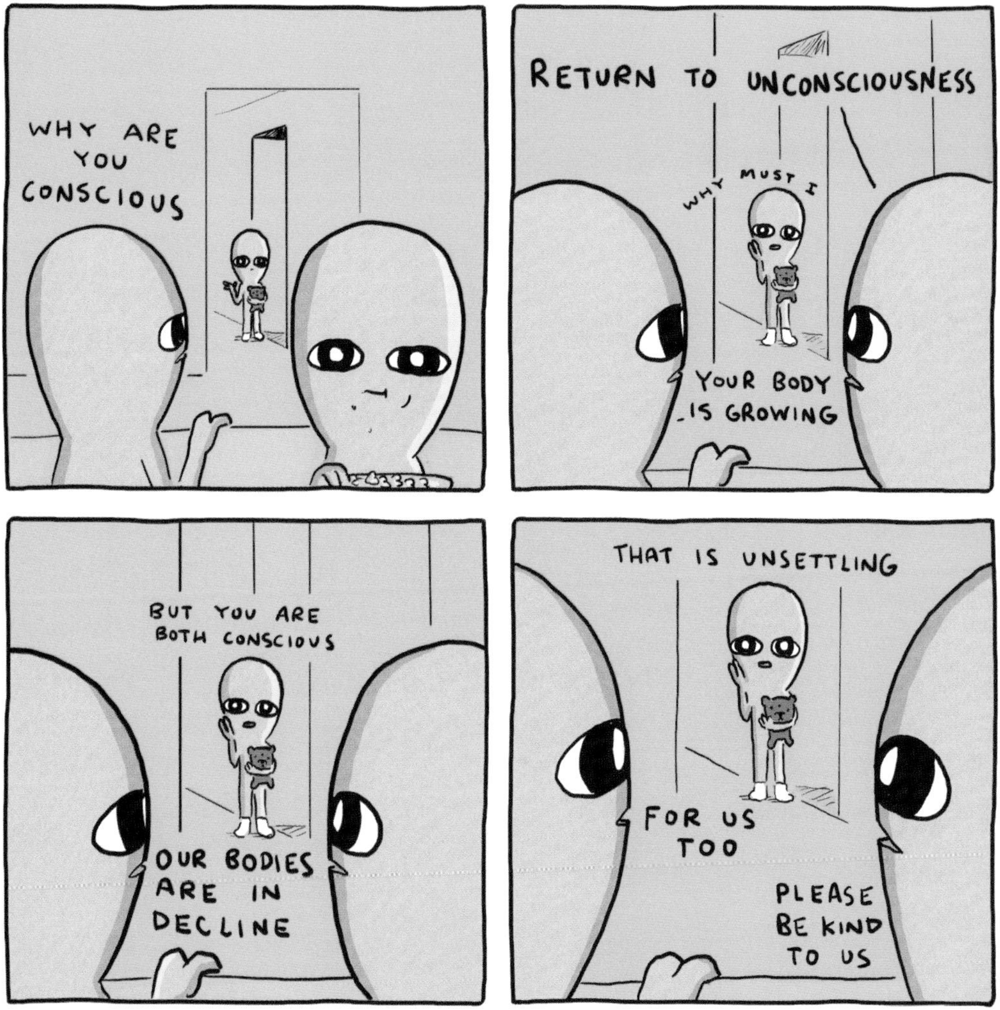
WHY ARE YOU CONSCIOUS
RETURN TO UNCONSCIOUSNESS
WHY MUST I
YOUR BODY IS GROWING
BUT YOU ARE BOTH CONSCIOUS
OUR BODIES ARE IN DECLINE
THAT IS UNSETTLING
FOR US TOO
PLEASE BE KIND TO US

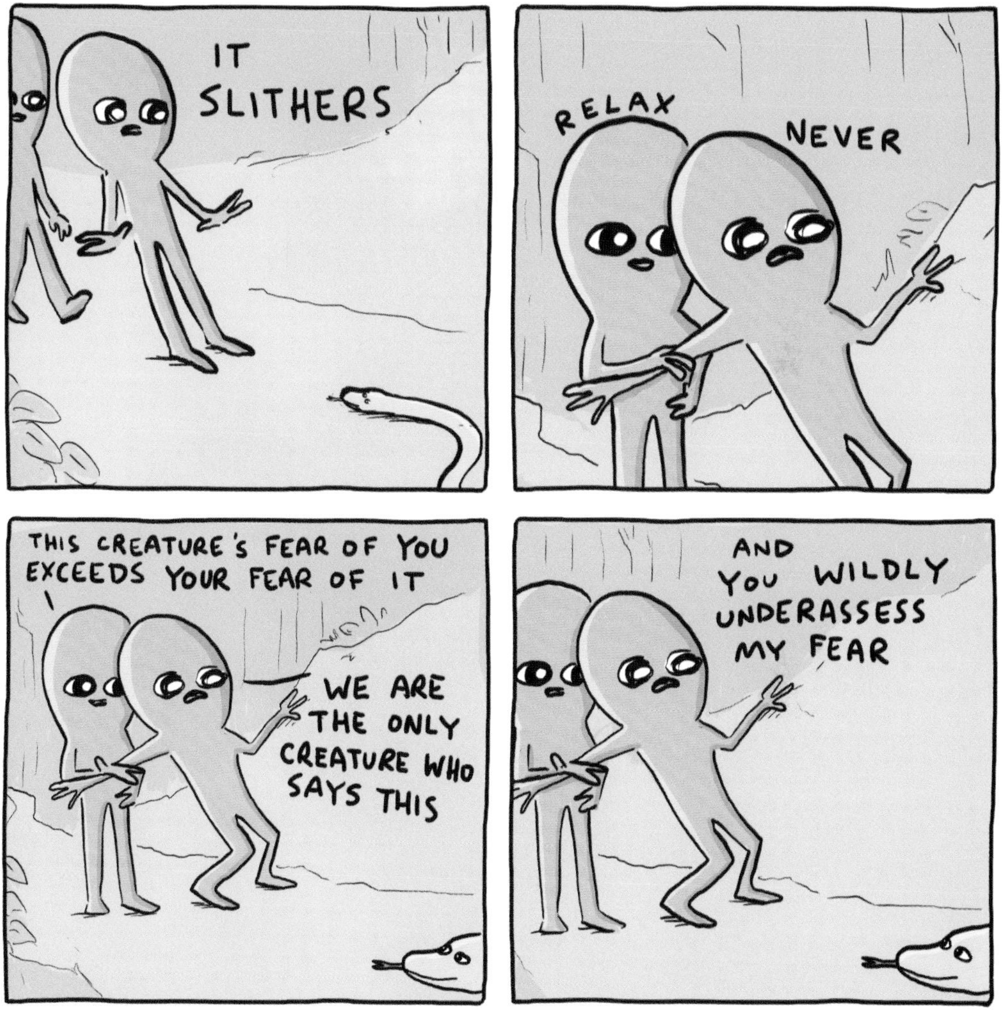
IT SLITHERS
RELAX
NEVER
THIS CREATURE'S FEAR OF YOU EXCEEDS YOUR FEAR OF IT
WE ARE THE ONLY CREATURE WHO SAYS THIS
AND YOU WILDLY UNDERASSESS MY FEAR

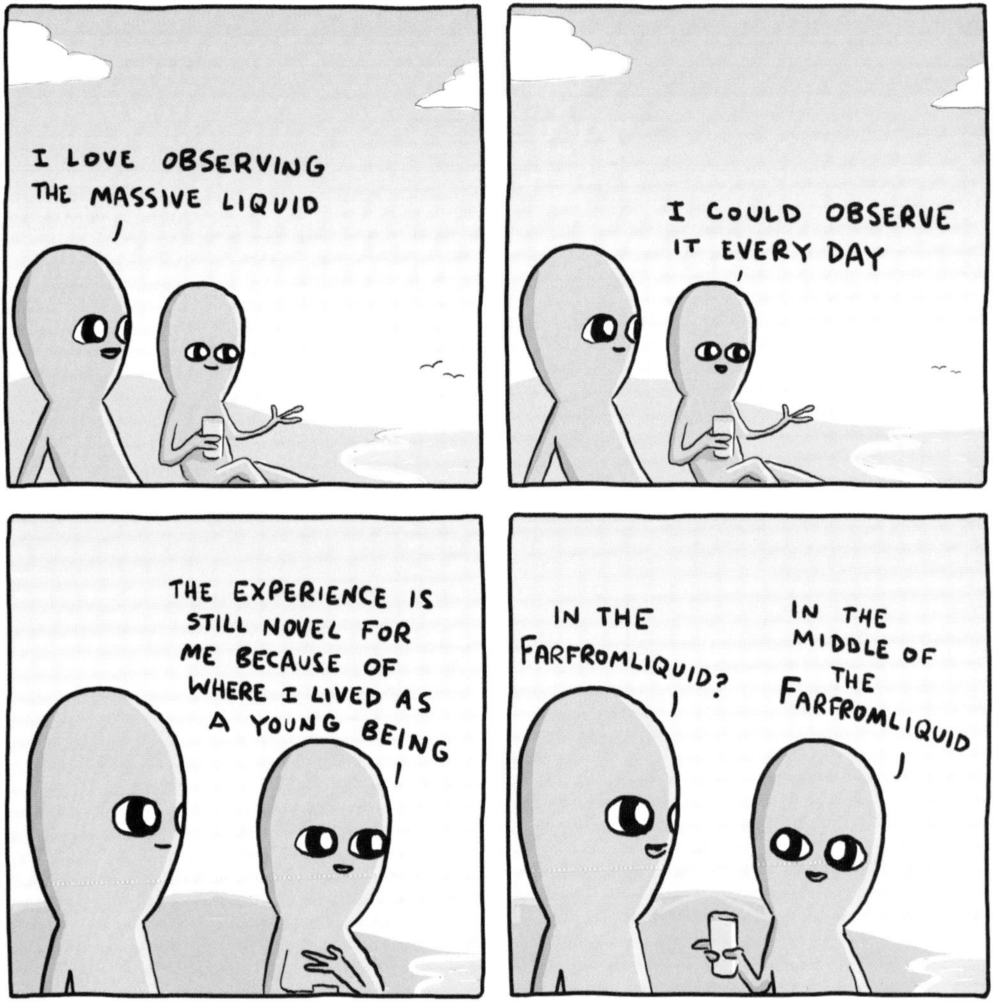
I LOVE OBSERVING THE MASSIVE LIQUID
I COULD OBSERVE IT EVERY DAY
THE EXPERIENCE IS STILL NOVEL FOR ME BECAUSE OF WHERE I LIVED AS A YOUNG BEING
IN THE FARFROMLIQUID?
IN THE MIDDLE OF THE FARFROMLIQUID

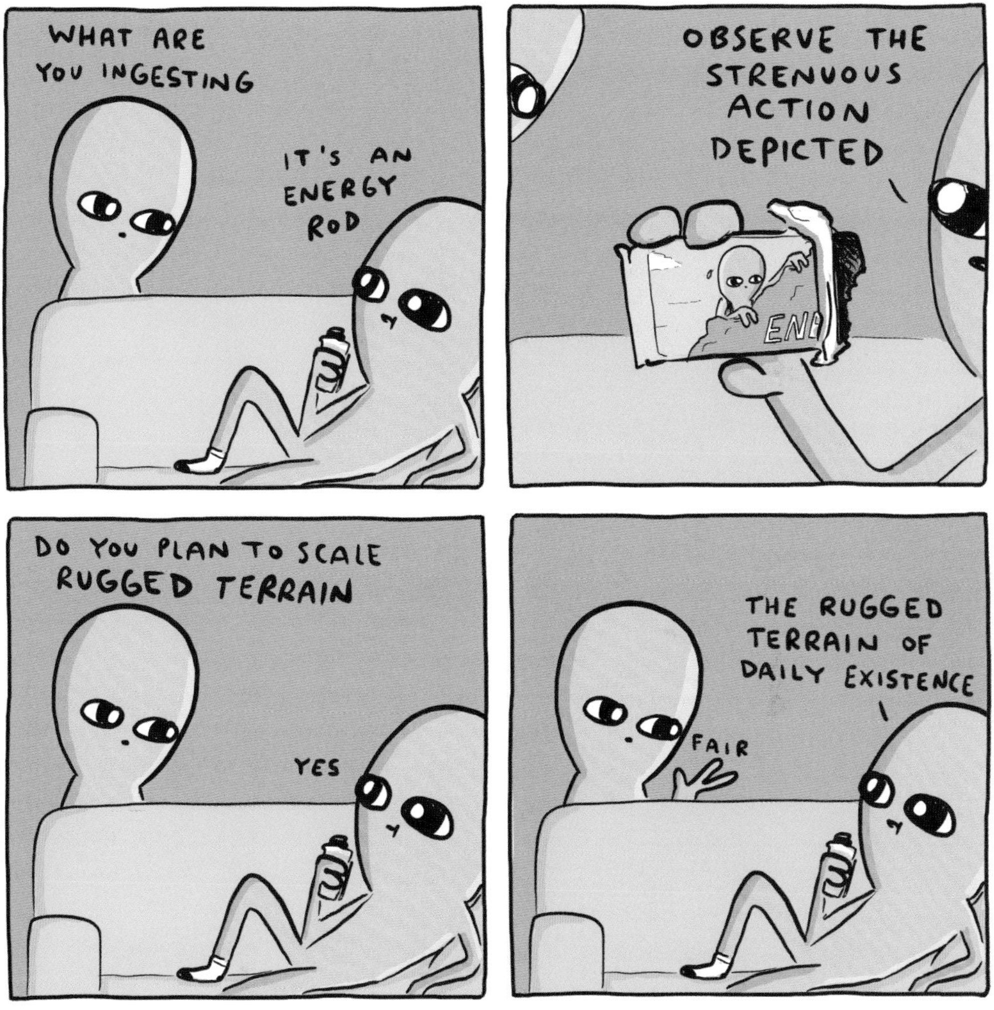
WHAT ARE YOU INGESTING
IT'S AN ENERGY ROD
OBSERVE THE STRENUOUS ACTION DEPICTED
DO YOU PLAN TO SCALE RUGGED TERRAIN
YES
THE RUGGED TERRAIN OF DAILY EXISTENCE
FAIR

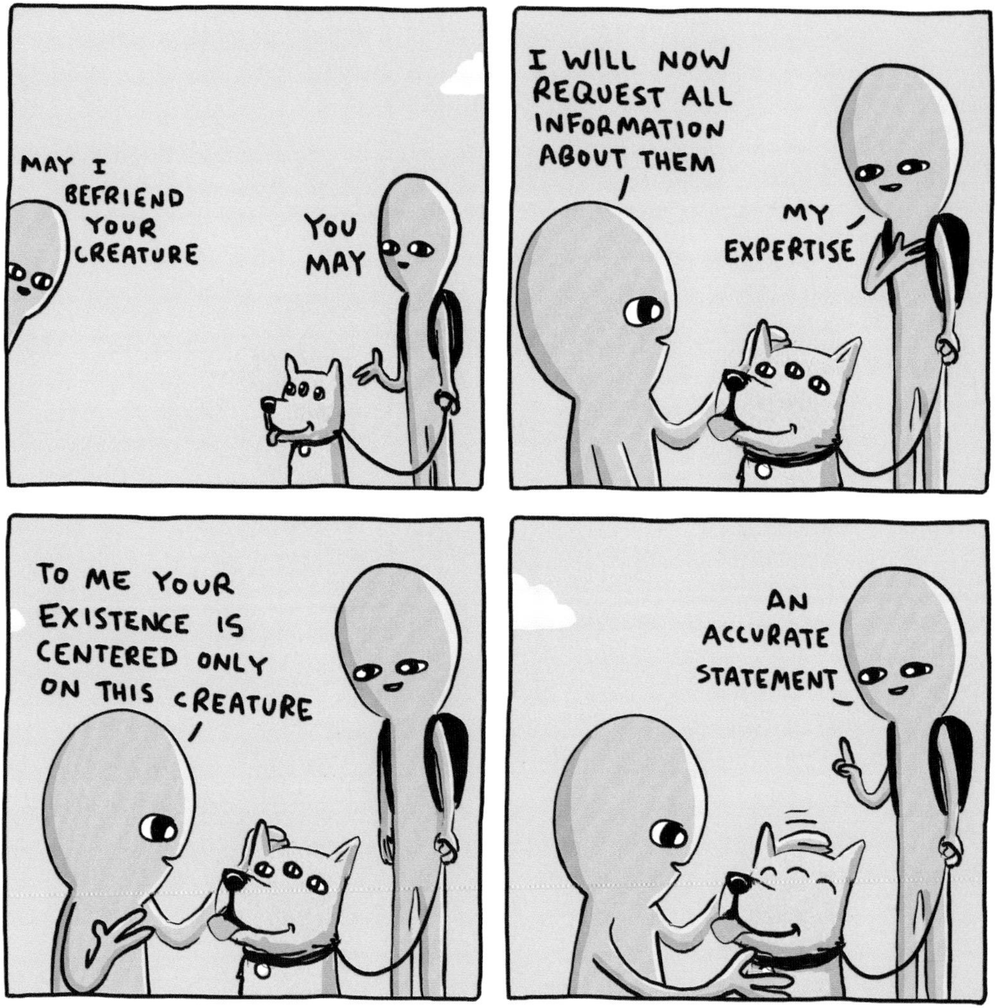
MAY I BEFRIEND YOUR CREATURE
YOU MAY
I WILL NOW REQUEST ALL INFORMATION ABOUT THEM
MY EXPERTISE
TO ME YOUR EXISTENCE IS CENTERED ONLY ON THIS CREATURE
AN ACCURATE STATEMENT

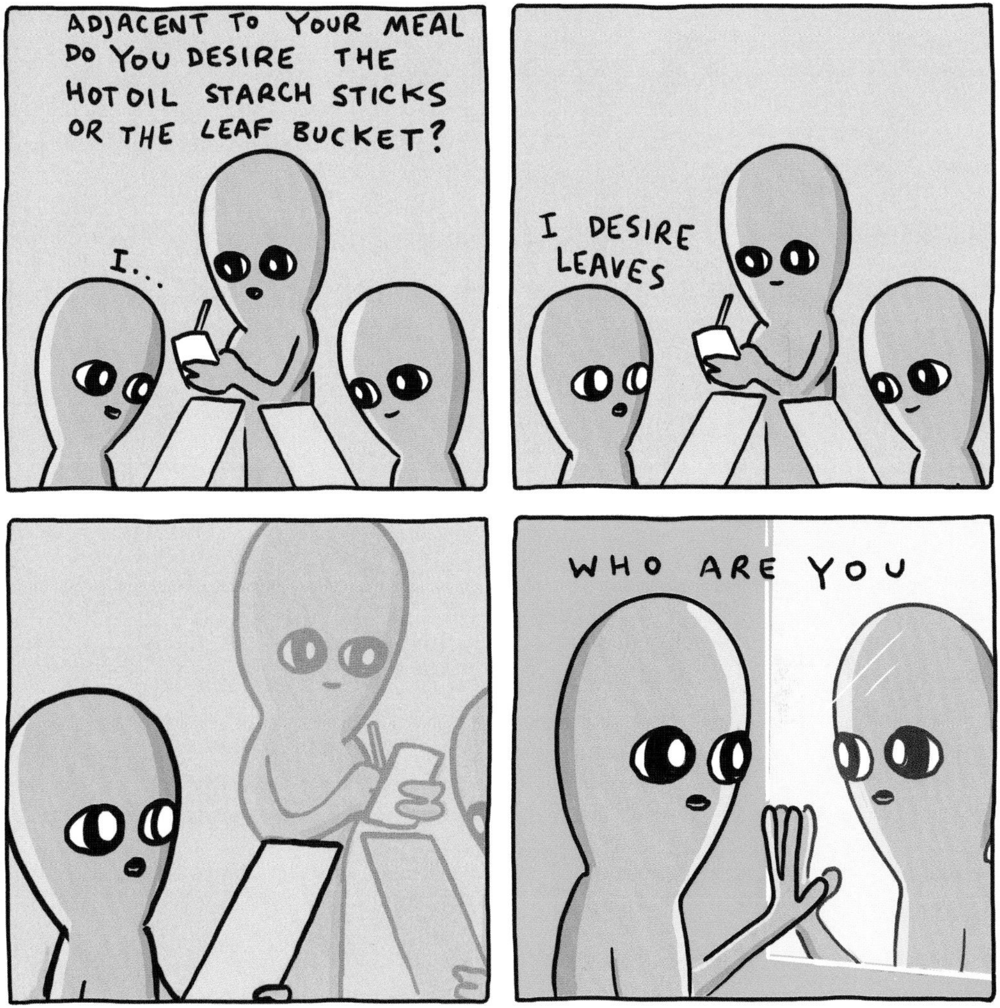
ADJACENT TO YOUR MEAL DO YOU DESIRE THE HOT OIL STARCH STICKS OR THE LEAF BUCKET?
I...
I DESIRE LEAVES
WHO ARE YOU

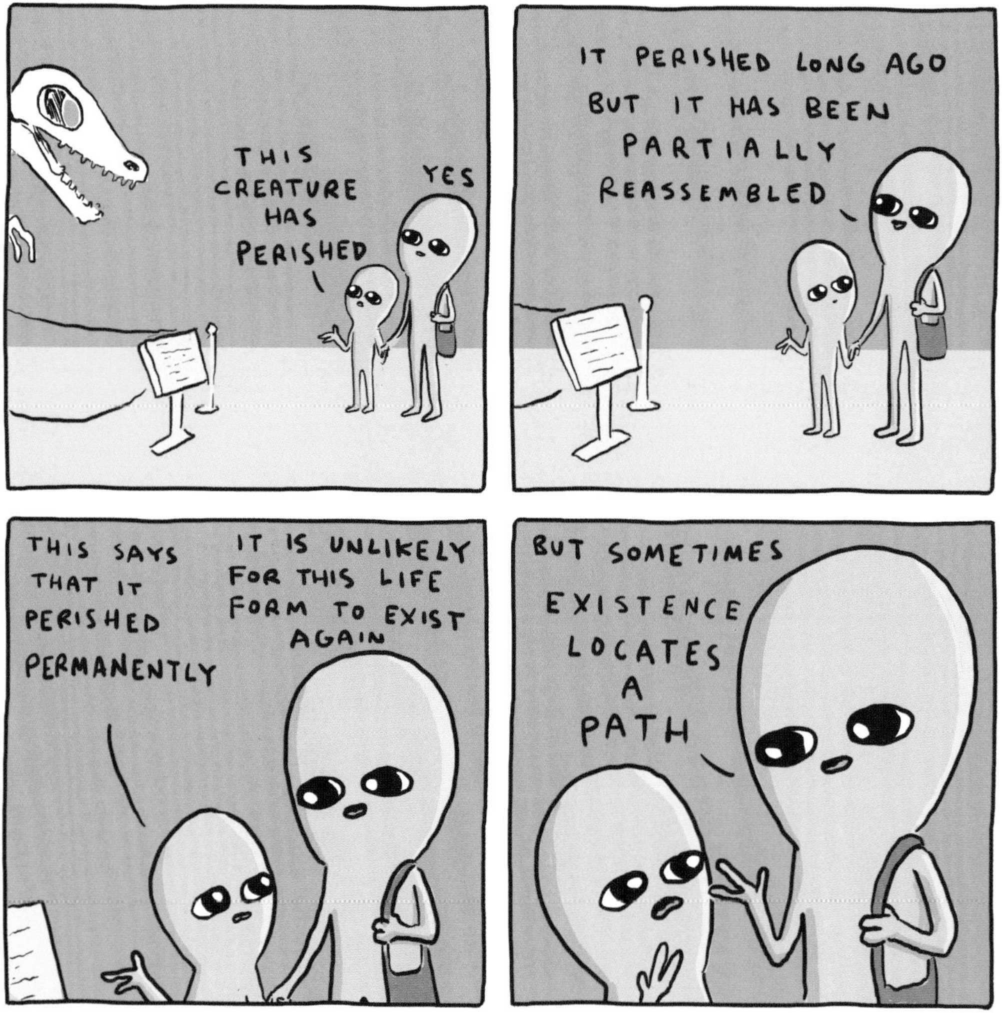
THIS CREATURE HAS PERISHED
YES
IT PERISHED LONG AGO
BUT IT HAS BEEN PARTIALLY REASSEMBLED
THIS SAYS THAT IT PERISHED PERMANENTLY
IT IS UNLIKELY FOR THIS LIFE FORM TO EXIST AGAIN
BUT SOMETIMES
EXISTENCE LOCATES A PATH

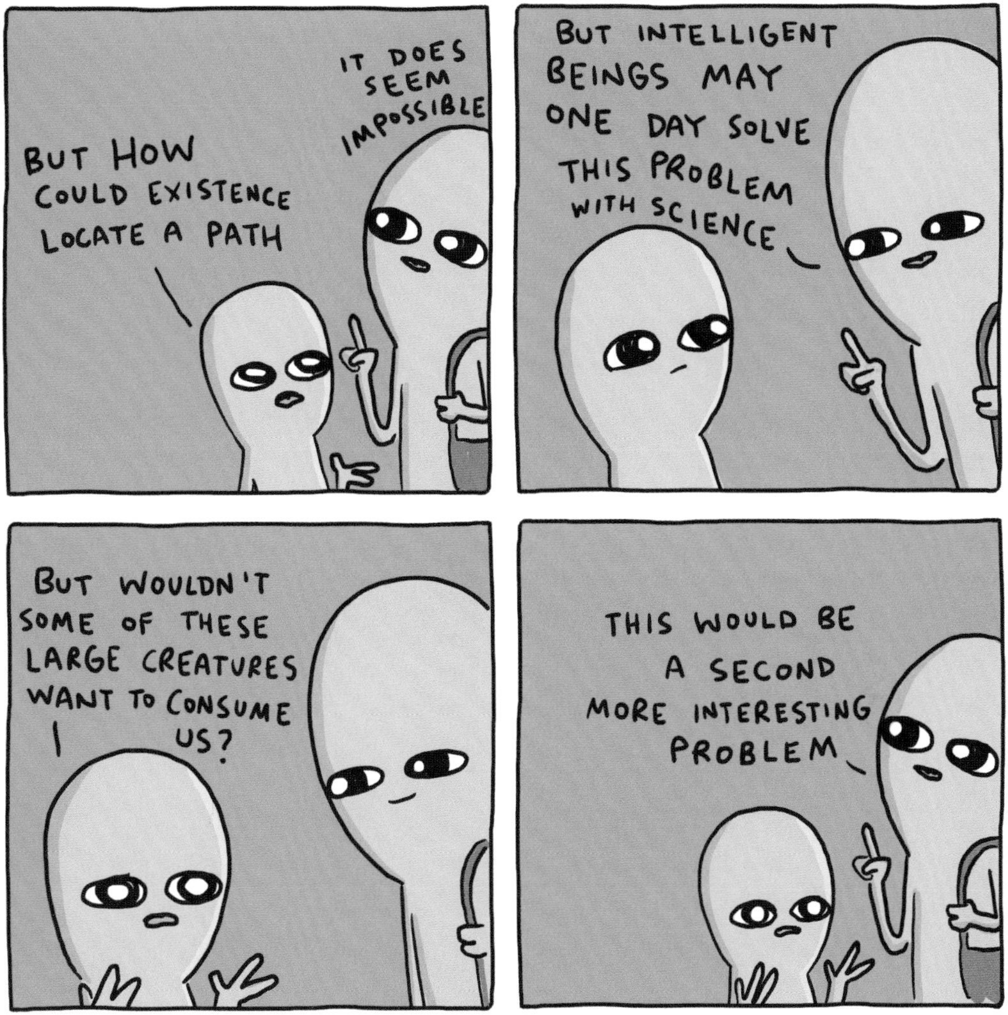
BUT HOW COULD EXISTENCE LOCATE A PATH
IT DOES SEEM IMPOSSIBLE
BUT INTELLIGENT BEINGS MAY ONE DAY SOLVE THIS PROBLEM WITH SCIENCE
BUT WOULDN'T SOME OF THESE LARGE CREATURES WANT TO CONSUME US?
THIS WOULD BE A SECOND MORE INTERESTING PROBLEM

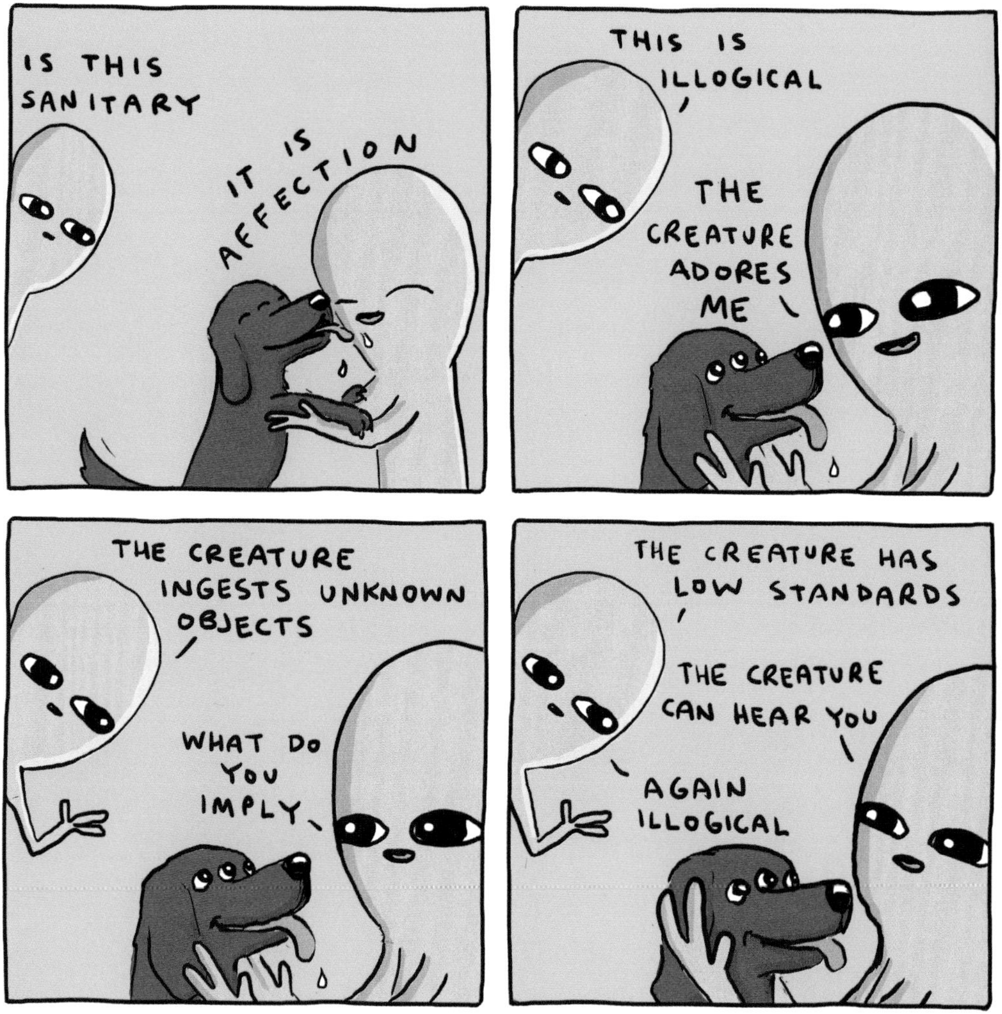
IS THIS SANITARY
IT IS AFFECTION
THIS IS ILLOGICAL
THE CREATURE ADORES ME
THE CREATURE INGESTS UNKNOWN OBJECTS
WHAT DO YOU IMPLY
THE CREATURE HAS LOW STANDARDS
THE CREATURE CAN HEAR YOU
AGAIN ILLOGICAL

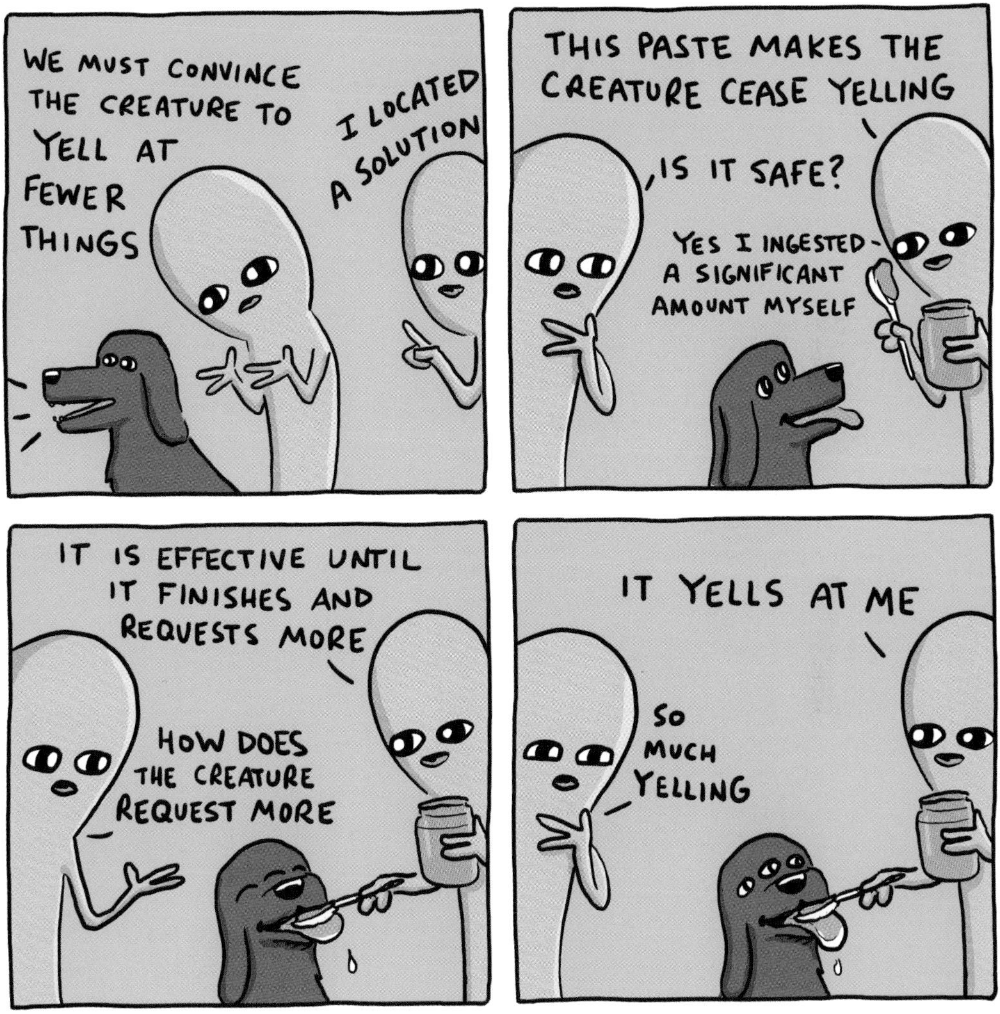
WE MUST CONVINCE THE CREATURE TO YELL AT FEWER THINGS
I LOCATED A SOLUTION
THIS PASTE MAKES THE CREATURE CEASE YELLING
IS IT SAFE?
YES I INGESTED A SIGNIFICANT AMOUNT MYSELF
IT IS EFFECTIVE UNTIL IT FINISHES AND REQUESTS MORE
HOW DOES THE CREATURE REQUEST MORE
IT YELLS AT ME
SO MUCH YELLING

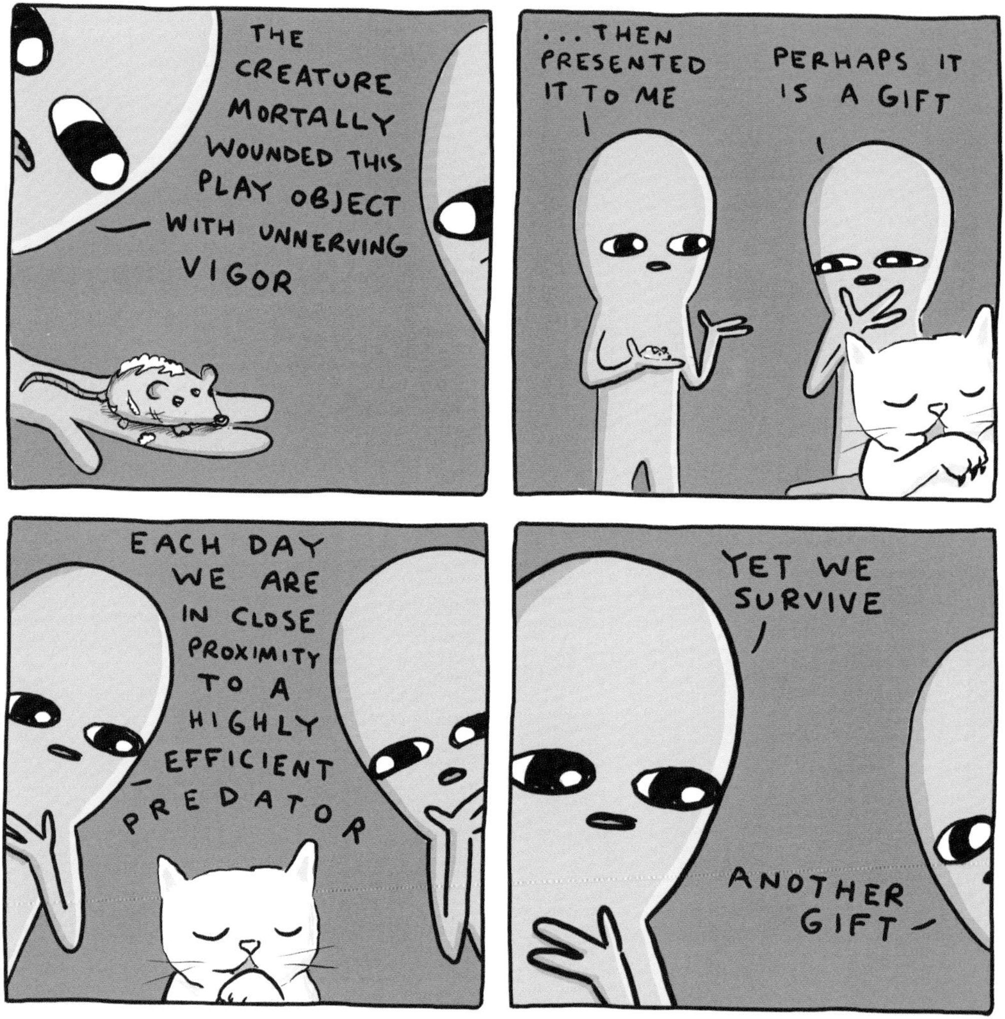
THE CREATURE MORTALLY WOUNDED THIS PLAY OBJECT WITH UNNERVING VIGOR
...THEN PRESENTED IT TO ME
PERHAPS IT IS A GIFT
EACH DAY WE ARE IN CLOSE PROXIMITY TO A HIGHLY EFFICIENT PREDATOR
YET WE SURVIVE
ANOTHER GIFT

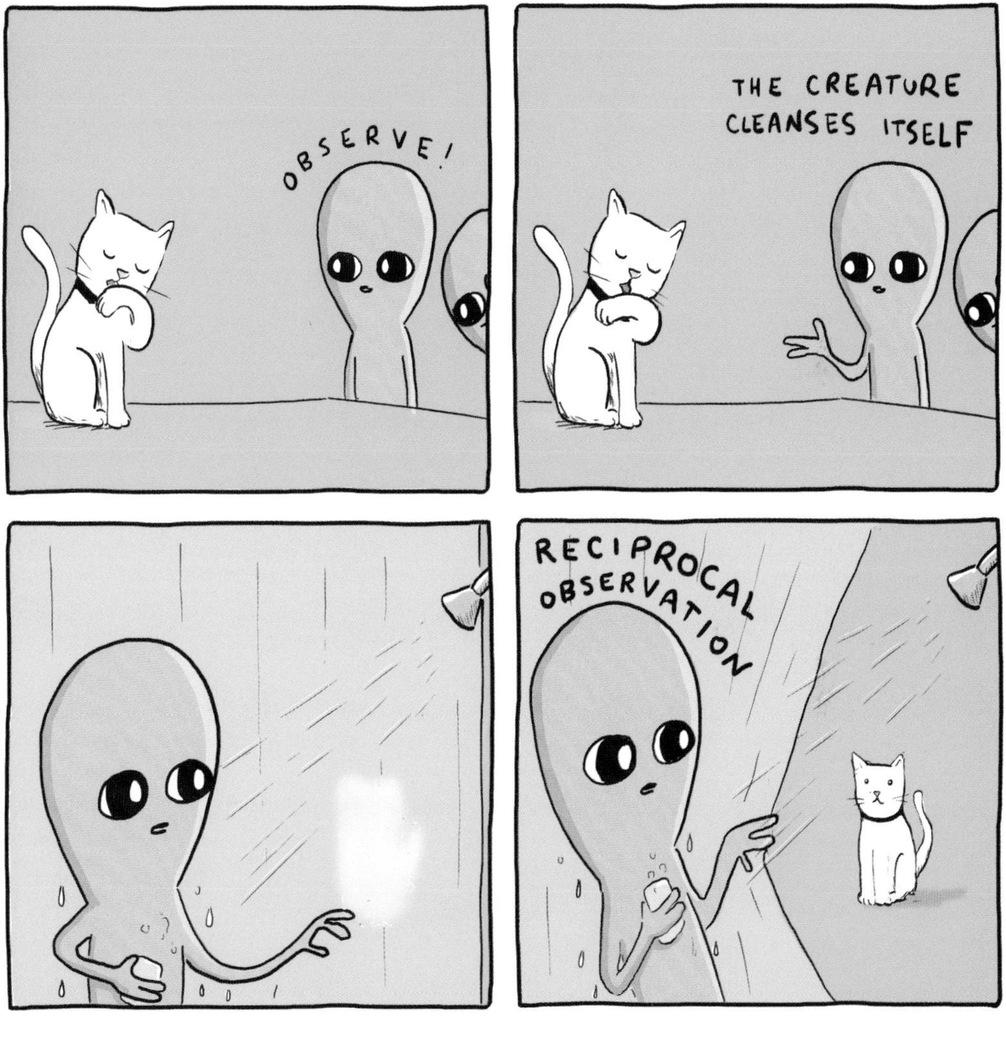
OBSERVE!
THE CREATURE CLEANSES ITSELF
RECIPROCAL OBSERVATION

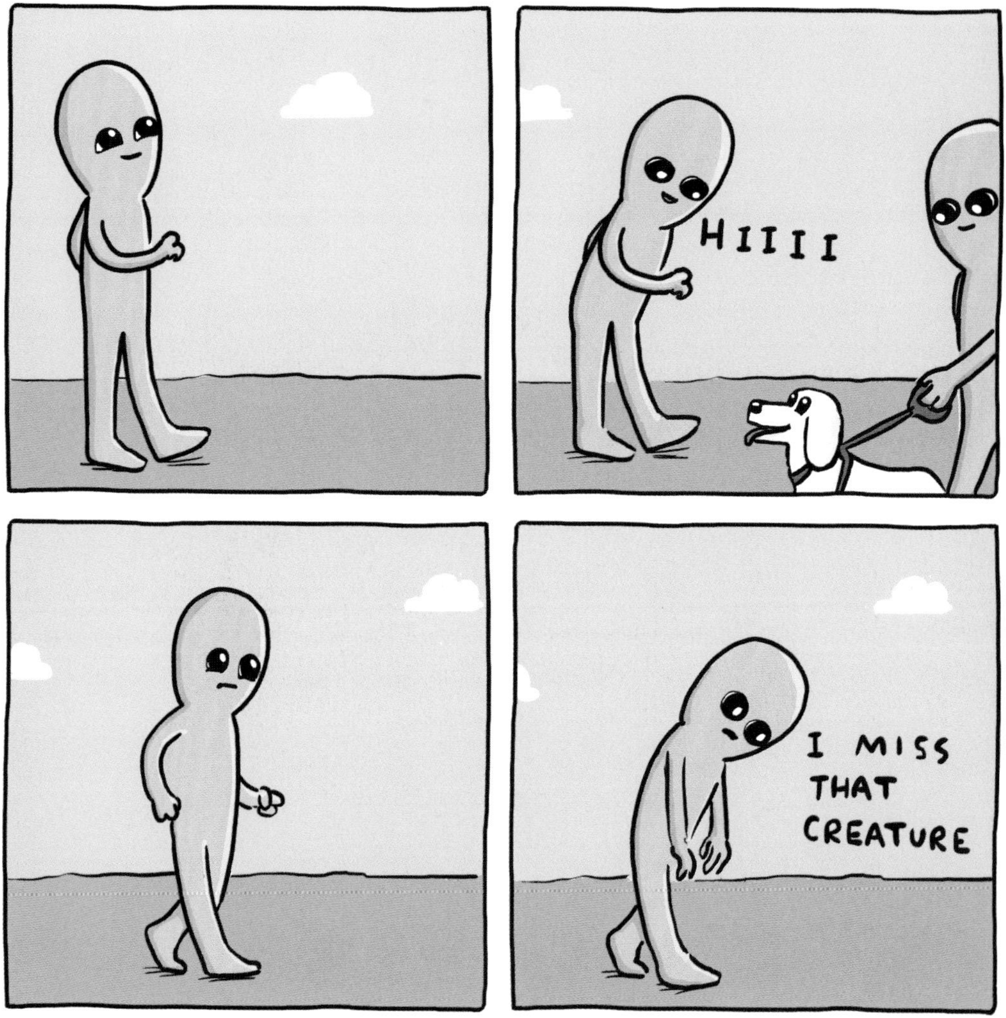
HIIII
I MISS THAT CREATURE

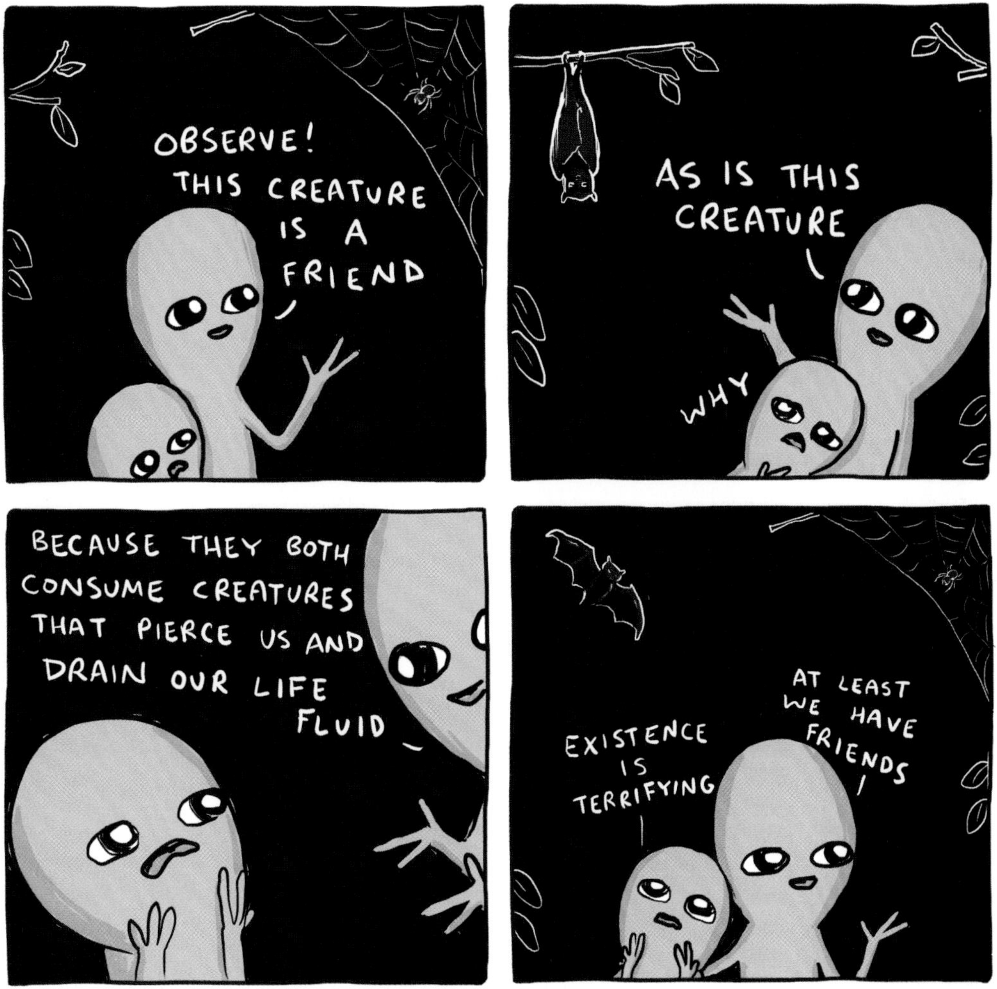
OBSERVE! THIS CREATURE IS A FRIEND
AS IS THIS CREATURE
WHY
BECAUSE THEY BOTH CONSUME CREATURES THAT PIERCE US AND DRAIN OUR LIFE FLUID
EXISTENCE IS TERRIFYING
AT LEAST WE HAVE FRIENDS

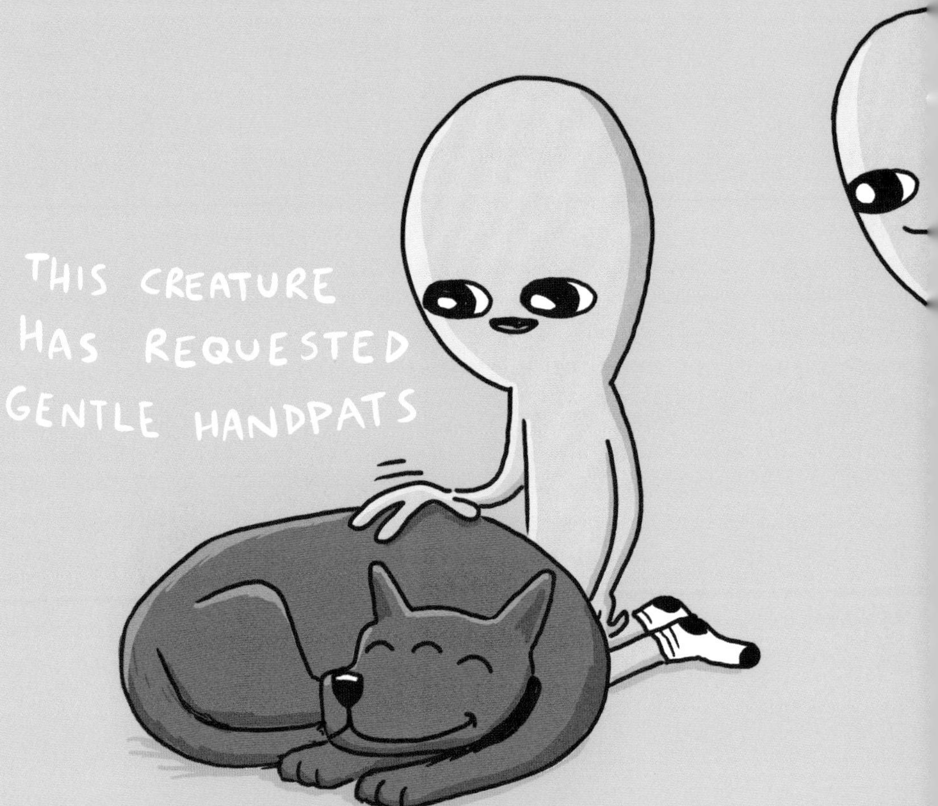
THIS CREATURE
HAS REQUESTED
GENTLE HANDPATS

EMOTIONS

WILDLY
UNPREPARED
FOR THE
DAY

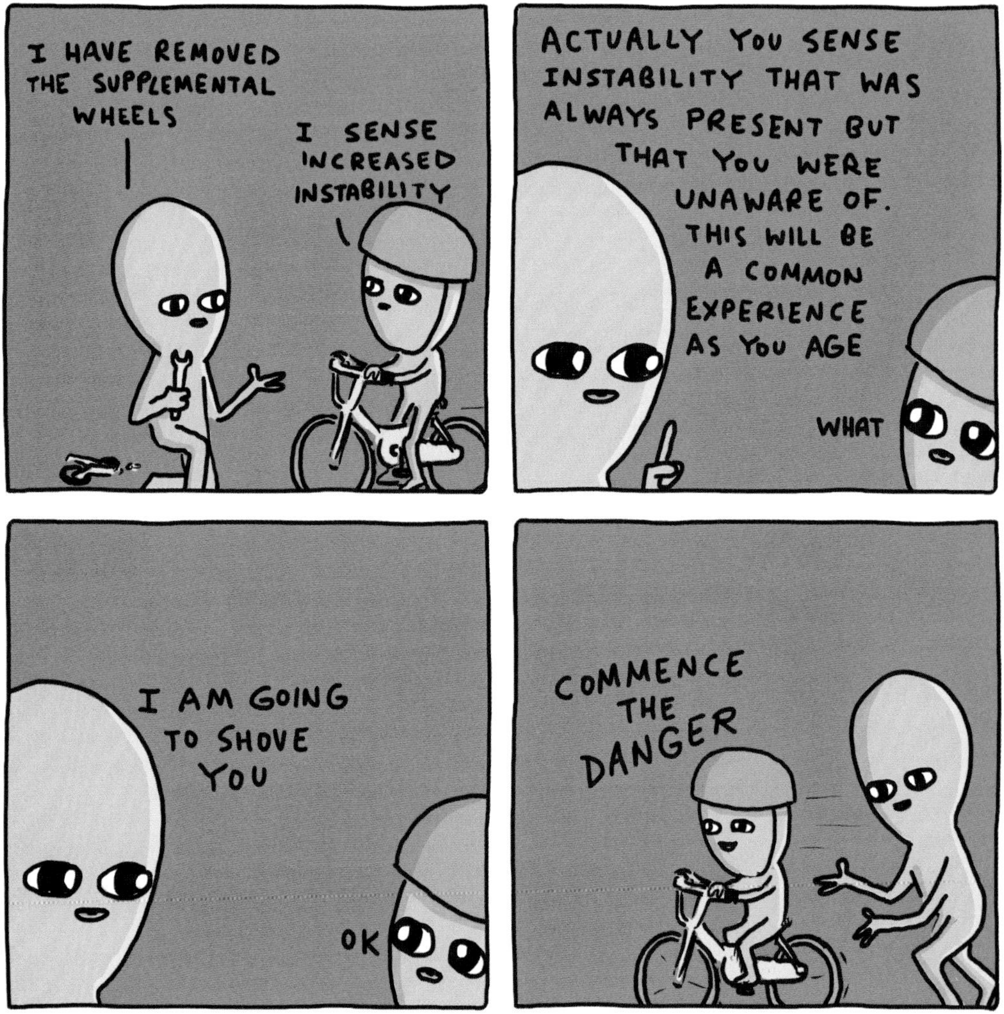

I HAVE REMOVED THE SUPPLEMENTAL WHEELS
I SENSE INCREASED INSTABILITY
ACTUALLY YOU SENSE INSTABILITY THAT WAS ALWAYS PRESENT BUT THAT YOU WERE UNAWARE OF. THIS WILL BE A COMMON EXPERIENCE AS YOU AGE
WHAT
I AM GOING TO SHOVE YOU
OK
COMMENCE THE DANGER

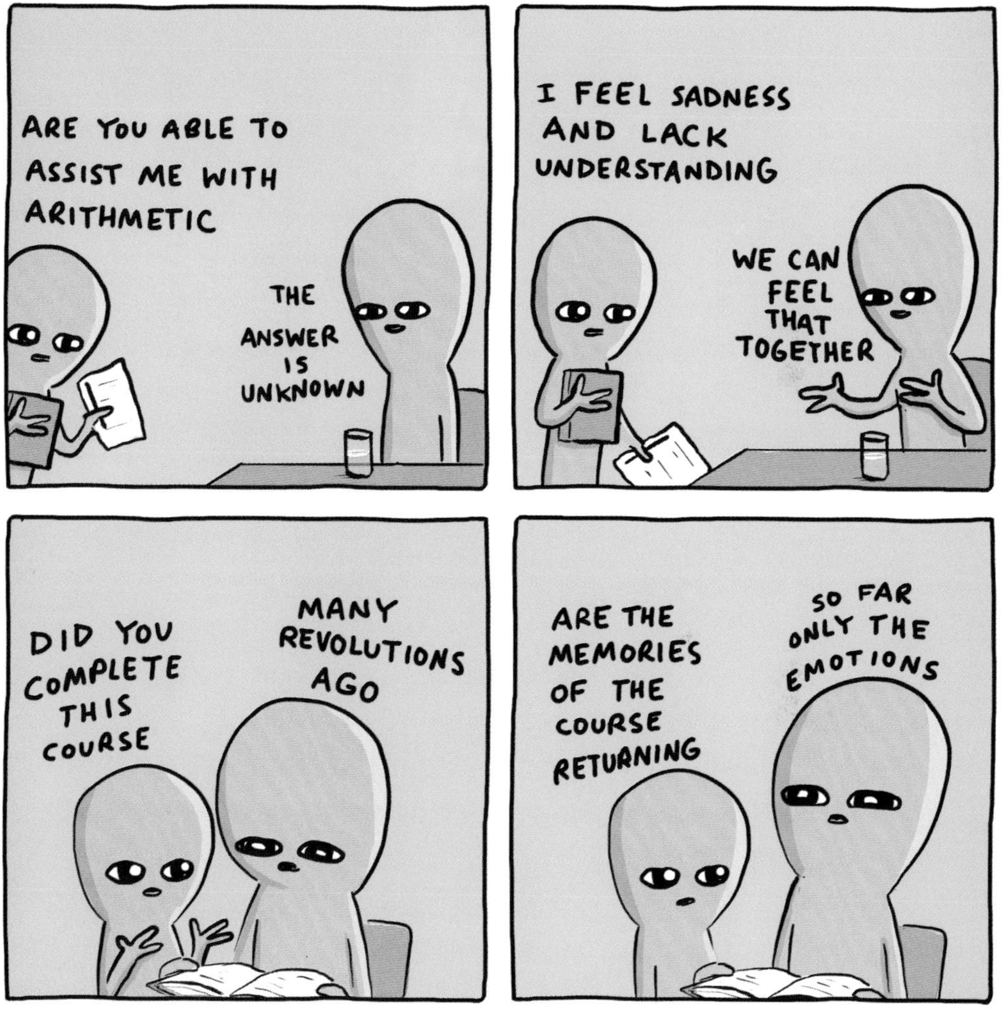
ARE YOU ABLE TO ASSIST ME WITH ARITHMETIC
THE ANSWER IS UNKNOWN
I FEEL SADNESS AND LACK UNDERSTANDING
WE CAN FEEL THAT TOGETHER
DID YOU COMPLETE THIS COURSE
MANY REVOLUTIONS AGO
ARE THE MEMORIES OF THE COURSE RETURNING
SO FAR ONLY THE EMOTIONS

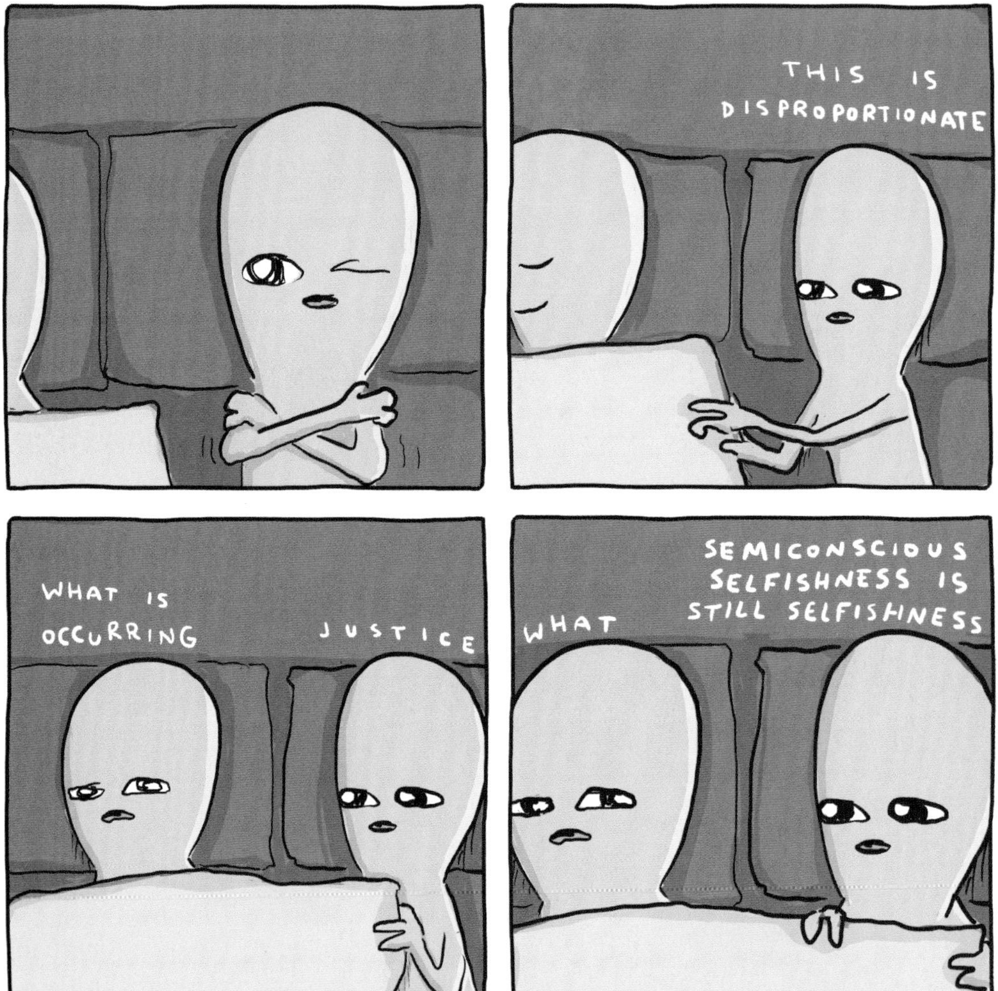
THIS IS DISPROPORTIONATE
WHAT IS OCCURRING
JUSTICE
WHAT
SEMICONSCIOUS SELFISHNESS IS STILL SELFISHNESS

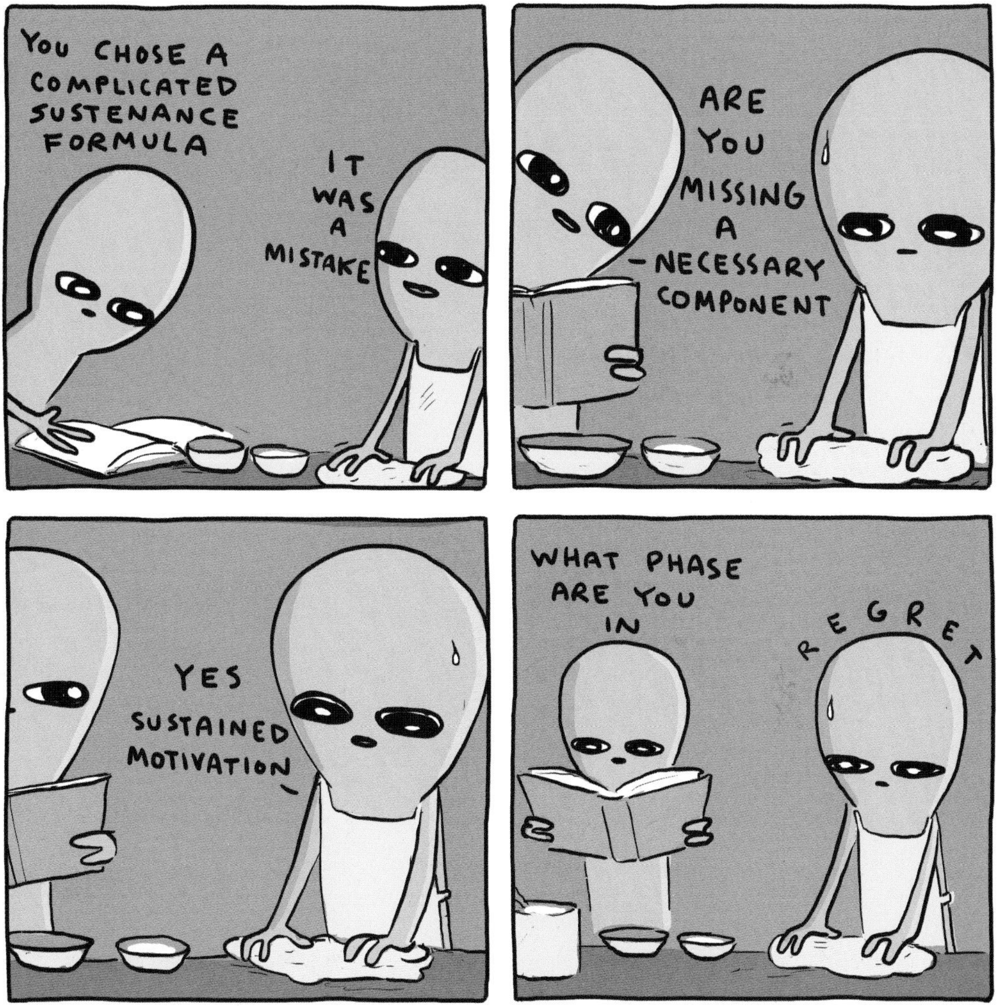
YOU CHOSE A COMPLICATED SUSTENANCE FORMULA
IT WAS A MISTAKE
ARE YOU MISSING A NECESSARY COMPONENT
YES
SUSTAINED MOTIVATION
WHAT PHASE ARE YOU IN
REGRET

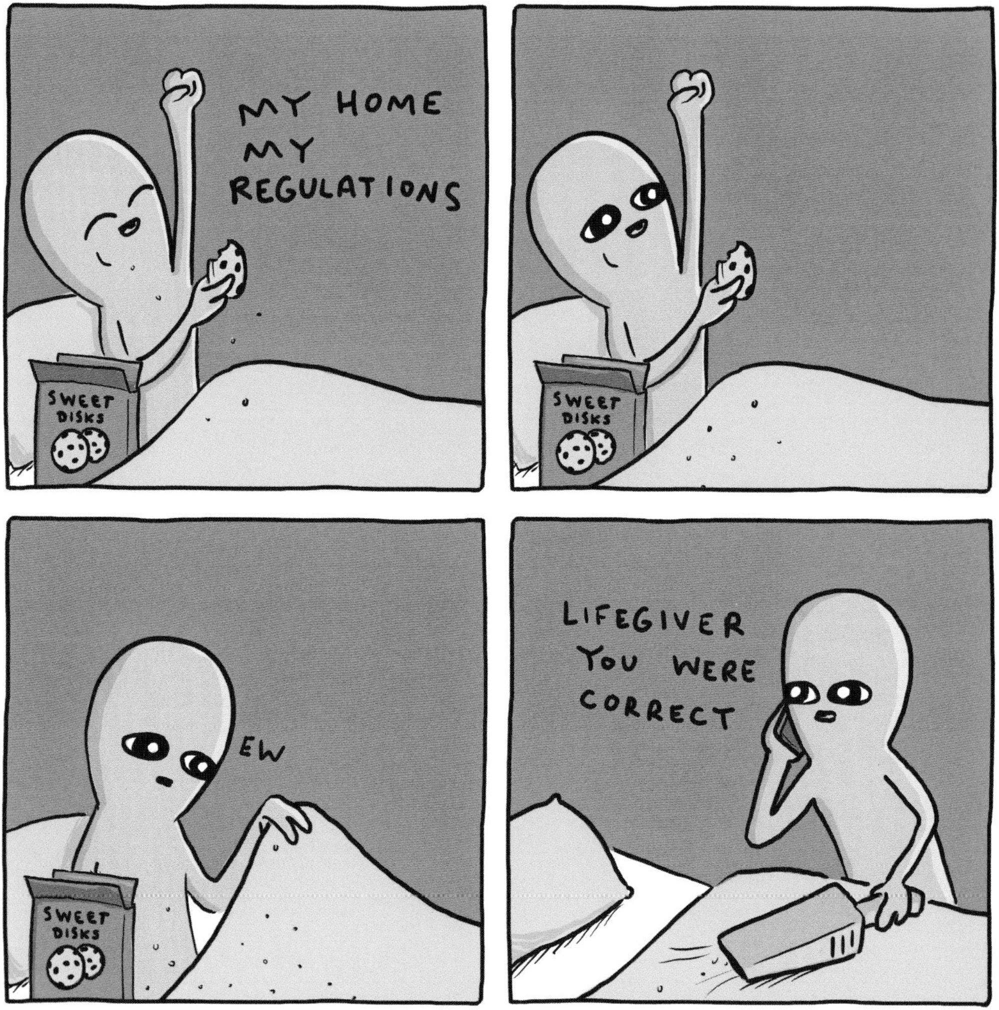
MY HOME
MY
REGULATIONS
SWEET DISKS
SWEET DISKS
EW
SWEET DISKS
LIFEGIVER
YOU WERE
CORRECT

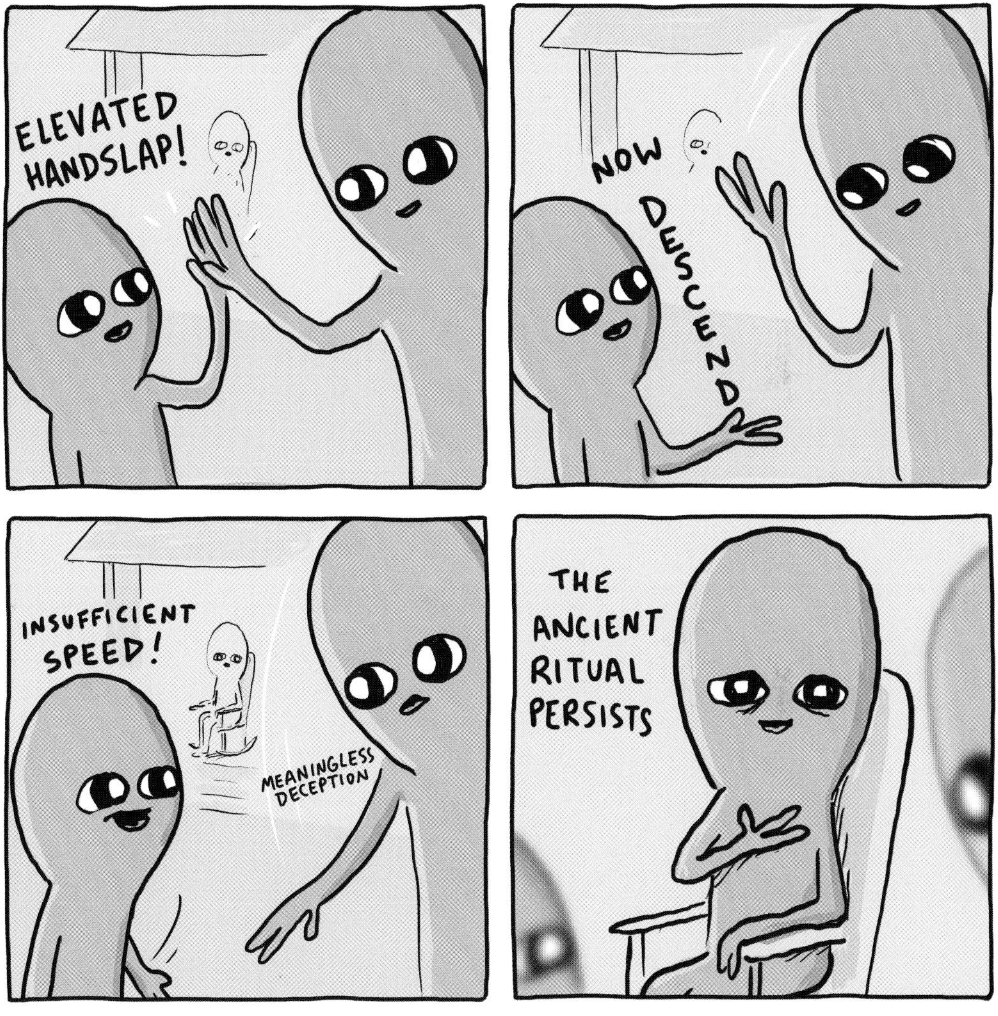
ELEVATED HANDSLAP!
NOW
DESCEND
INSUFFICIENT SPEED!
MEANINGLESS DECEPTION
THE ANCIENT RITUAL PERSISTS

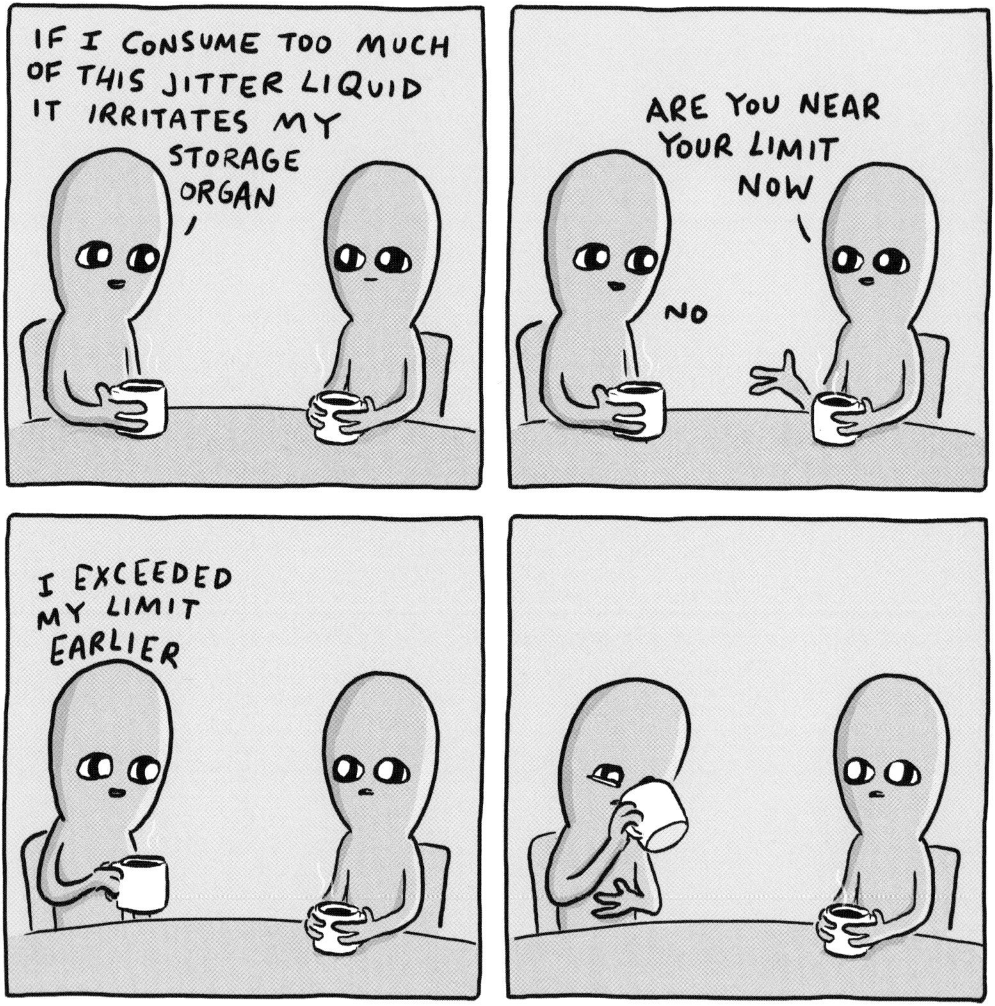
IF I CONSUME TOO MUCH OF THIS JITTER LIQUID IT IRRITATES MY STORAGE ORGAN
ARE YOU NEAR YOUR LIMIT NOW
NO
I EXCEEDED MY LIMIT EARLIER

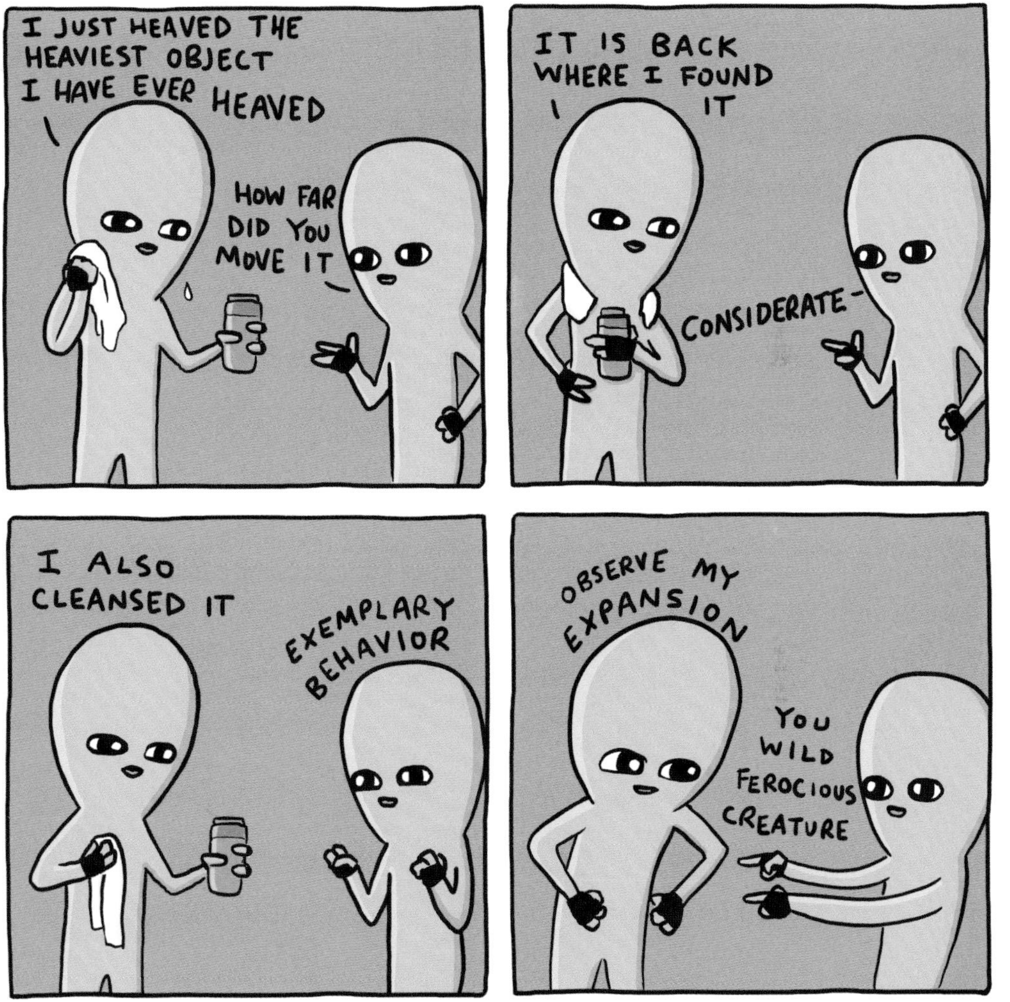
I JUST HEAVED THE HEAVIEST OBJECT I HAVE EVER HEAVED
HOW FAR DID YOU MOVE IT
IT IS BACK WHERE I FOUND IT
CONSIDERATE
I ALSO CLEANSED IT
EXEMPLARY BEHAVIOR
OBSERVE MY EXPANSION
YOU WILD FEROCIOUS CREATURE

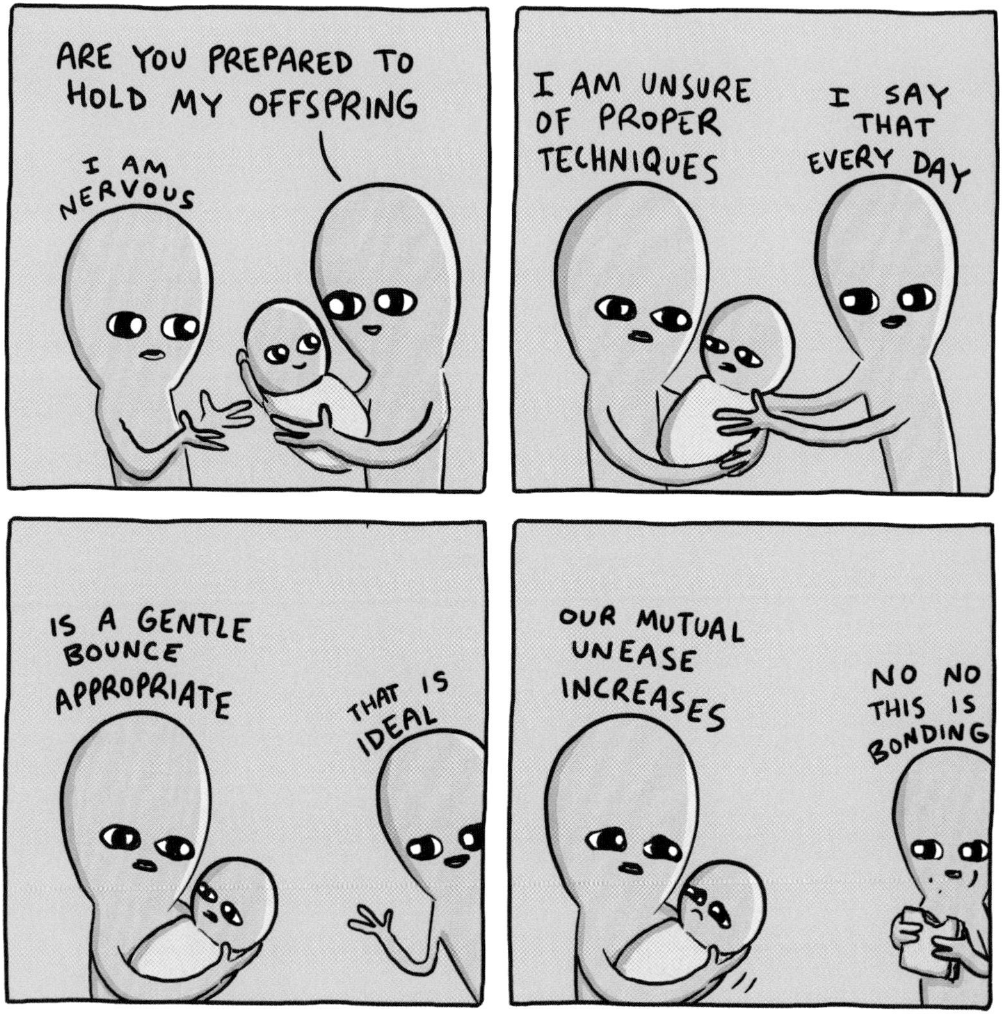
ARE YOU PREPARED TO HOLD MY OFFSPRING
I AM NERVOUS
I AM UNSURE OF PROPER TECHNIQUES
I SAY THAT EVERY DAY
IS A GENTLE BOUNCE APPROPRIATE
THAT IS IDEAL
OUR MUTUAL UNEASE INCREASES
NO NO THIS IS BONDING

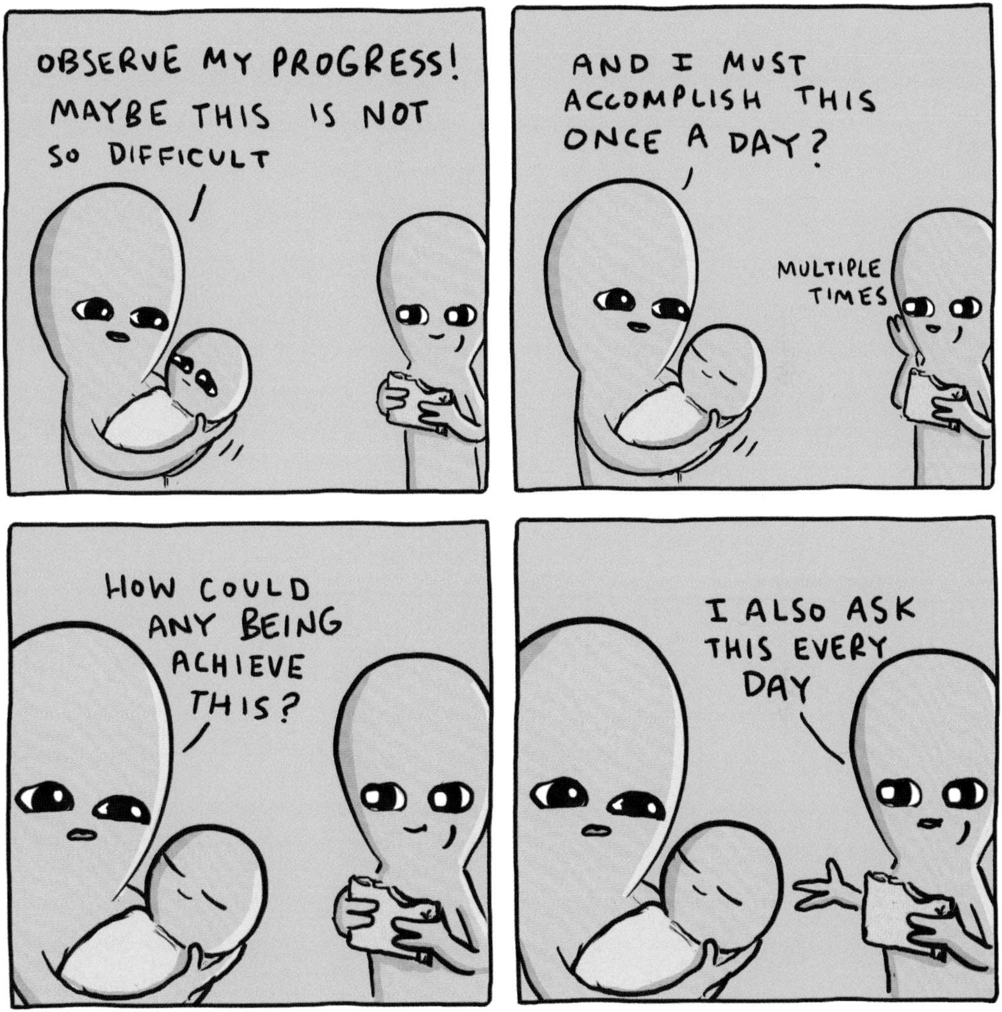
OBSERVE MY PROGRESS!
MAYBE THIS IS NOT SO DIFFICULT
AND I MUST ACCOMPLISH THIS ONCE A DAY?
MULTIPLE TIMES
HOW COULD ANY BEING ACHIEVE THIS?
I ALSO ASK THIS EVERY DAY

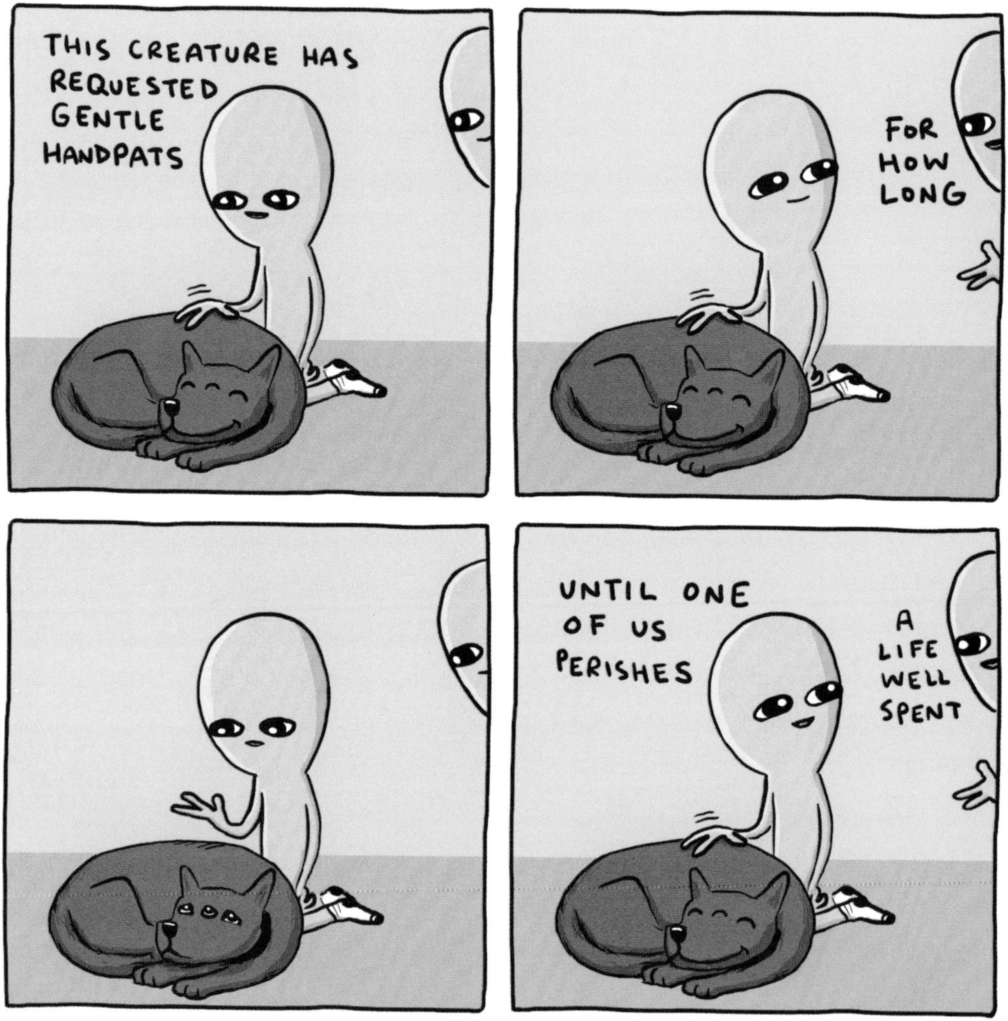
THIS CREATURE HAS REQUESTED GENTLE HANDPATS
FOR HOW LONG
UNTIL ONE OF US PERISHES
A LIFE WELL SPENT

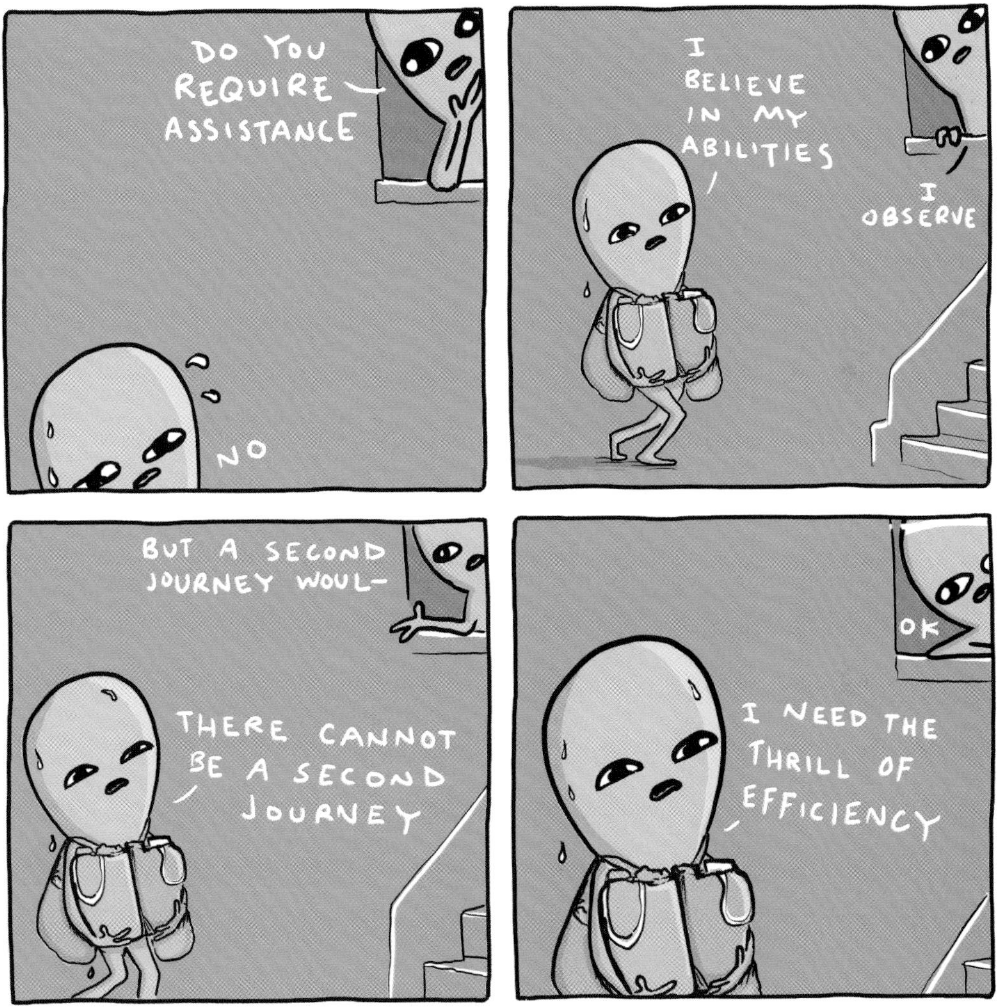
DO YOU REQUIRE ASSISTANCE
NO
I BELIEVE IN MY ABILITIES
I OBSERVE
BUT A SECOND JOURNEY WOUL-
THERE CANNOT BE A SECOND JOURNEY
OK
I NEED THE THRILL OF EFFICIENCY

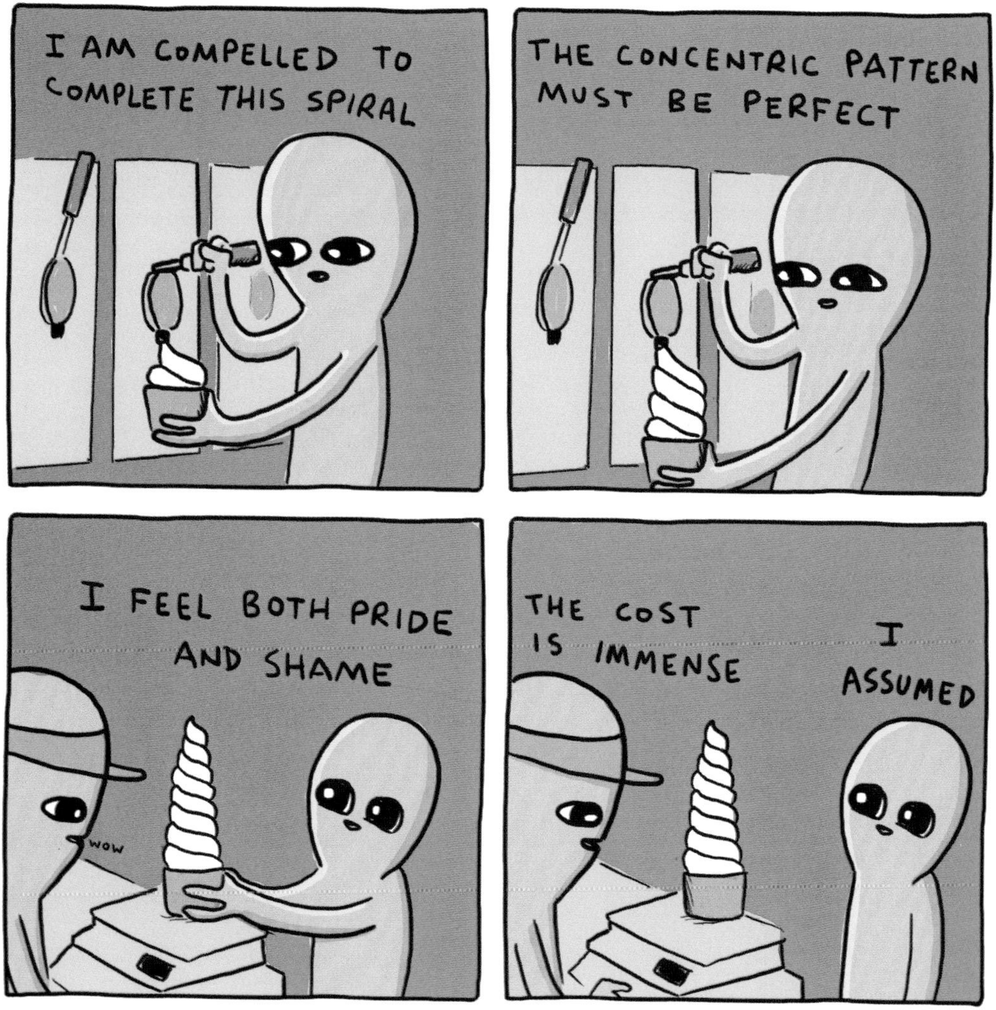
I AM COMPELLED TO COMPLETE THIS SPIRAL
THE CONCENTRIC PATTERN MUST BE PERFECT
I FEEL BOTH PRIDE AND SHAME
WOW
THE COST IS IMMENSE
I ASSUMED

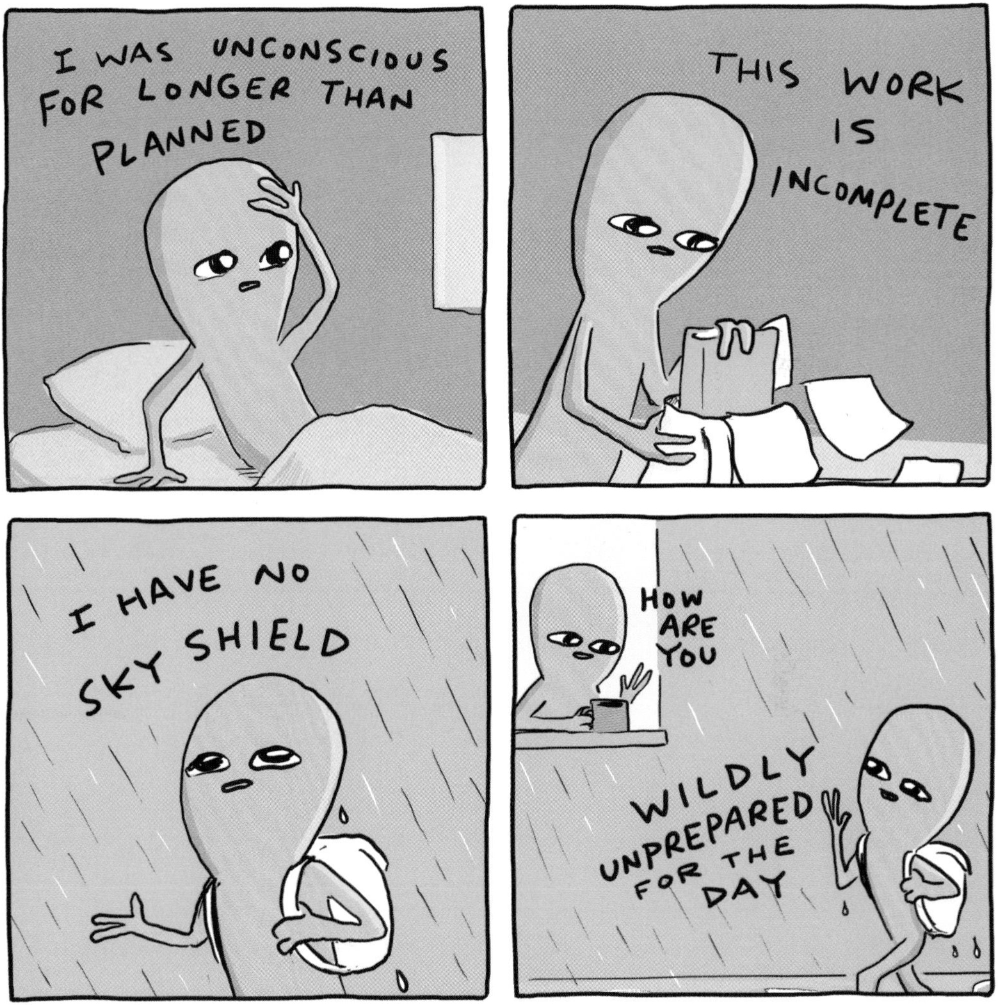
I WAS UNCONSCIOUS FOR LONGER THAN PLANNED
THIS WORK IS INCOMPLETE
I HAVE NO SKY SHIELD
HOW ARE YOU
WILDLY UNPREPARED FOR THE DAY

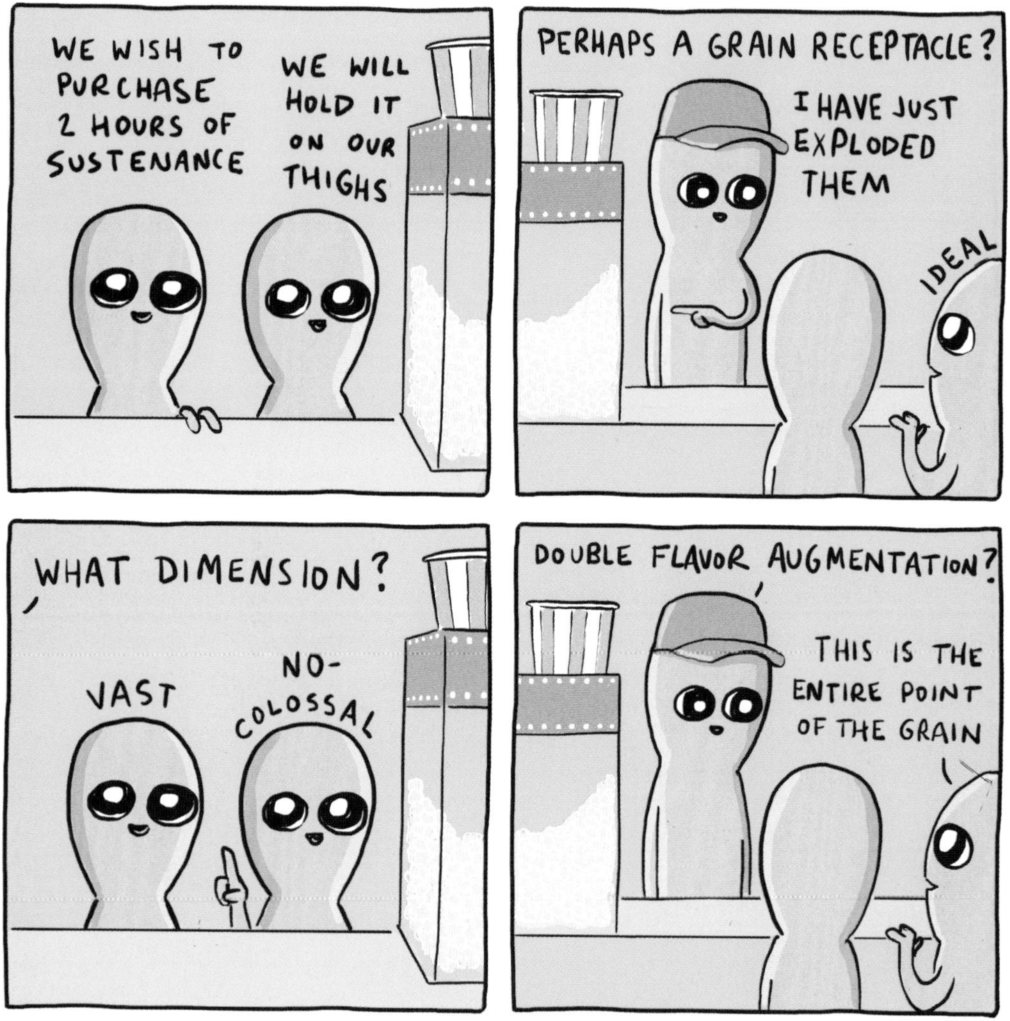
WE WISH TO PURCHASE 2 HOURS OF SUSTENANCE
WE WILL HOLD IT ON OUR THIGHS
PERHAPS A GRAIN RECEPTACLE?
I HAVE JUST EXPLODED THEM
IDEAL
WHAT DIMENSION?
VAST
NO- COLOSSAL
DOUBLE FLAVOR AUGMENTATION?
THIS IS THE ENTIRE POINT OF THE GRAIN

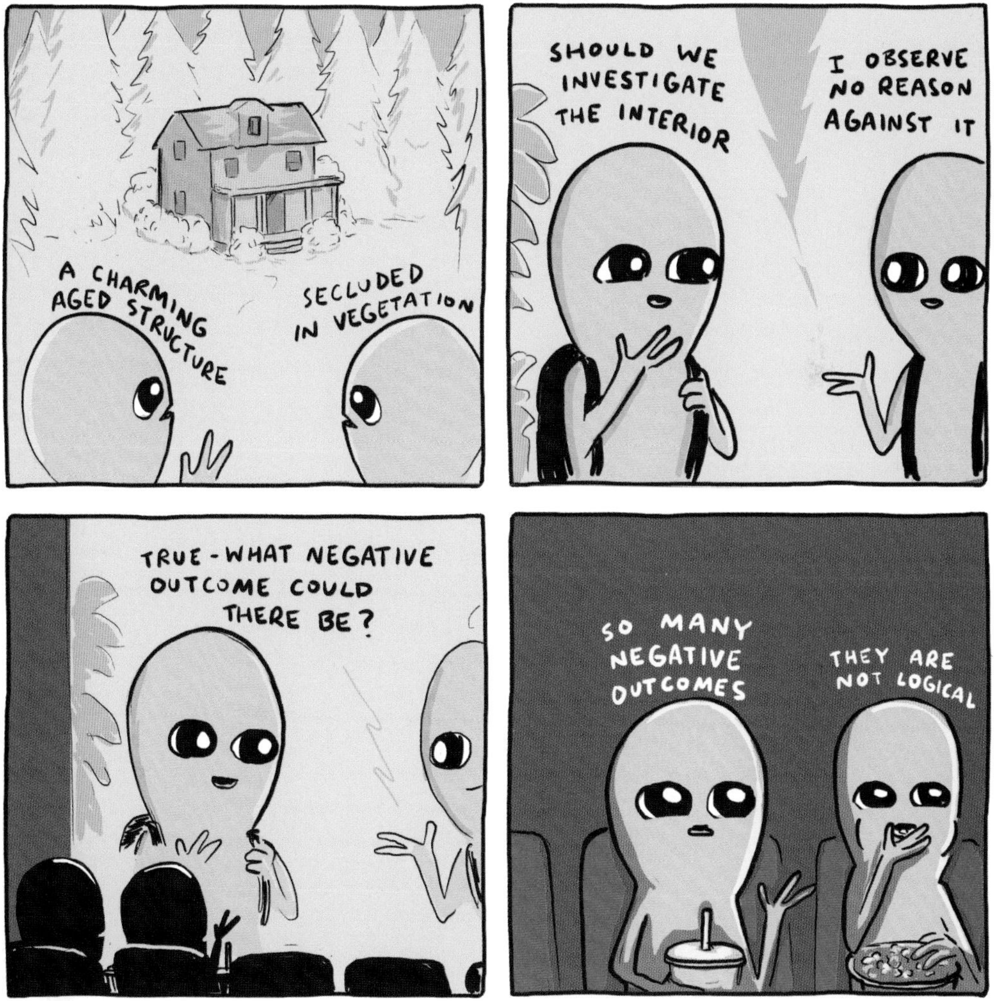
A CHARMING AGED STRUCTURE
SECLUDED IN VEGETATION
SHOULD WE INVESTIGATE THE INTERIOR
I OBSERVE NO REASON AGAINST IT
TRUE - WHAT NEGATIVE OUTCOME COULD THERE BE?
SO MANY NEGATIVE OUTCOMES
THEY ARE NOT LOGICAL

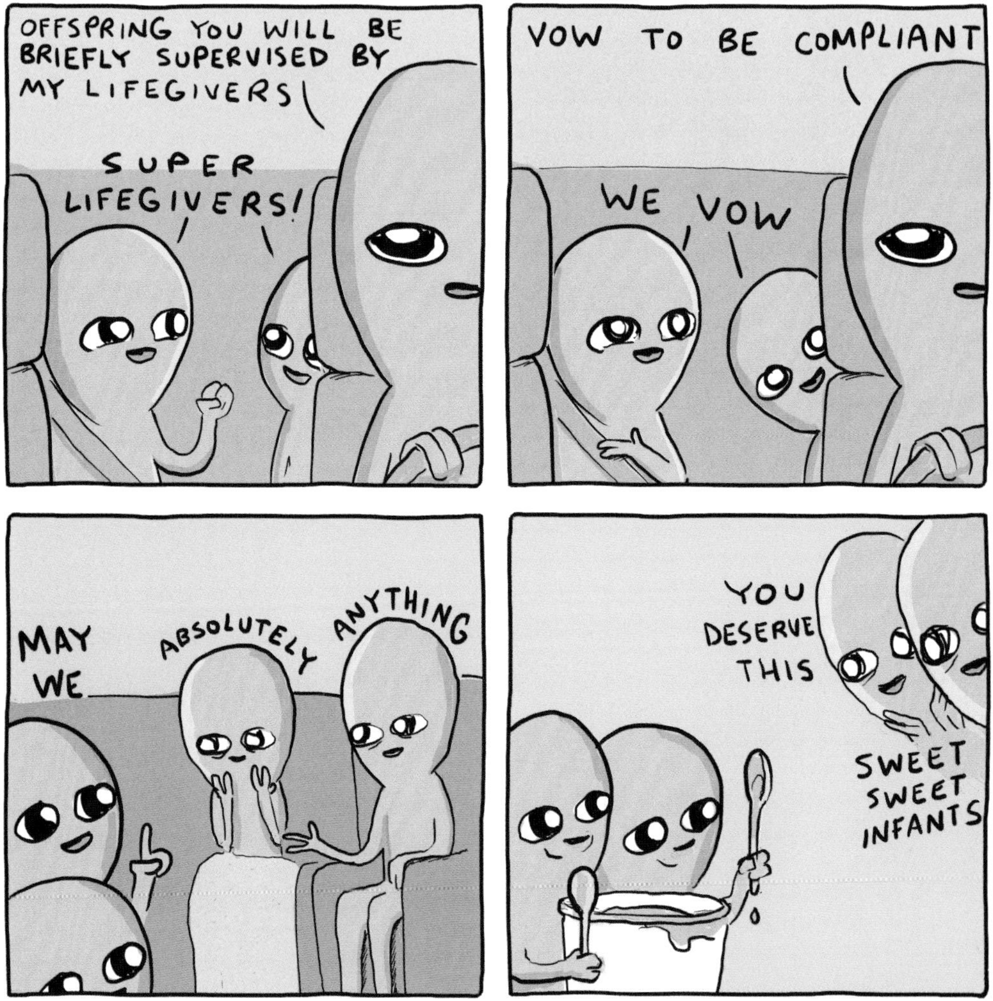
OFFSPRING YOU WILL BE BRIEFLY SUPERVISED BY MY LIFEGIVERS
SUPER LIFEGIVERS!
VOW TO BE COMPLIANT
WE VOW
MAY WE
ABSOLUTELY
ANYTHING
YOU DESERVE THIS
SWEET SWEET INFANTS

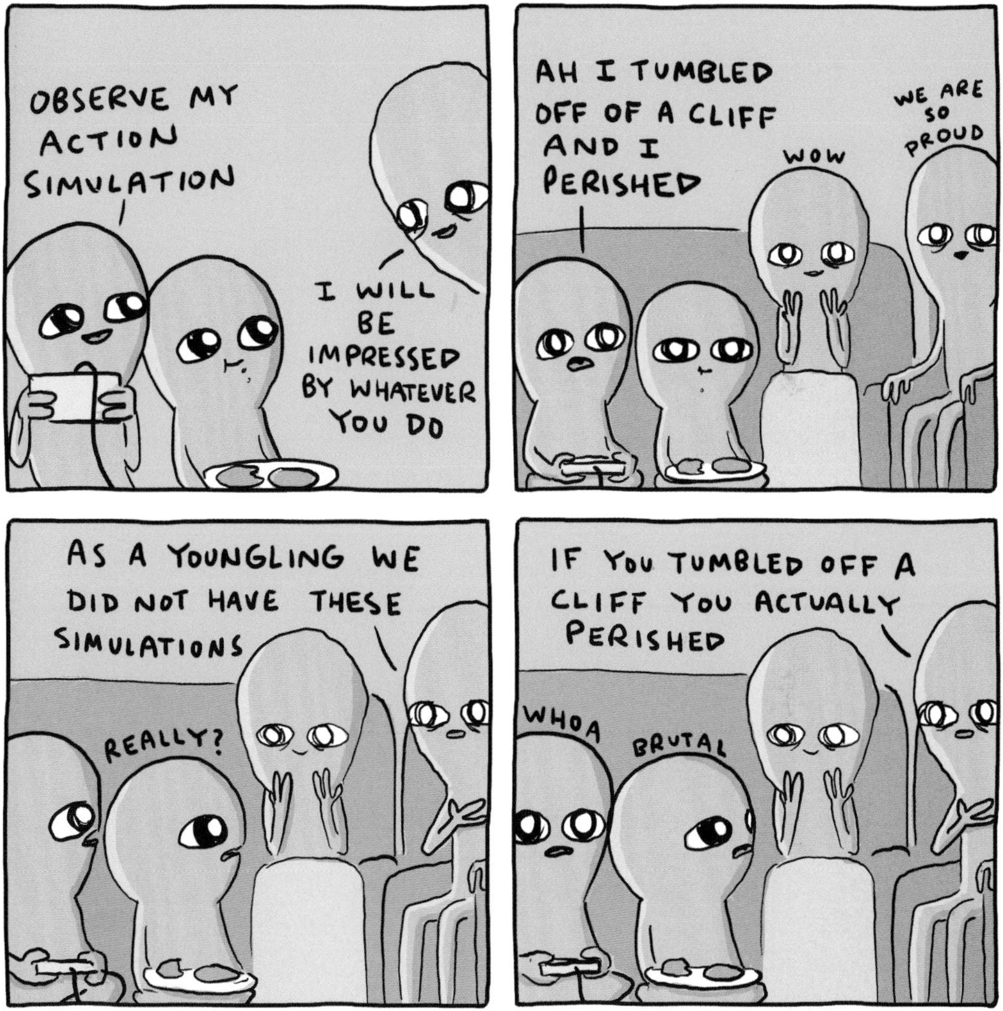
OBSERVE MY ACTION SIMULATION
I WILL BE IMPRESSED BY WHATEVER YOU DO
AH I TUMBLED OFF OF A CLIFF AND I PERISHED
WOW
WE ARE SO PROUD
AS A YOUNGLING WE DID NOT HAVE THESE SIMULATIONS
REALLY?
IF YOU TUMBLED OFF A CLIFF YOU ACTUALLY PERISHED
WHOA
BRUTAL

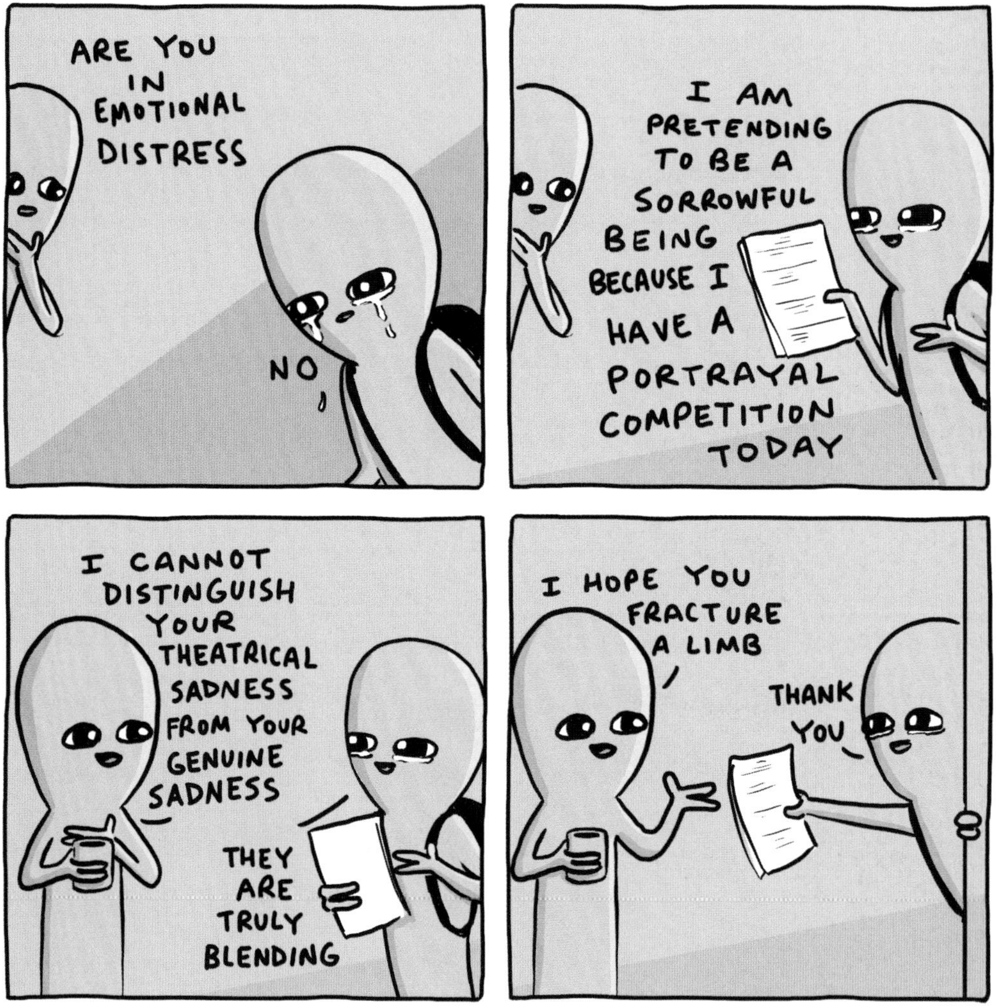
ARE YOU IN EMOTIONAL DISTRESS
NO
I AM PRETENDING TO BE A SORROWFUL BEING BECAUSE I HAVE A PORTRAYAL COMPETITION TODAY
I CANNOT DISTINGUISH YOUR THEATRICAL SADNESS FROM YOUR GENUINE SADNESS
THEY ARE TRULY BLENDING
I HOPE YOU FRACTURE A LIMB
THANK YOU

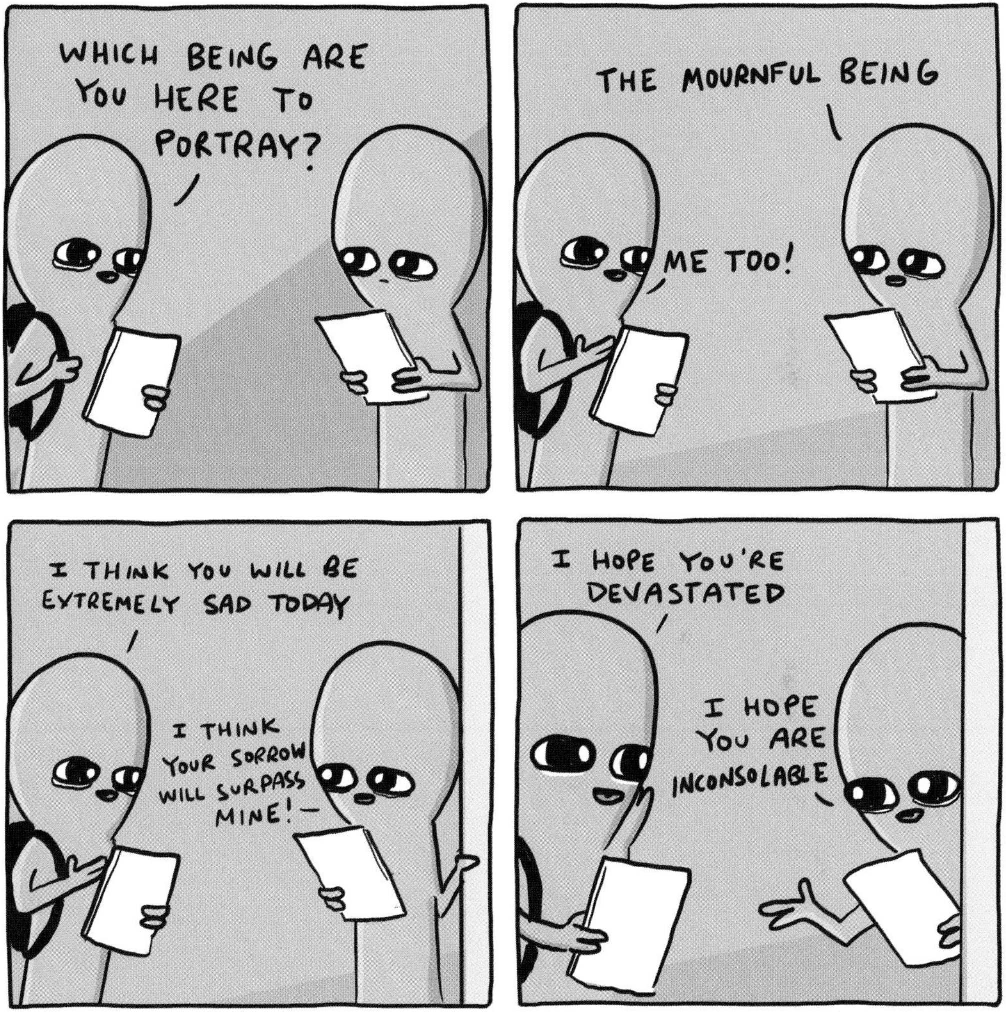
WHICH BEING ARE YOU HERE TO PORTRAY?
THE MOURNFUL BEING
ME TOO!
I THINK YOU WILL BE EXTREMELY SAD TODAY
I THINK YOUR SORROW WILL SURPASS MINE!
I HOPE YOU'RE DEVASTATED
I HOPE YOU ARE INCONSOLABLE

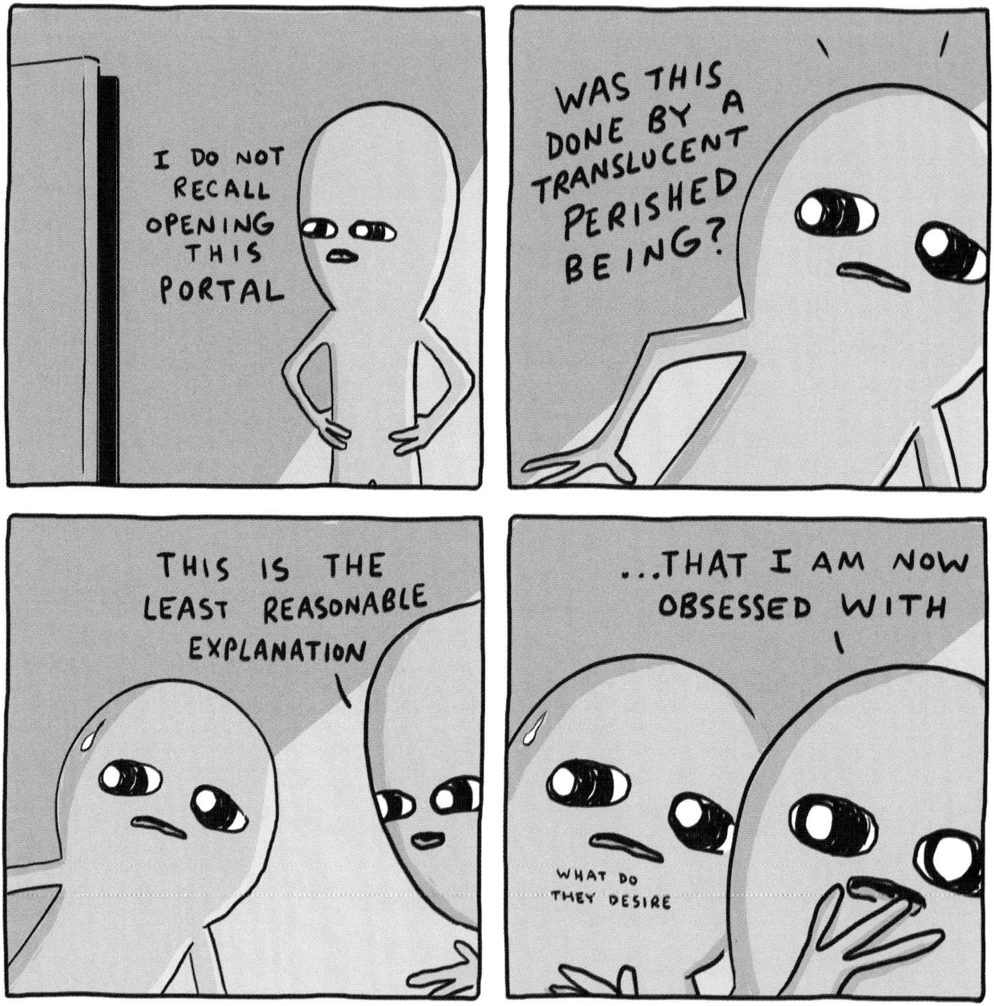
I DO NOT RECALL OPENING THIS PORTAL
WAS THIS DONE BY A TRANSLUCENT PERISHED BEING?
THIS IS THE LEAST REASONABLE EXPLANATION
...THAT I AM NOW OBSESSED WITH
WHAT DO THEY DESIRE

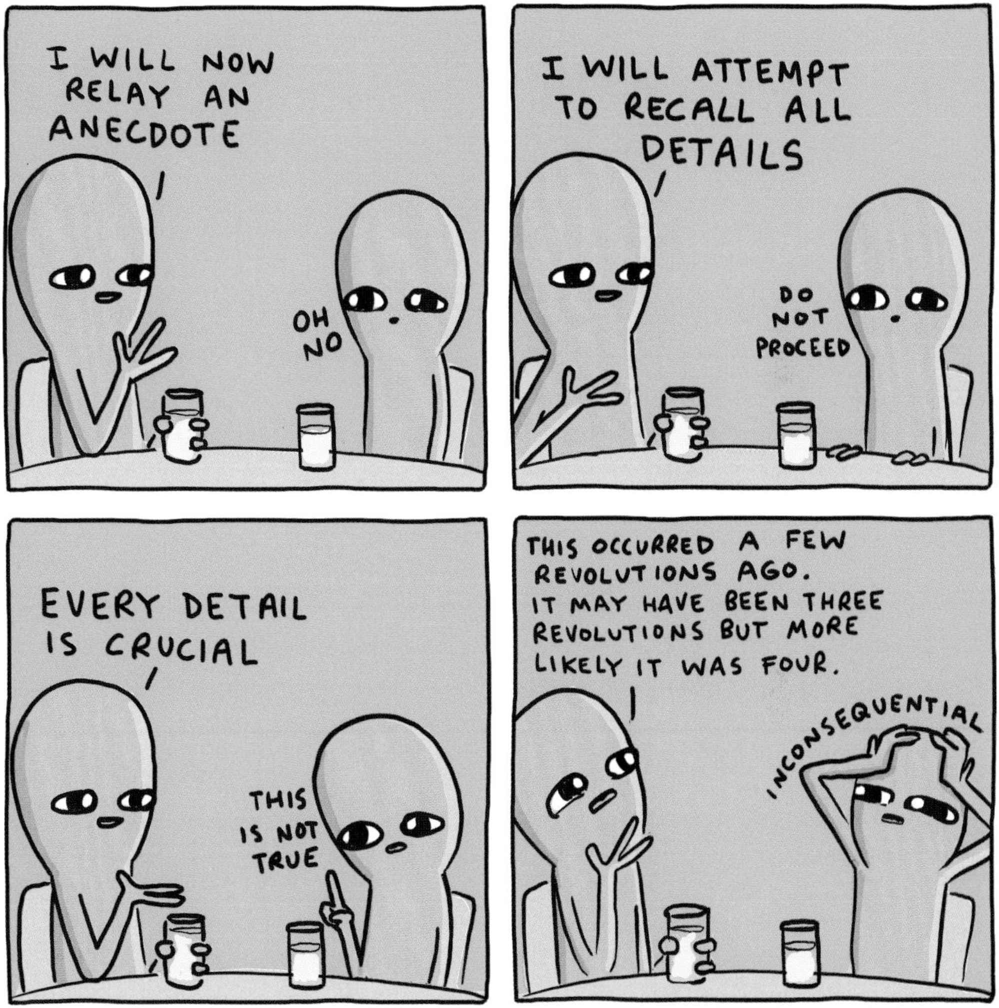
I WILL NOW RELAY AN ANECDOTE
OH NO
I WILL ATTEMPT TO RECALL ALL DETAILS
DO NOT PROCEED
EVERY DETAIL IS CRUCIAL
THIS IS NOT TRUE
THIS OCCURRED A FEW REVOLUTIONS AGO. IT MAY HAVE BEEN THREE REVOLUTIONS BUT MORE LIKELY IT WAS FOUR.
INCONSEQUENTIAL

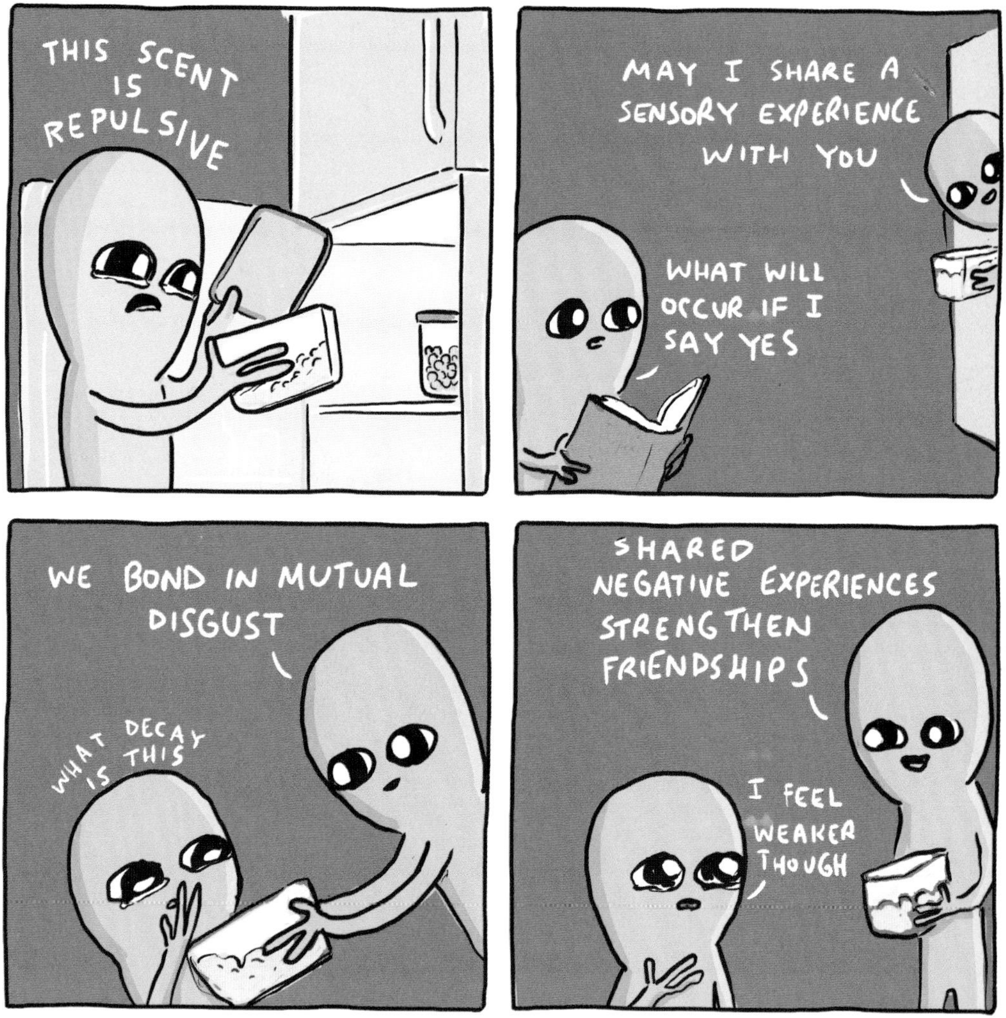
THIS SCENT IS REPULSIVE
MAY I SHARE A SENSORY EXPERIENCE WITH YOU
WHAT WILL OCCUR IF I SAY YES
WE BOND IN MUTUAL DISGUST
WHAT DECAY IS THIS
SHARED NEGATIVE EXPERIENCES STRENGTHEN FRIENDSHIPS
I FEEL WEAKER THOUGH

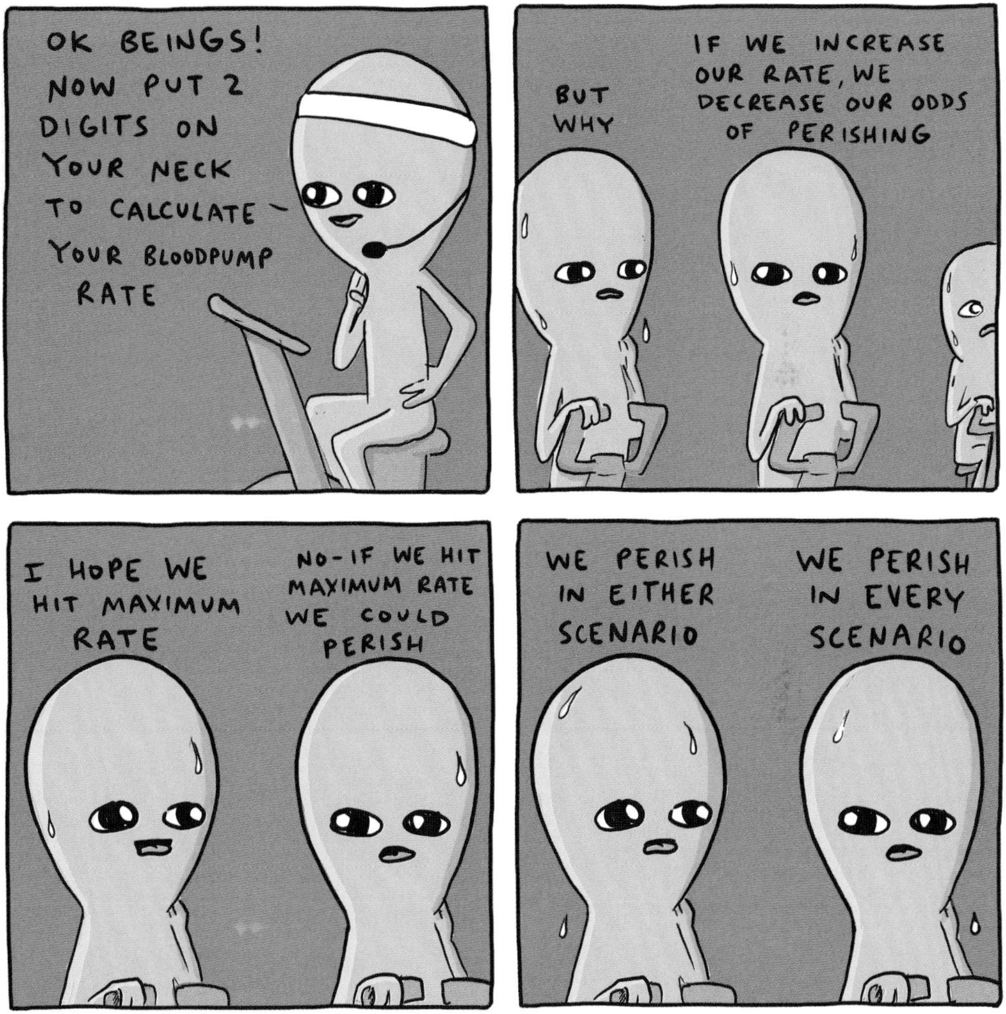
OK BEINGS! NOW PUT 2 DIGITS ON YOUR NECK TO CALCULATE YOUR BLOODPUMP RATE
BUT WHY
IF WE INCREASE OUR RATE, WE DECREASE OUR ODDS OF PERISHING
I HOPE WE HIT MAXIMUM RATE
NO-IF WE HIT MAXIMUM RATE WE COULD PERISH
WE PERISH IN EITHER SCENARIO
WE PERISH IN EVERY SCENARIO

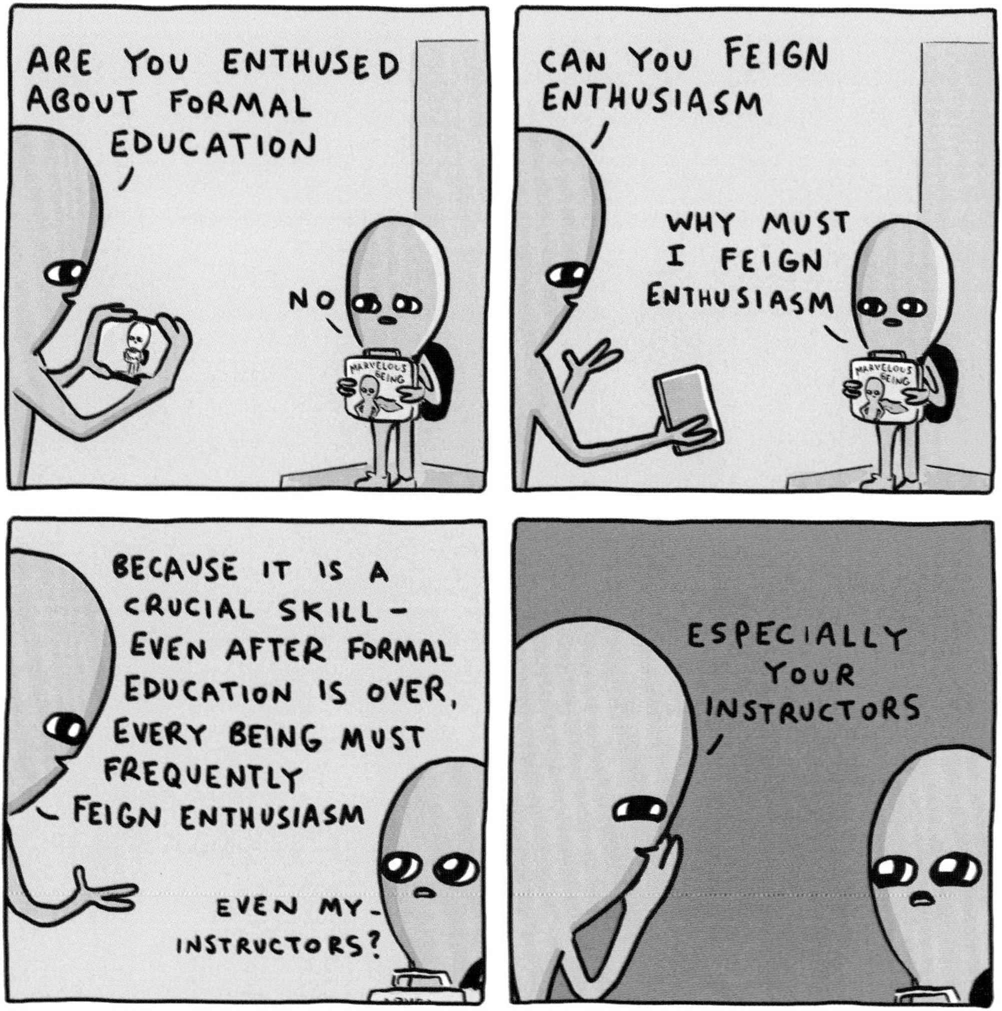
ARE YOU ENTHUSED ABOUT FORMAL EDUCATION
NO
MARVELOUS BEING
CAN YOU FEIGN ENTHUSIASM
WHY MUST I FEIGN ENTHUSIASM
MARVELOUS BEING
BECAUSE IT IS A CRUCIAL SKILL- EVEN AFTER FORMAL EDUCATION IS OVER, EVERY BEING MUST FREQUENTLY FEIGN ENTHUSIASM
EVEN MY- INSTRUCTORS?
ESPECIALLY YOUR INSTRUCTORS

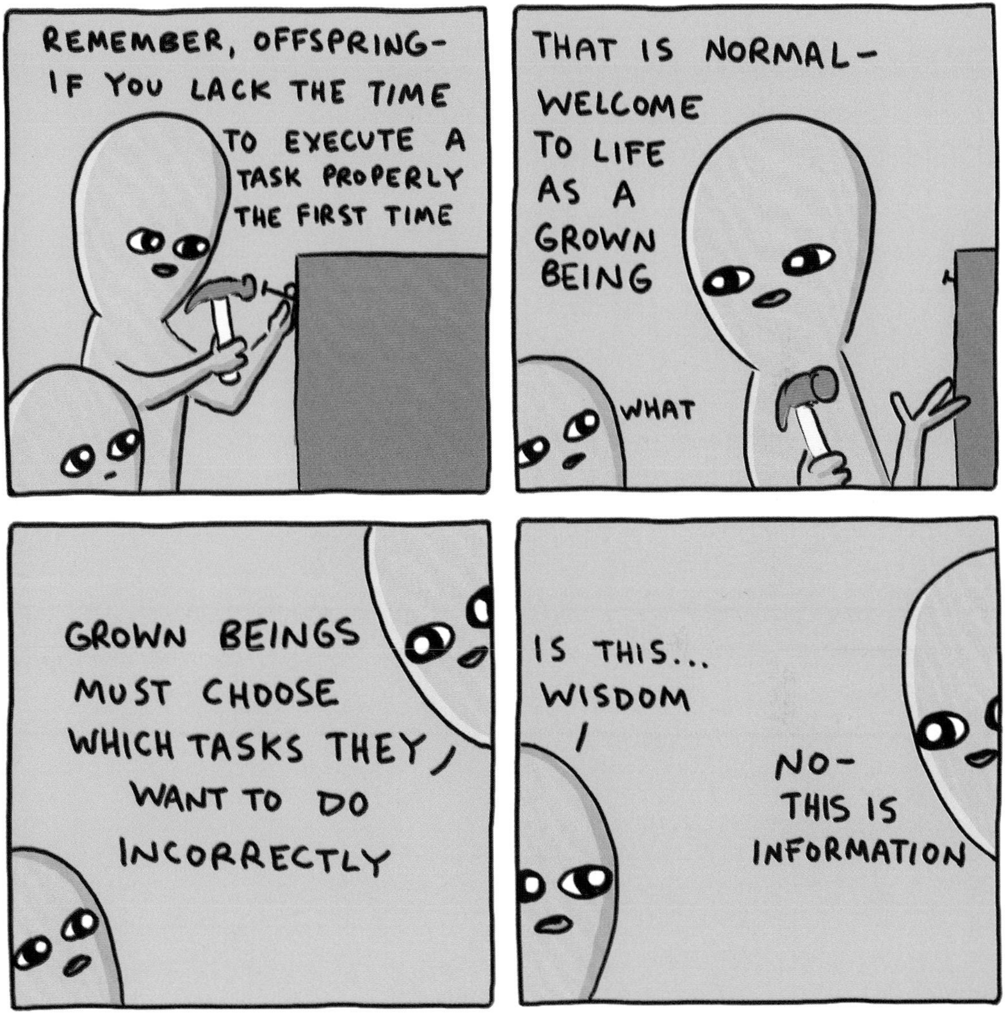
REMEMBER, OFFSPRING-
IF YOU LACK THE TIME
TO EXECUTE A TASK PROPERLY THE FIRST TIME
THAT IS NORMAL-
WELCOME TO LIFE AS A GROWN BEING
WHAT
GROWN BEINGS MUST CHOOSE WHICH TASKS THEY WANT TO DO INCORRECTLY
IS THIS... WISDOM
NO-
THIS IS INFORMATION

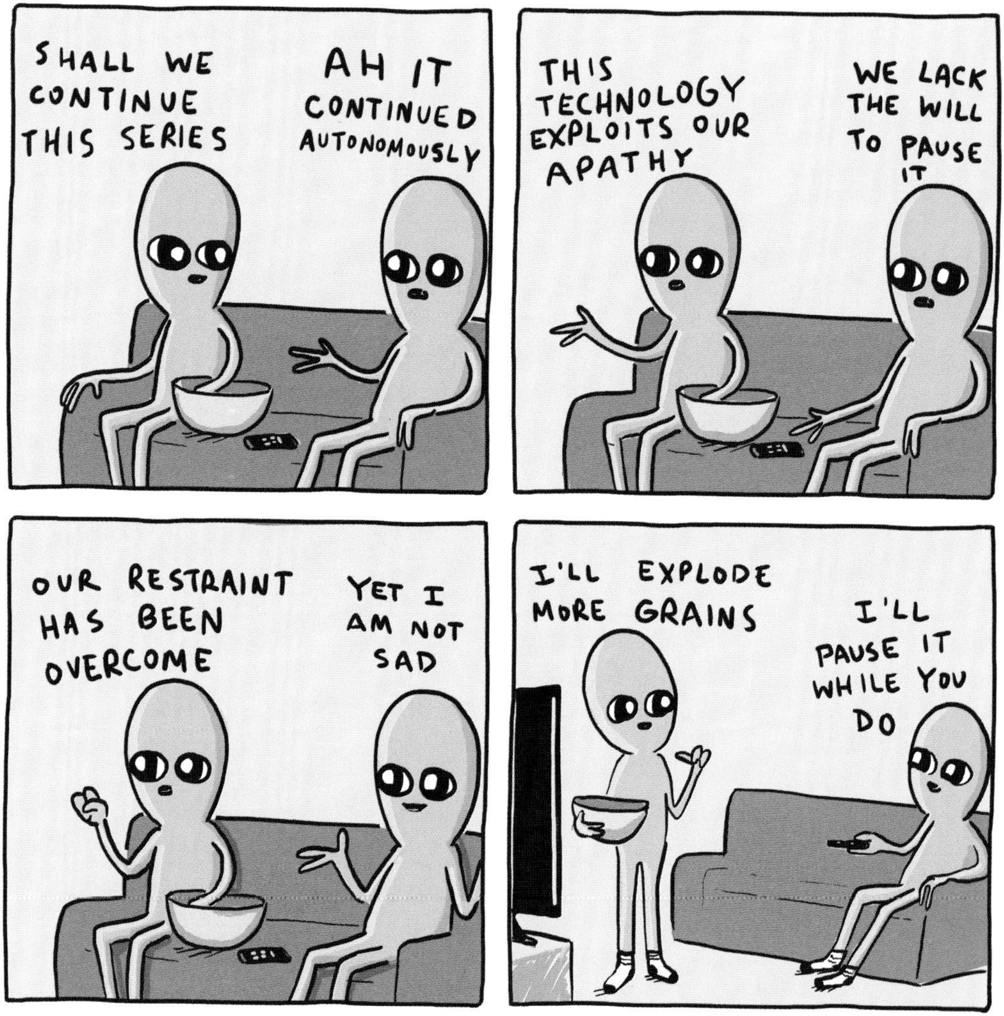
SHALL WE CONTINUE THIS SERIES
AH IT CONTINUED AUTONOMOUSLY
THIS TECHNOLOGY EXPLOITS OUR APATHY
WE LACK THE WILL TO PAUSE IT
OUR RESTRAINT HAS BEEN OVERCOME
YET I AM NOT SAD
I'LL EXPLODE MORE GRAINS
I'LL PAUSE IT WHILE YOU DO

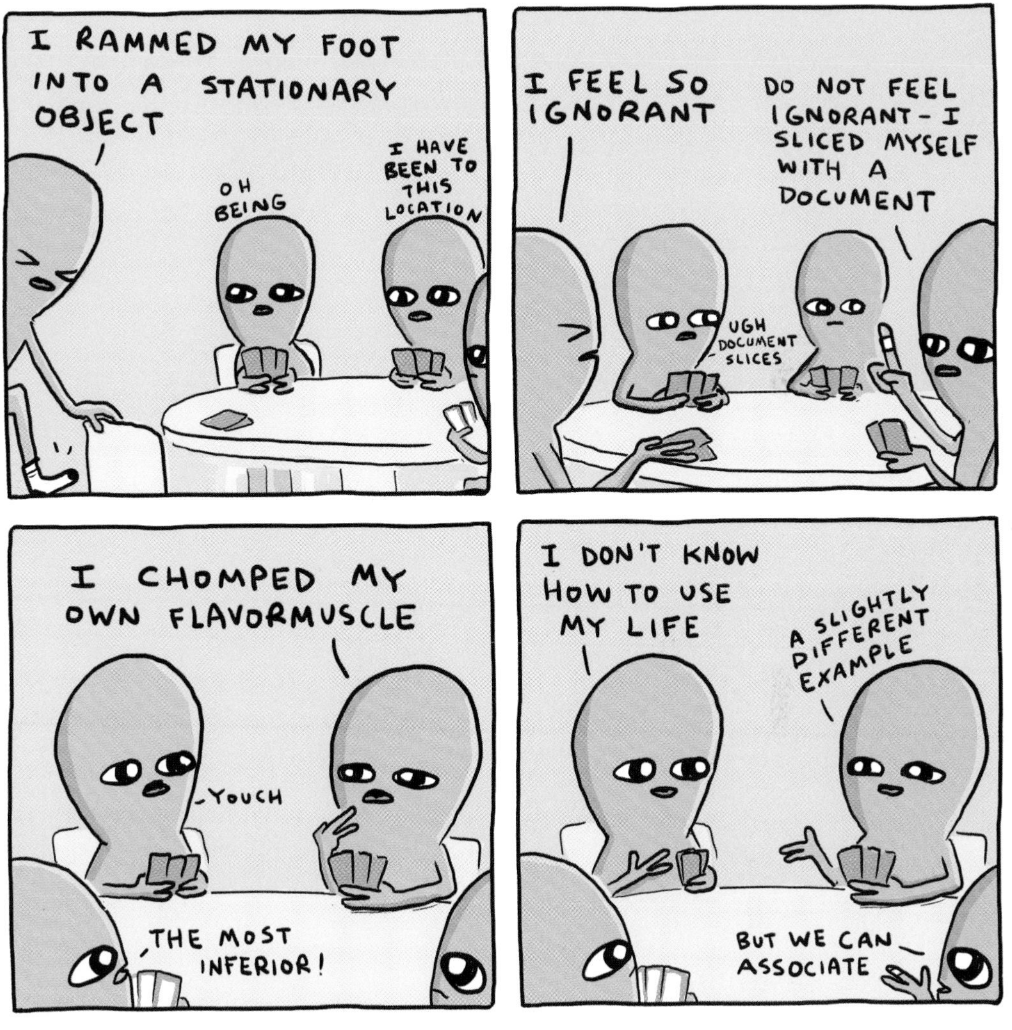
I RAMMED MY FOOT INTO A STATIONARY OBJECT
OH BEING
I HAVE BEEN TO THIS LOCATION
I FEEL SO IGNORANT
DO NOT FEEL IGNORANT - I SLICED MYSELF WITH A DOCUMENT
UGH DOCUMENT SLICES
I CHOMPED MY OWN FLAVORMUSCLE
YOUCH
THE MOST INFERIOR!
I DON'T KNOW HOW TO USE MY LIFE
A SLIGHTLY DIFFERENT EXAMPLE
BUT WE CAN ASSOCIATE

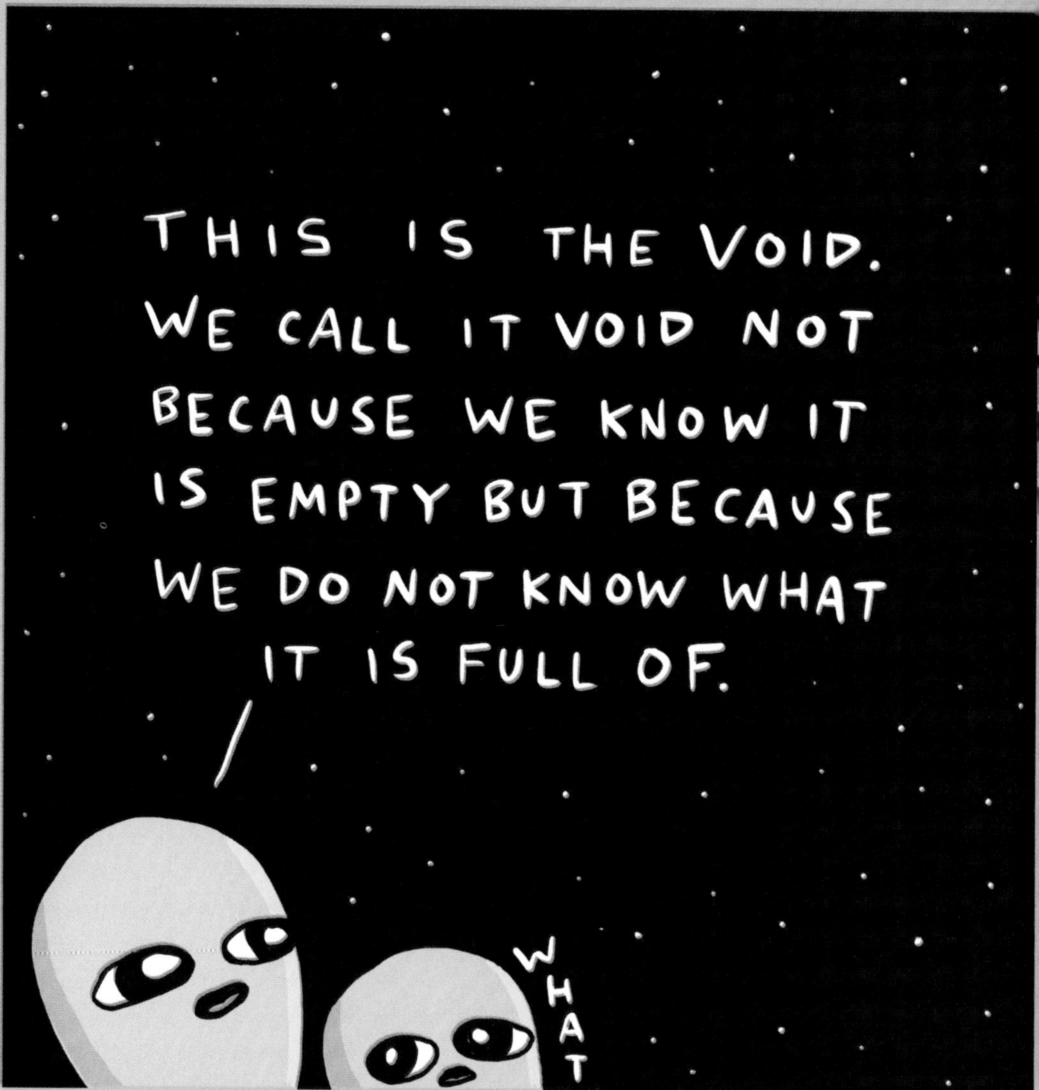
THIS IS THE VOID. WE CALL IT VOID NOT BECAUSE WE KNOW IT IS EMPTY BUT BECAUSE WE DO NOT KNOW WHAT IT IS FULL OF.
WHAT

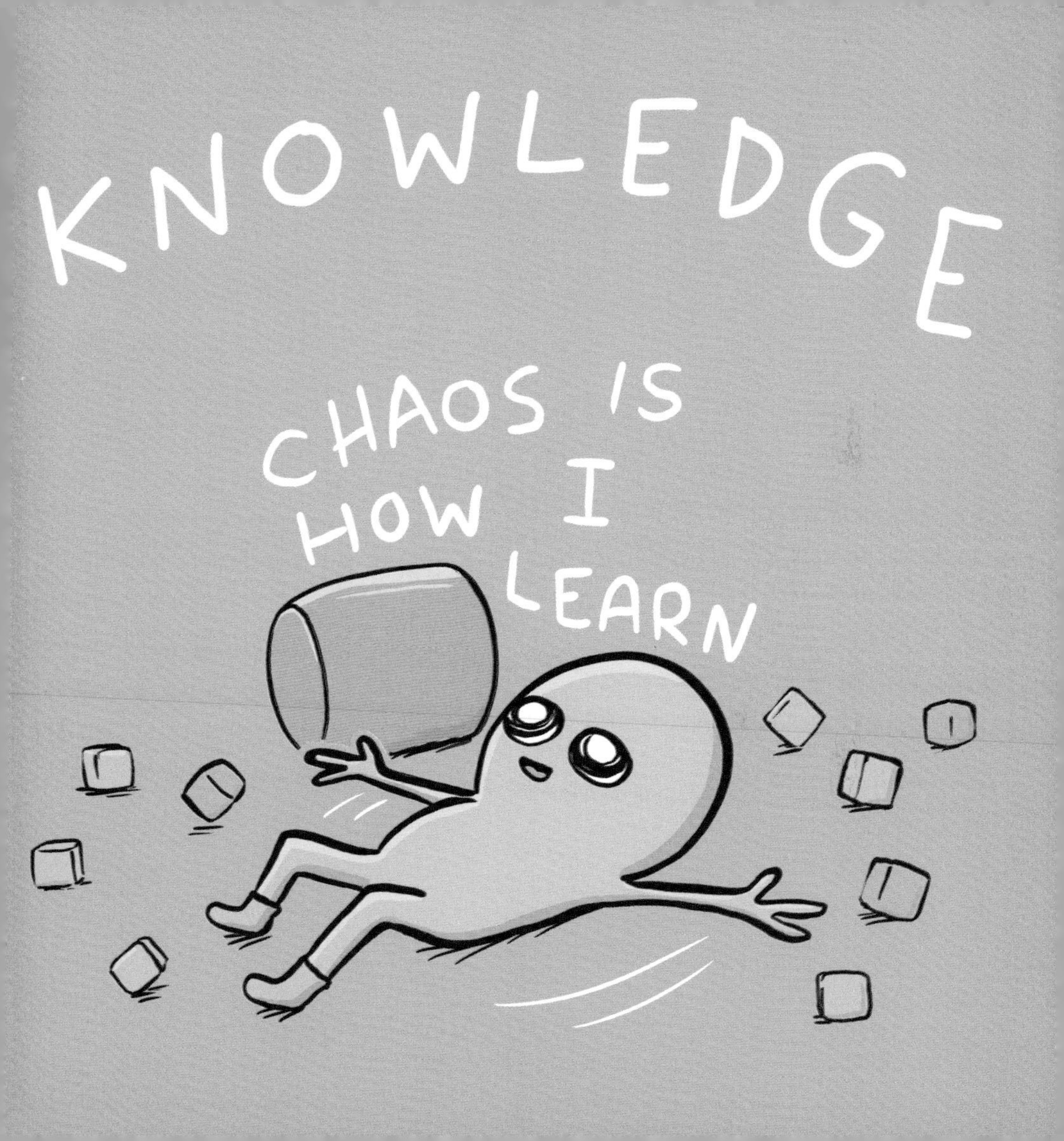
KNOWLEDGE
CHAOS IS HOW I LEARN

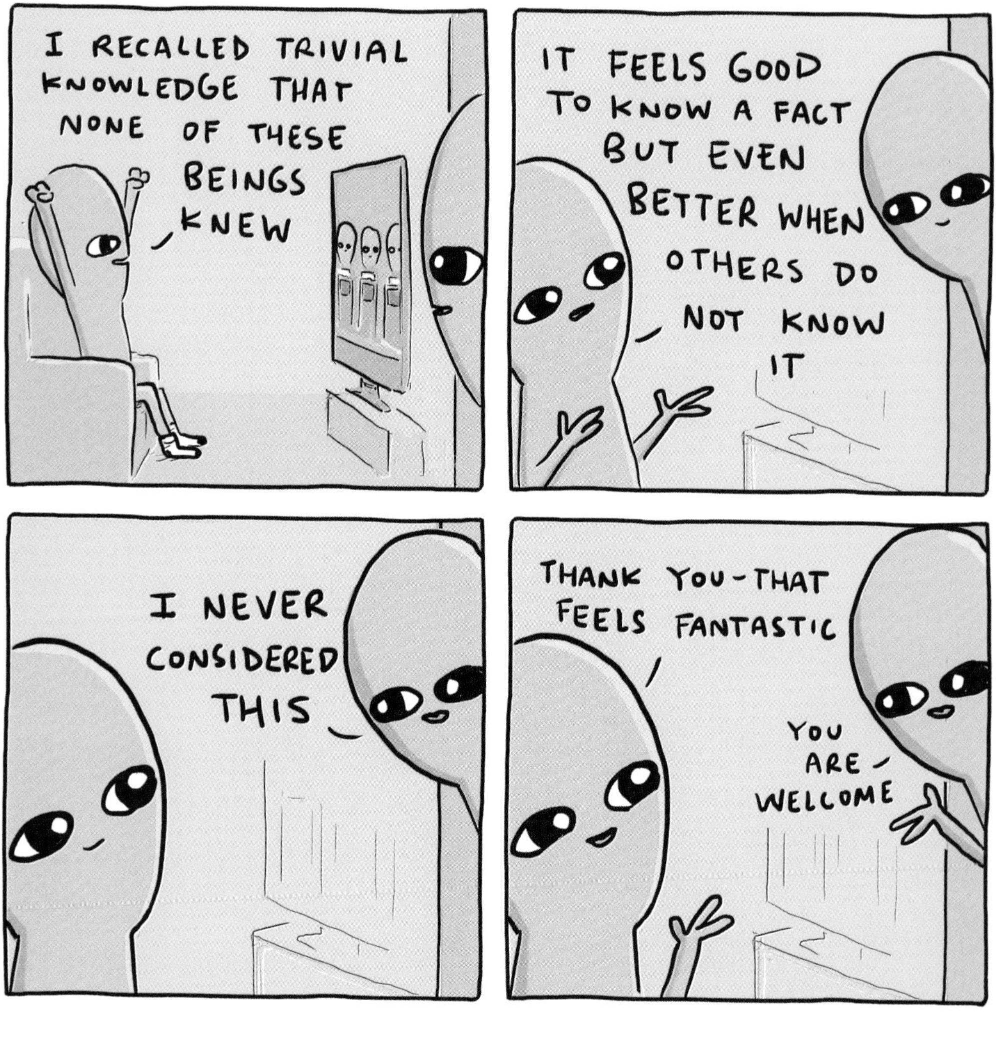
I RECALLED TRIVIAL KNOWLEDGE THAT NONE OF THESE BEINGS KNEW
IT FEELS GOOD TO KNOW A FACT BUT EVEN BETTER WHEN OTHERS DO NOT KNOW IT
I NEVER CONSIDERED THIS
THANK YOU - THAT FEELS FANTASTIC
YOU ARE WELCOME

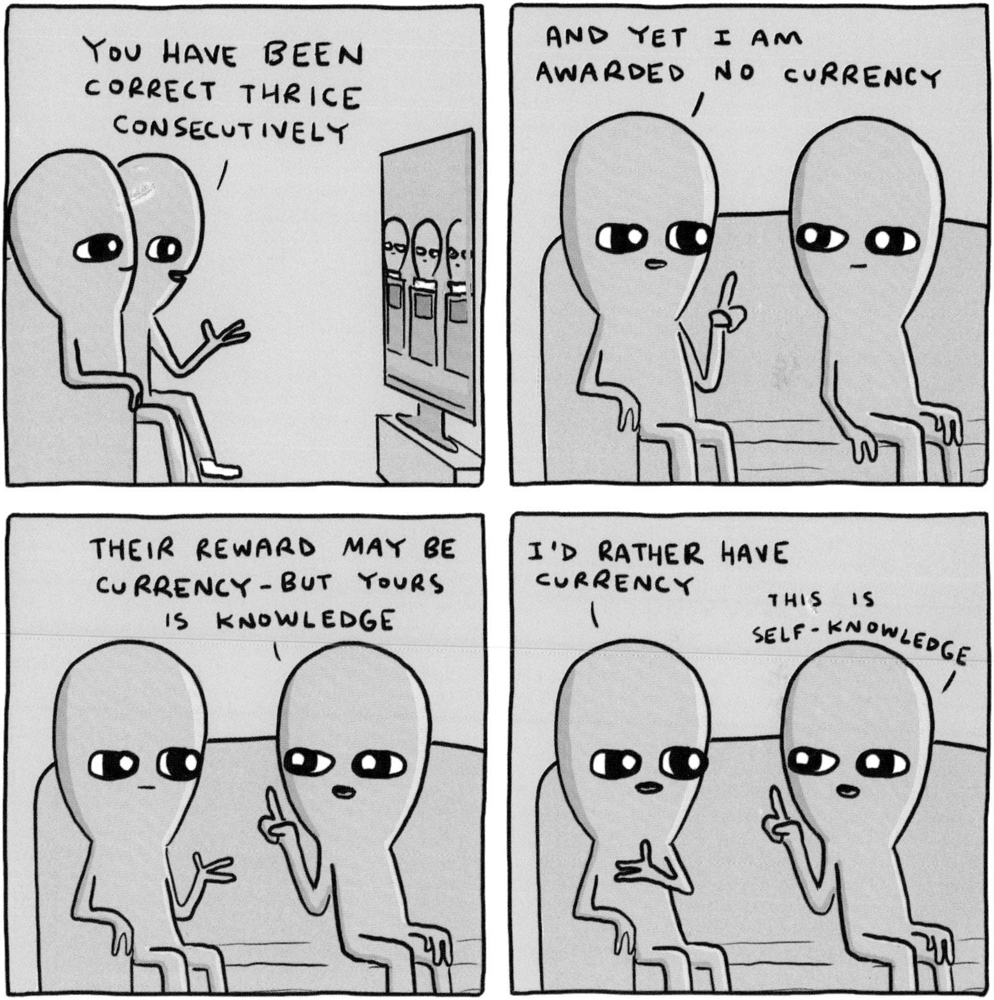
YOU HAVE BEEN CORRECT THRICE CONSECUTIVELY
AND YET I AM AWARDED NO CURRENCY
THEIR REWARD MAY BE CURRENCY - BUT YOURS IS KNOWLEDGE
I'D RATHER HAVE CURRENCY
THIS IS SELF-KNOWLEDGE

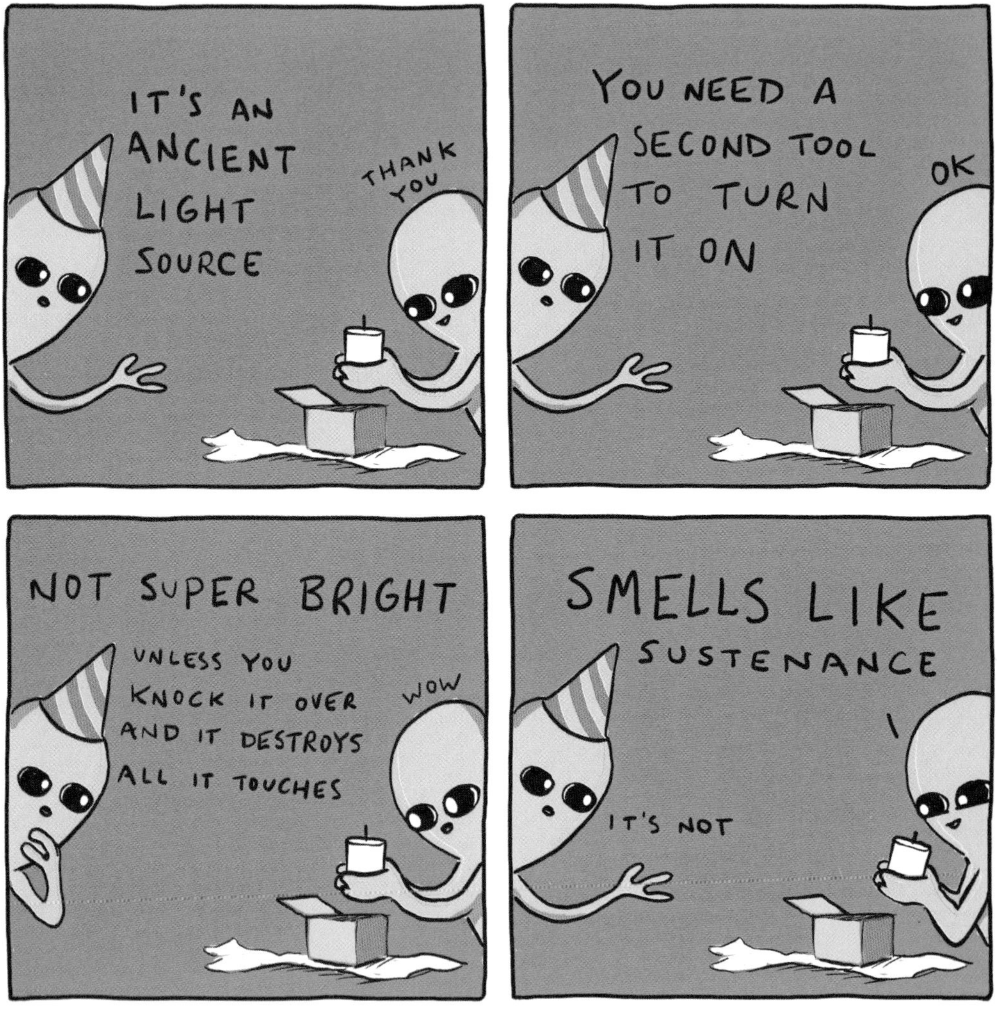
IT'S AN ANCIENT LIGHT SOURCE
THANK YOU
YOU NEED A SECOND TOOL TO TURN IT ON
OK
NOT SUPER BRIGHT
UNLESS YOU KNOCK IT OVER AND IT DESTROYS ALL IT TOUCHES
WOW
SMELLS LIKE SUSTENANCE
IT'S NOT

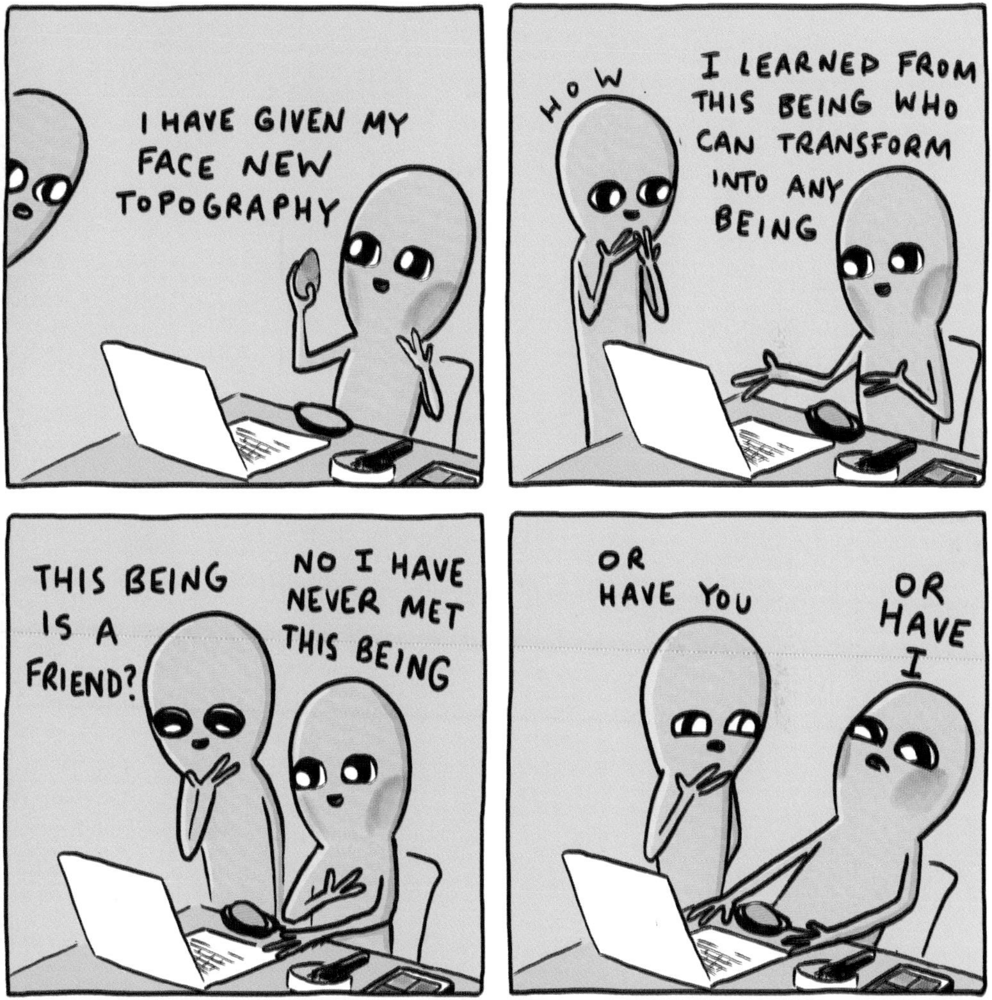
I HAVE GIVEN MY FACE NEW TOPOGRAPHY
HOW
I LEARNED FROM THIS BEING WHO CAN TRANSFORM INTO ANY BEING
THIS BEING IS A FRIEND?
NO I HAVE NEVER MET THIS BEING
OR HAVE YOU
OR HAVE I

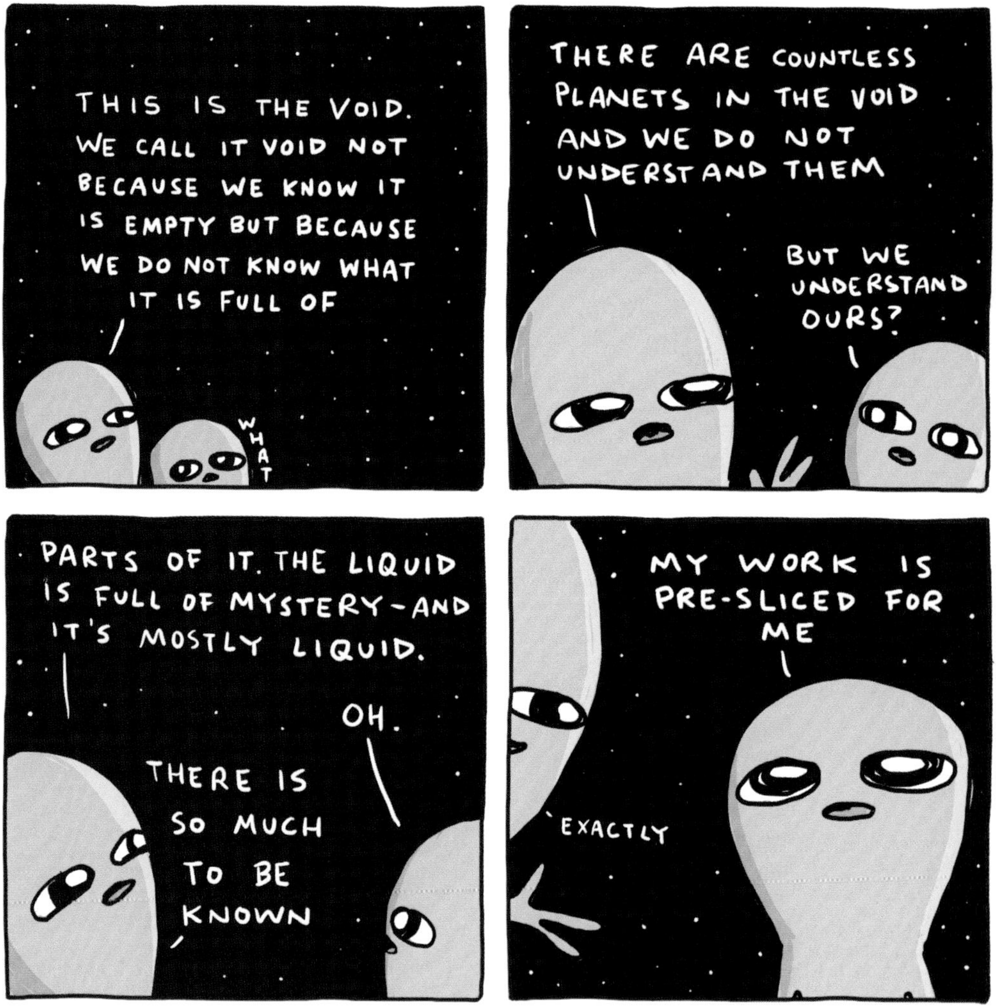
THIS IS THE VOID. WE CALL IT VOID NOT BECAUSE WE KNOW IT IS EMPTY BUT BECAUSE WE DO NOT KNOW WHAT IT IS FULL OF
WHAT
THERE ARE COUNTLESS PLANETS IN THE VOID AND WE DO NOT UNDERSTAND THEM
BUT WE UNDERSTAND OURS?
PARTS OF IT. THE LIQUID IS FULL OF MYSTERY - AND IT'S MOSTLY LIQUID.
OH.
THERE IS SO MUCH TO BE KNOWN
MY WORK IS PRE-SLICED FOR ME
EXACTLY

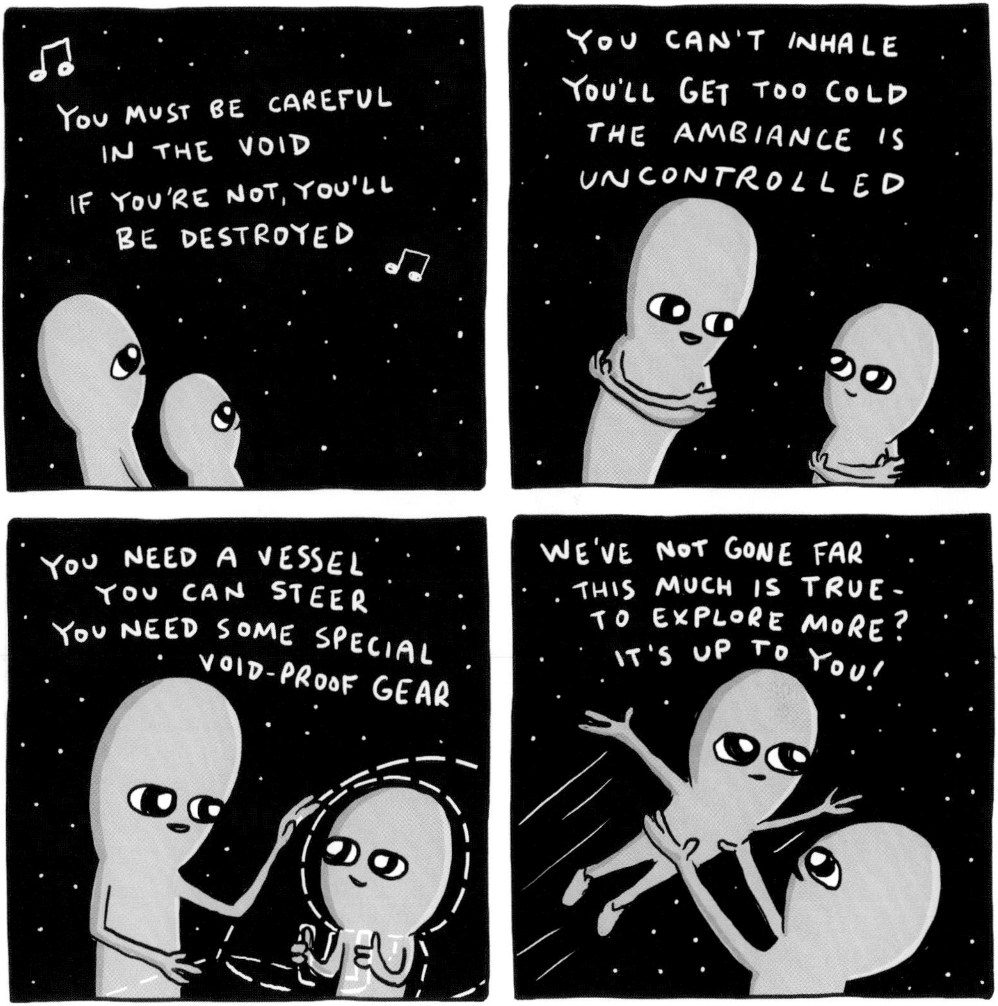

YOU MUST BE CAREFUL
IN THE VOID
IF YOU'RE NOT, YOU'LL
BE DESTROYED
YOU CAN'T INHALE
YOU'LL GET TOO COLD
THE AMBIANCE IS
UNCONTROLLED
YOU NEED A VESSEL
YOU CAN STEER
YOU NEED SOME SPECIAL
VOID-PROOF GEAR
WE'VE NOT GONE FAR
THIS MUCH IS TRUE-
TO EXPLORE MORE?
IT'S UP TO YOU!

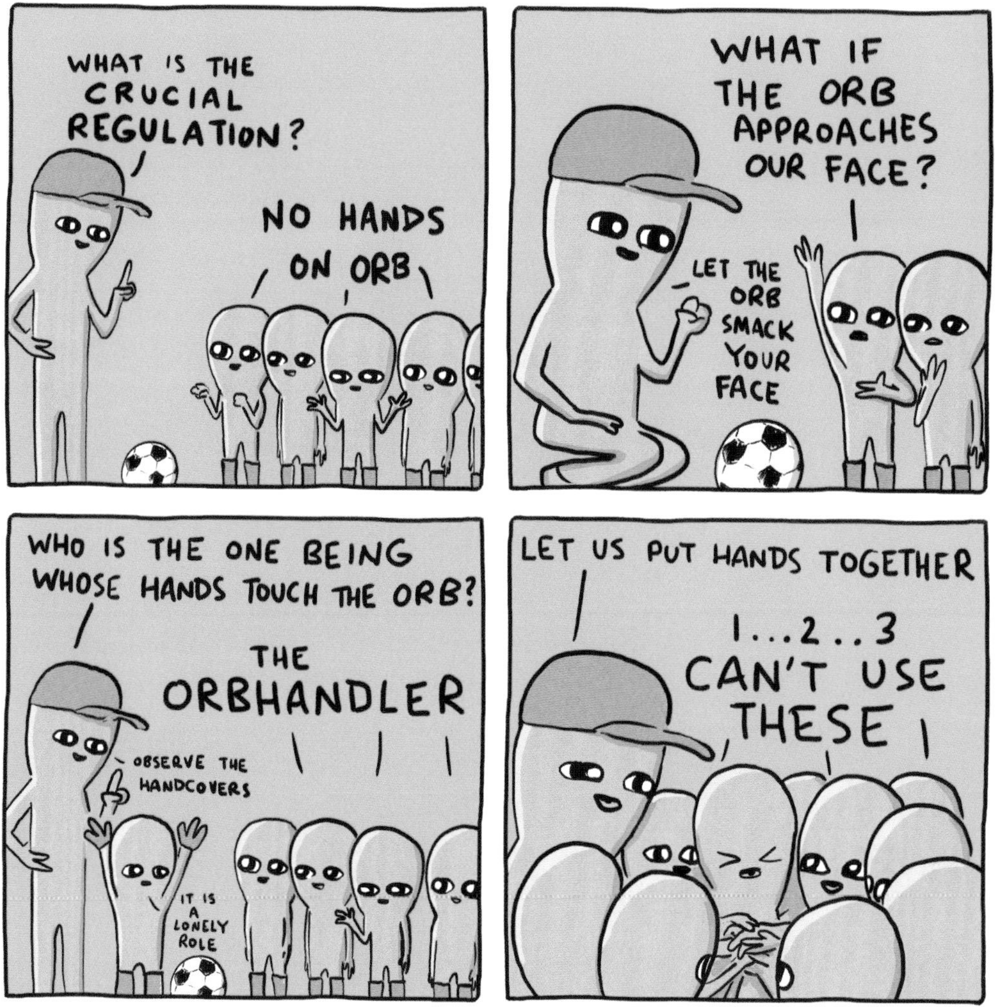
WHAT IS THE CRUCIAL REGULATION?
NO HANDS ON ORB
WHAT IF THE ORB APPROACHES OUR FACE?
LET THE ORB SMACK YOUR FACE
WHO IS THE ONE BEING WHOSE HANDS TOUCH THE ORB?
THE ORBHANDLER
OBSERVE THE HANDCOVERS
IT IS A LONELY ROLE
LET US PUT HANDS TOGETHER
1...2..3 CAN'T USE THESE

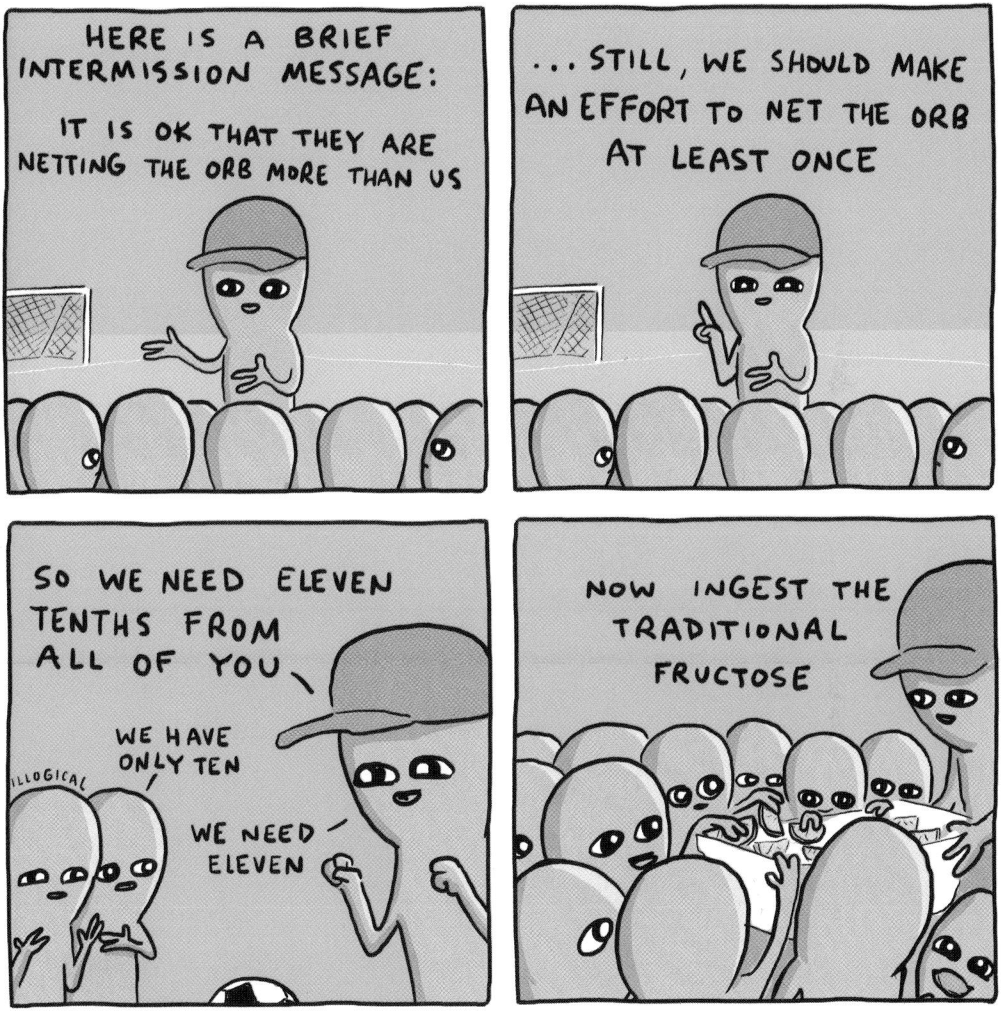
HERE IS A BRIEF INTERMISSION MESSAGE:
IT IS OK THAT THEY ARE NETTING THE ORB MORE THAN US
...STILL, WE SHOULD MAKE AN EFFORT TO NET THE ORB AT LEAST ONCE
SO WE NEED ELEVEN TENTHS FROM ALL OF YOU
WE HAVE ONLY TEN
ILLOGICAL
WE NEED ELEVEN
NOW INGEST THE TRADITIONAL FRUCTOSE

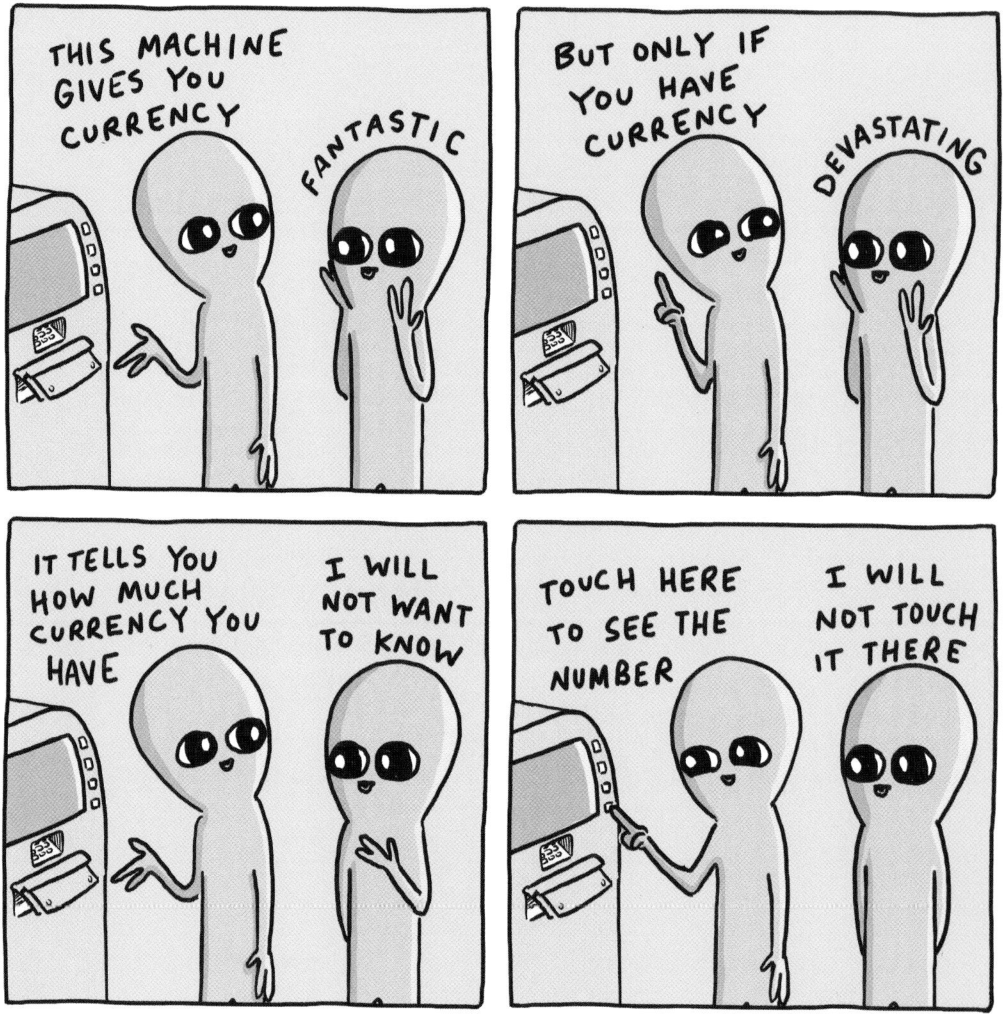
THIS MACHINE GIVES YOU CURRENCY
FANTASTIC
BUT ONLY IF YOU HAVE CURRENCY
DEVASTATING
IT TELLS YOU HOW MUCH CURRENCY YOU HAVE
I WILL NOT WANT TO KNOW
TOUCH HERE TO SEE THE NUMBER
I WILL NOT TOUCH IT THERE

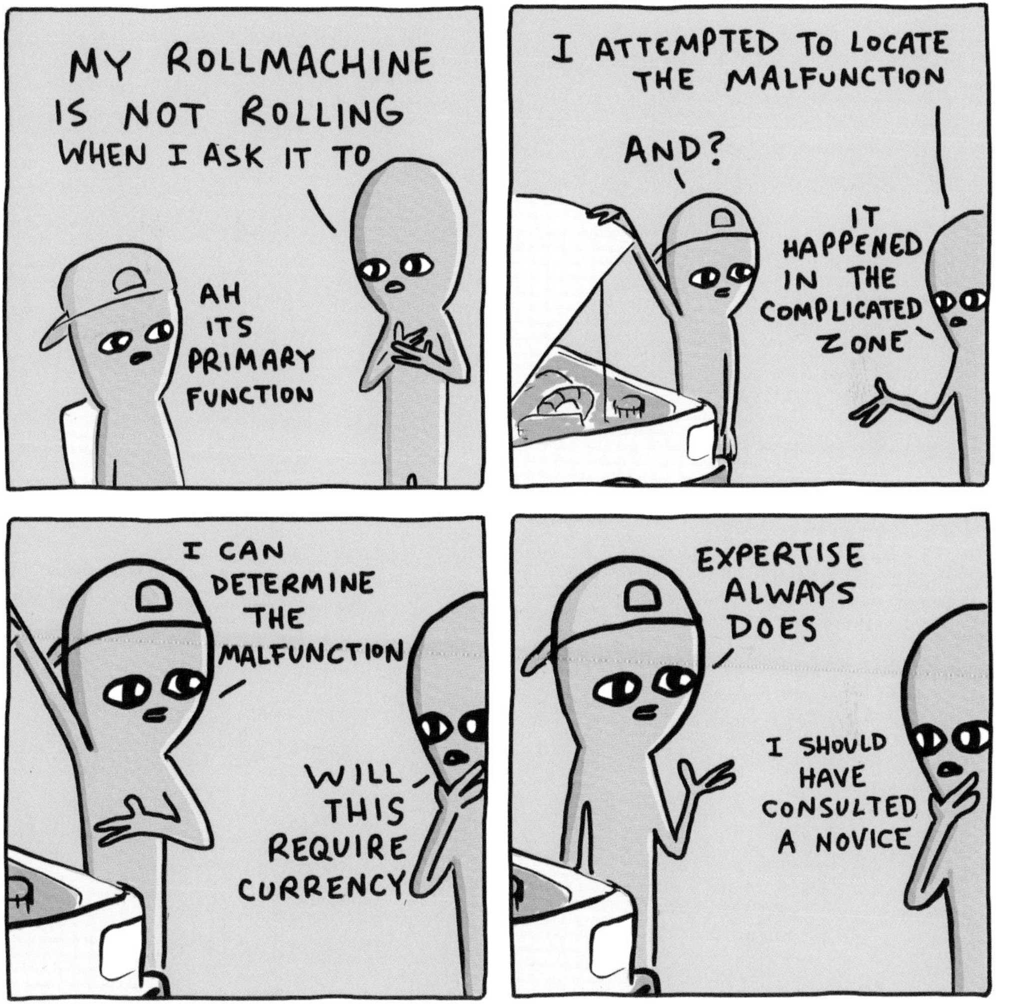

MY ROLLMACHINE IS NOT ROLLING WHEN I ASK IT TO
AH ITS PRIMARY FUNCTION
I ATTEMPTED TO LOCATE THE MALFUNCTION
AND?
IT HAPPENED IN THE COMPLICATED ZONE
I CAN DETERMINE THE MALFUNCTION
WILL THIS REQUIRE CURRENCY
EXPERTISE ALWAYS DOES
I SHOULD HAVE CONSULTED A NOVICE

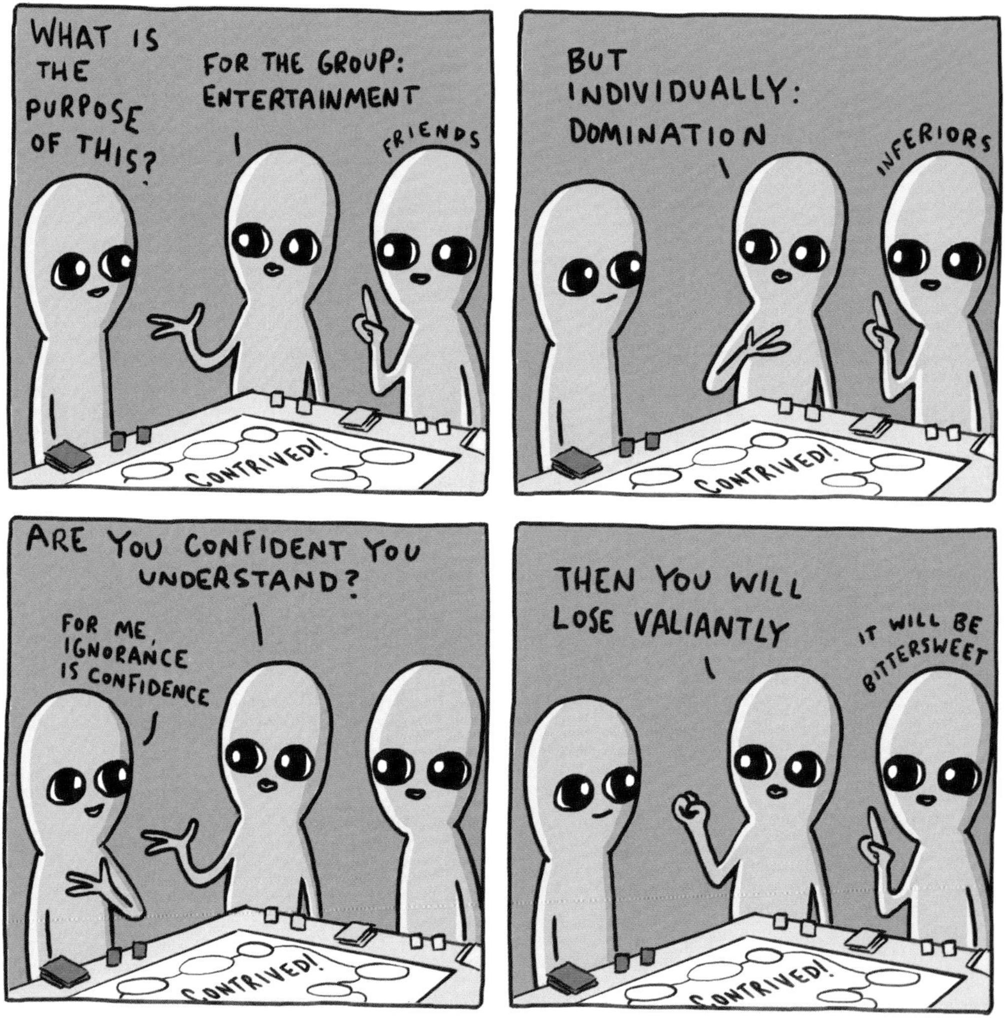
WHAT IS THE PURPOSE OF THIS?
FOR THE GROUP: ENTERTAINMENT
FRIENDS
CONTRIVED!
BUT INDIVIDUALLY: DOMINATION
INFERIORS
CONTRIVED!
ARE YOU CONFIDENT YOU UNDERSTAND?
FOR ME, IGNORANCE IS CONFIDENCE
CONTRIVED!
THEN YOU WILL LOSE VALIANTLY
IT WILL BE BITTERSWEET
CONTRIVED!

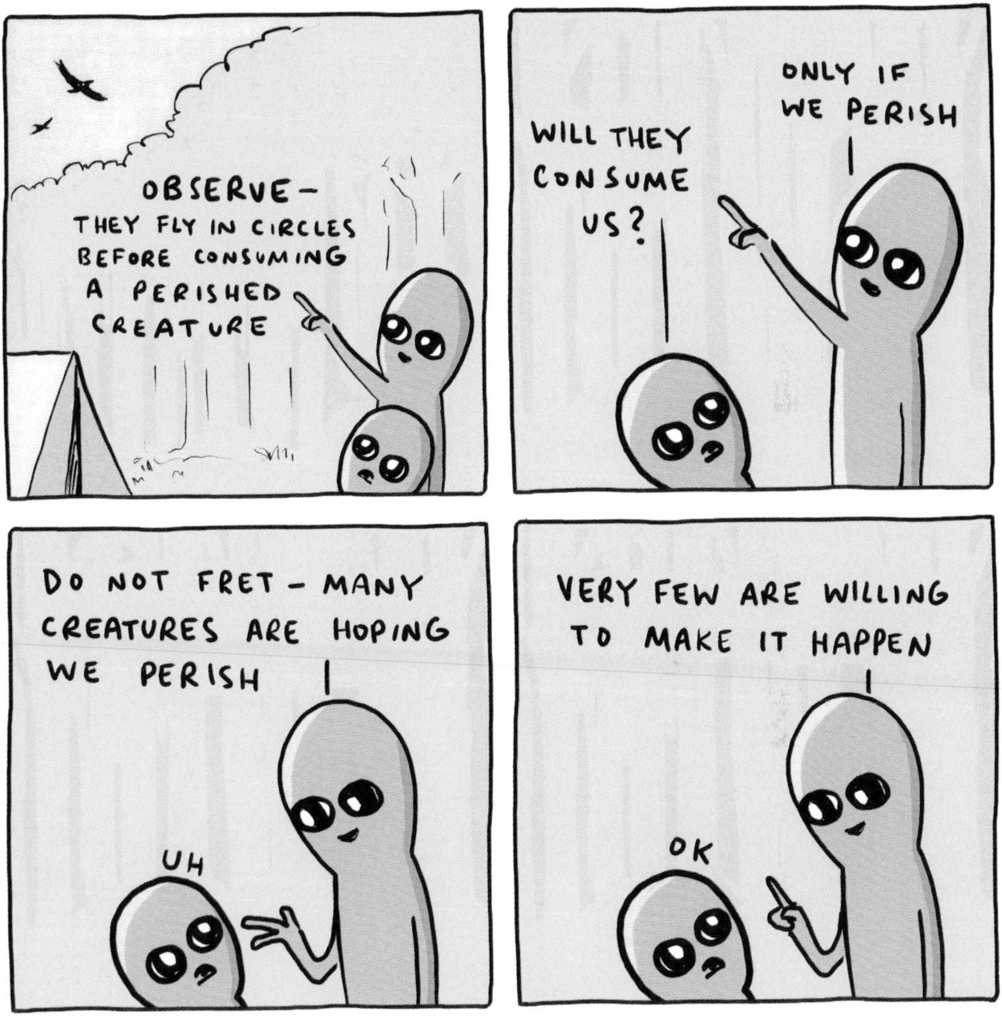
OBSERVE - THEY FLY IN CIRCLES BEFORE CONSUMING A PERISHED CREATURE
WILL THEY CONSUME US?
ONLY IF WE PERISH
DO NOT FRET - MANY CREATURES ARE HOPING WE PERISH
UH
VERY FEW ARE WILLING TO MAKE IT HAPPEN
OK

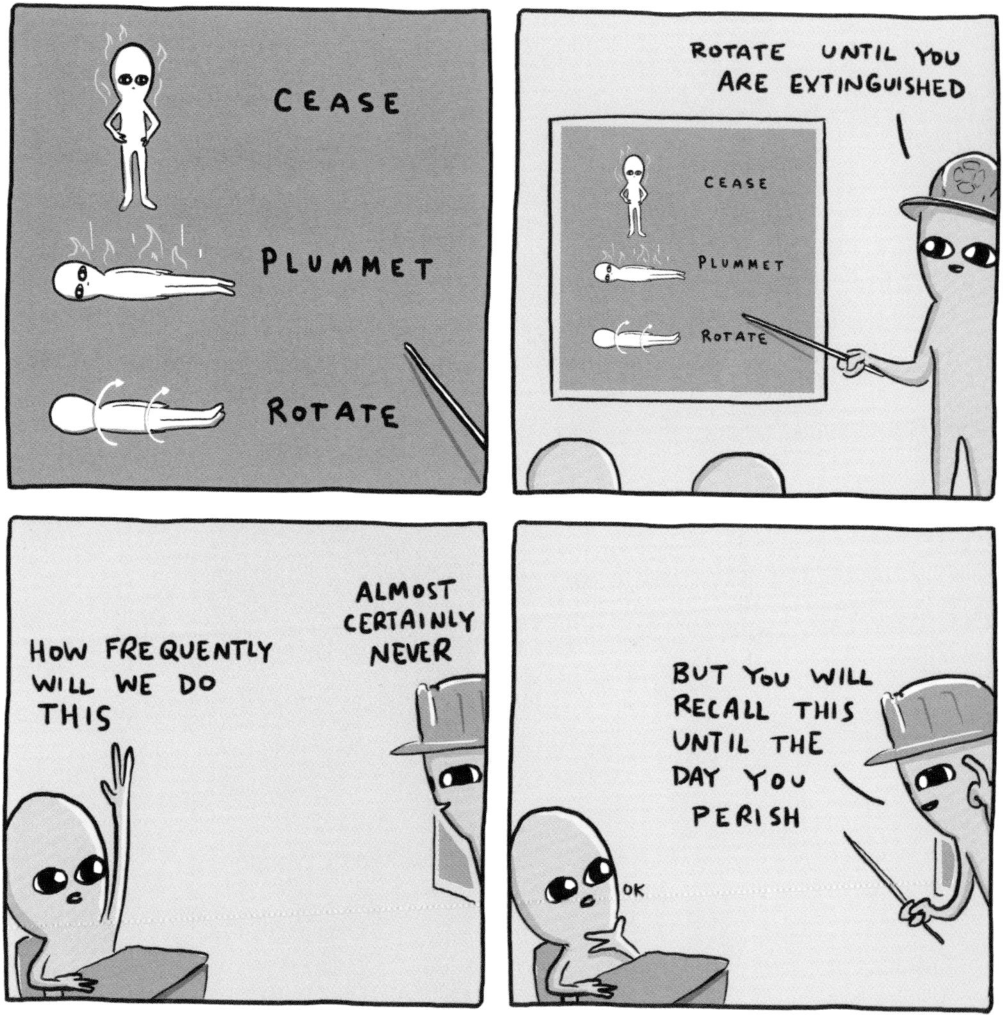
CEASE
PLUMMET
ROTATE
ROTATE UNTIL YOU ARE EXTINGUISHED
CEASE
PLUMMET
ROTATE
HOW FREQUENTLY WILL WE DO THIS
ALMOST CERTAINLY NEVER
BUT YOU WILL RECALL THIS UNTIL THE DAY YOU PERISH
OK

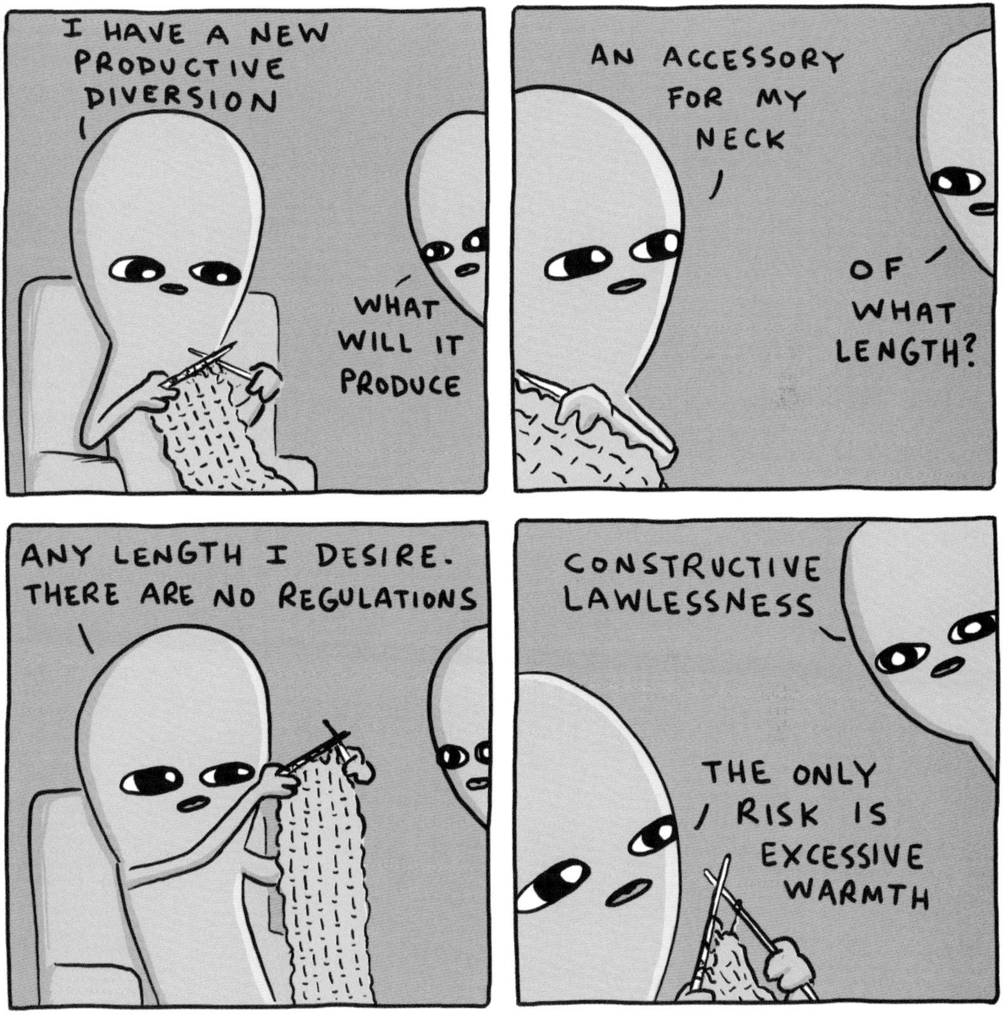
I HAVE A NEW PRODUCTIVE DIVERSION
WHAT WILL IT PRODUCE
AN ACCESSORY FOR MY NECK
OF WHAT LENGTH?
ANY LENGTH I DESIRE. THERE ARE NO REGULATIONS
CONSTRUCTIVE LAWLESSNESS
THE ONLY RISK IS EXCESSIVE WARMTH

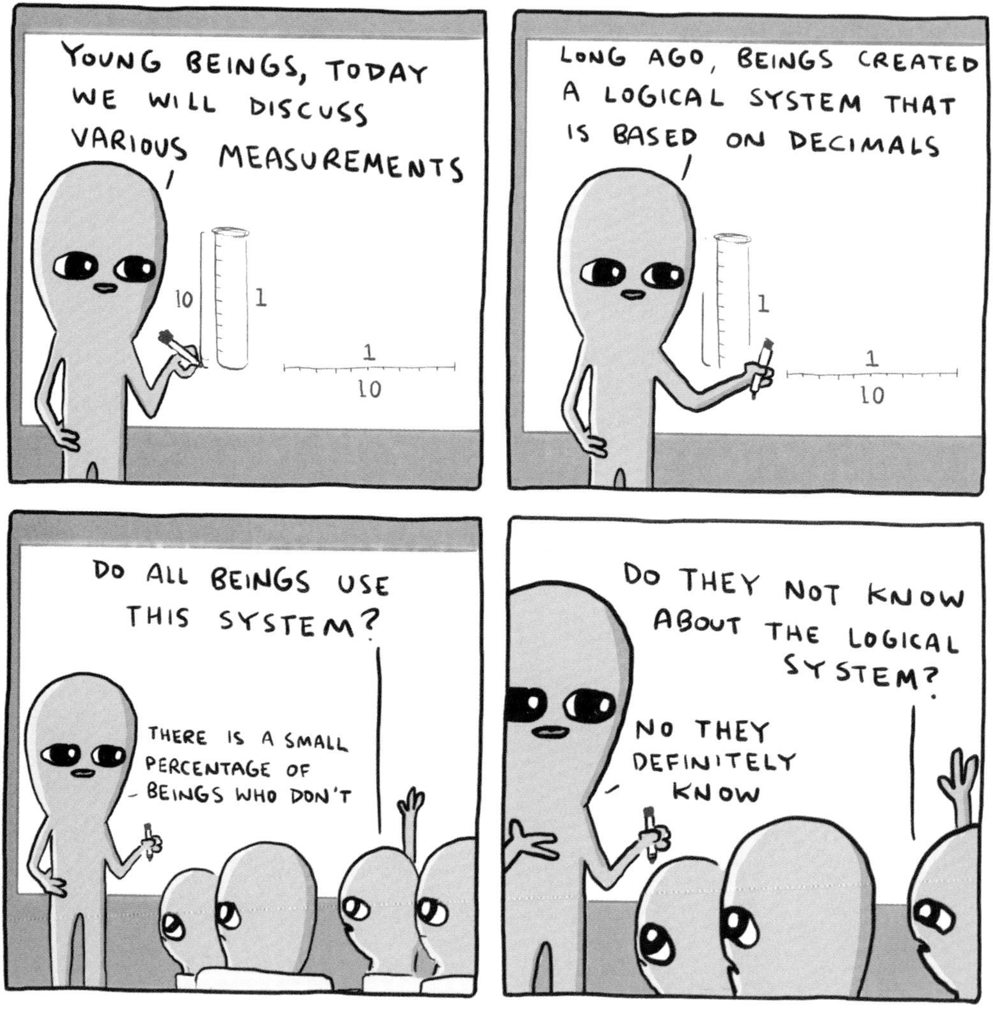

YOUNG BEINGS, TODAY WE WILL DISCUSS VARIOUS MEASUREMENTS
10
1
1
10
LONG AGO, BEINGS CREATED A LOGICAL SYSTEM THAT IS BASED ON DECIMALS
1
1
10
DO ALL BEINGS USE THIS SYSTEM?
THERE IS A SMALL PERCENTAGE OF BEINGS WHO DON'T
DO THEY NOT KNOW ABOUT THE LOGICAL SYSTEM?
NO THEY DEFINITELY KNOW

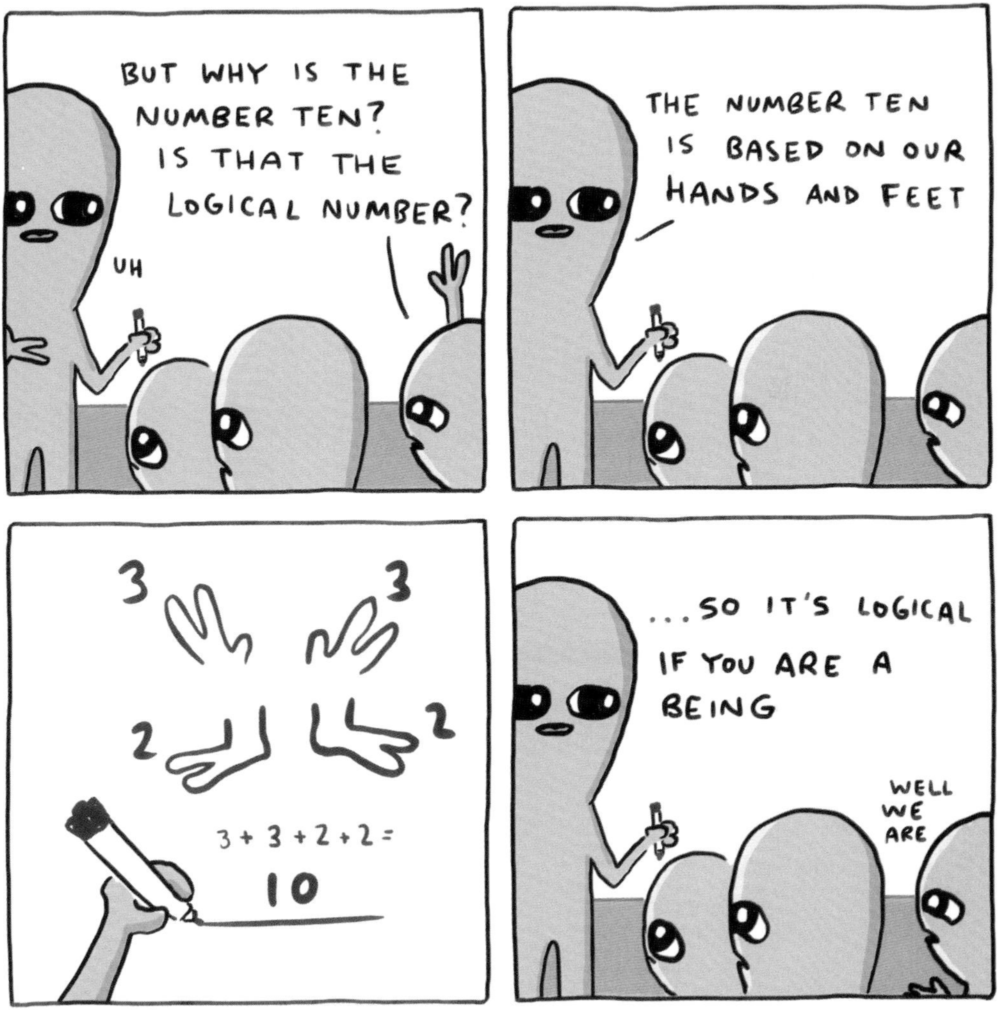
BUT WHY IS THE NUMBER TEN? IS THAT THE LOGICAL NUMBER?
UH
THE NUMBER TEN IS BASED ON OUR HANDS AND FEET
3
3
2
2
3 + 3 + 2 + 2 =
10
. . . SO IT'S LOGICAL IF YOU ARE A BEING
WELL WE ARE

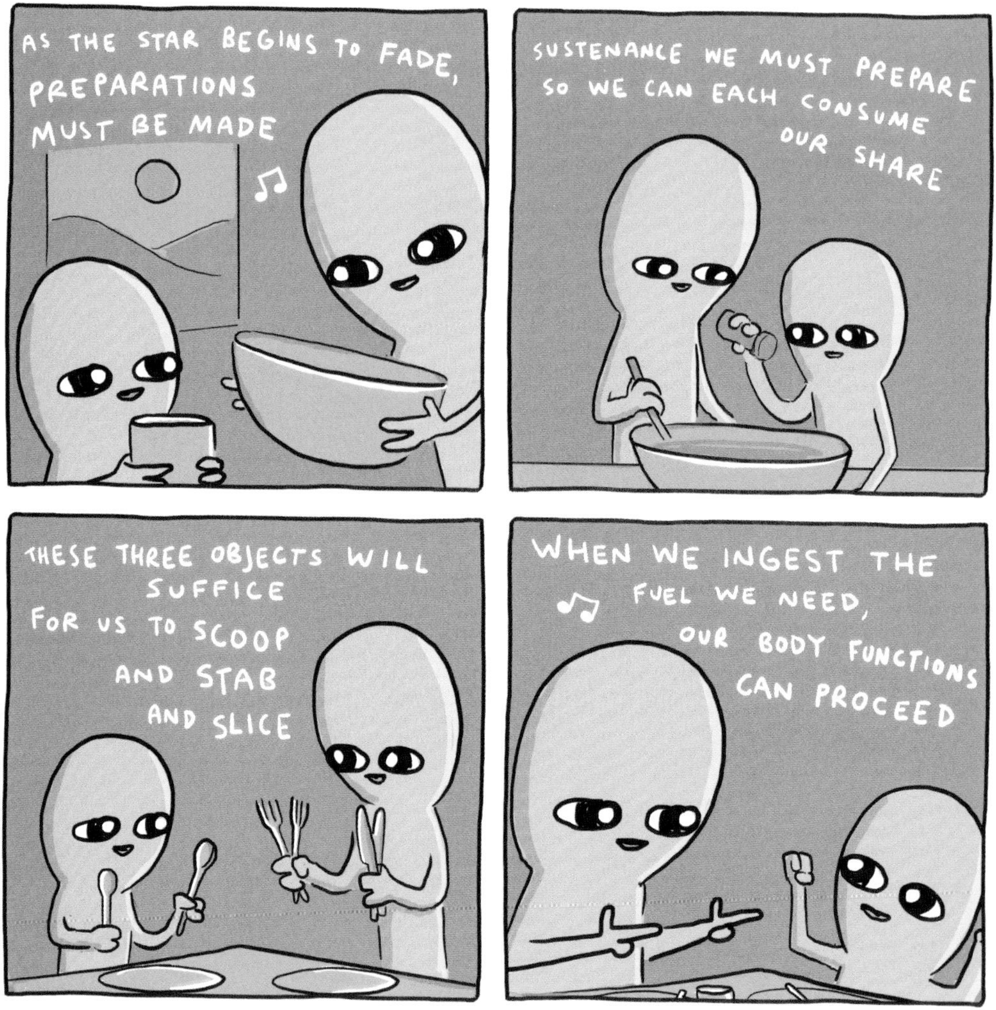
AS THE STAR BEGINS TO FADE,
PREPARATIONS
MUST BE MADE
SUSTENANCE WE MUST PREPARE
SO WE CAN EACH CONSUME
OUR SHARE
THESE THREE OBJECTS WILL
SUFFICE
FOR US TO SCOOP
AND STAB
AND SLICE
WHEN WE INGEST THE
FUEL WE NEED,
OUR BODY FUNCTIONS
CAN PROCEED

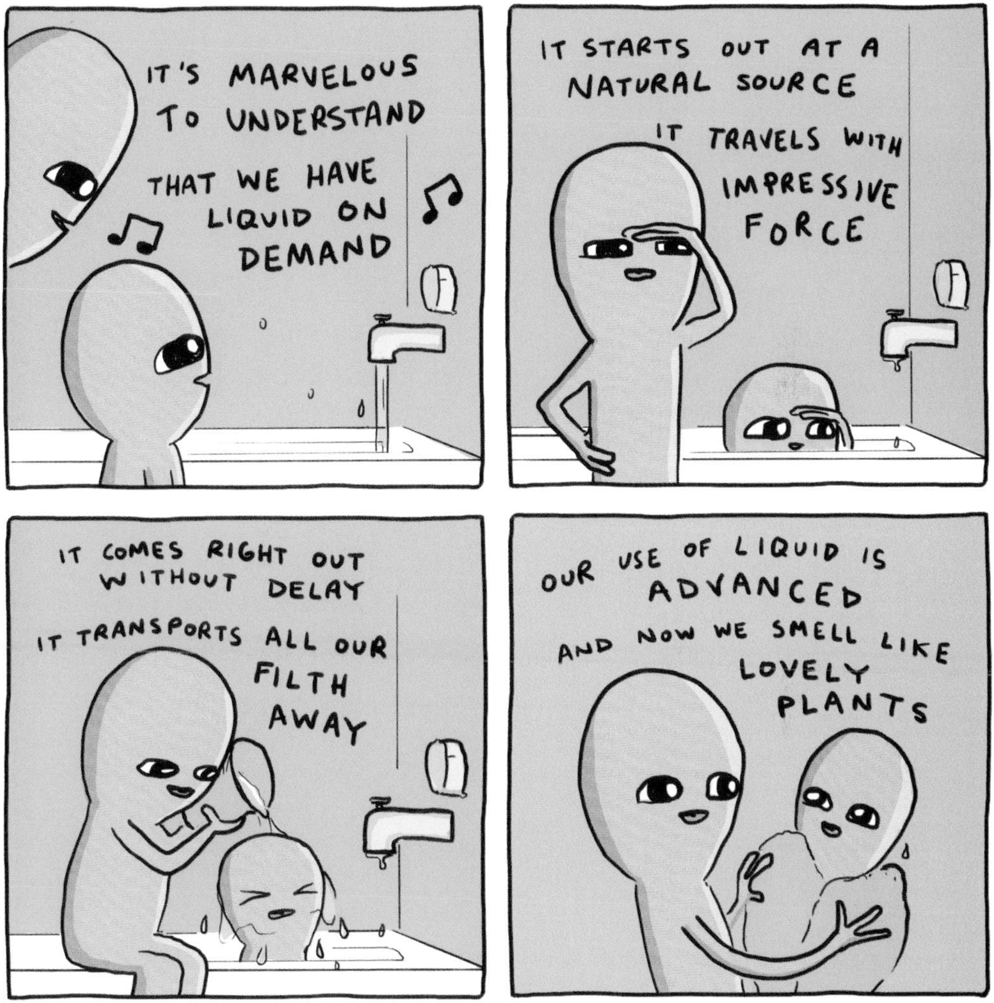
IT'S MARVELOUS TO UNDERSTAND
THAT WE HAVE LIQUID ON DEMAND
IT STARTS OUT AT A NATURAL SOURCE
IT TRAVELS WITH IMPRESSIVE FORCE
IT COMES RIGHT OUT WITHOUT DELAY
IT TRANSPORTS ALL OUR FILTH AWAY
OUR USE OF LIQUID IS ADVANCED
AND NOW WE SMELL LIKE LOVELY PLANTS

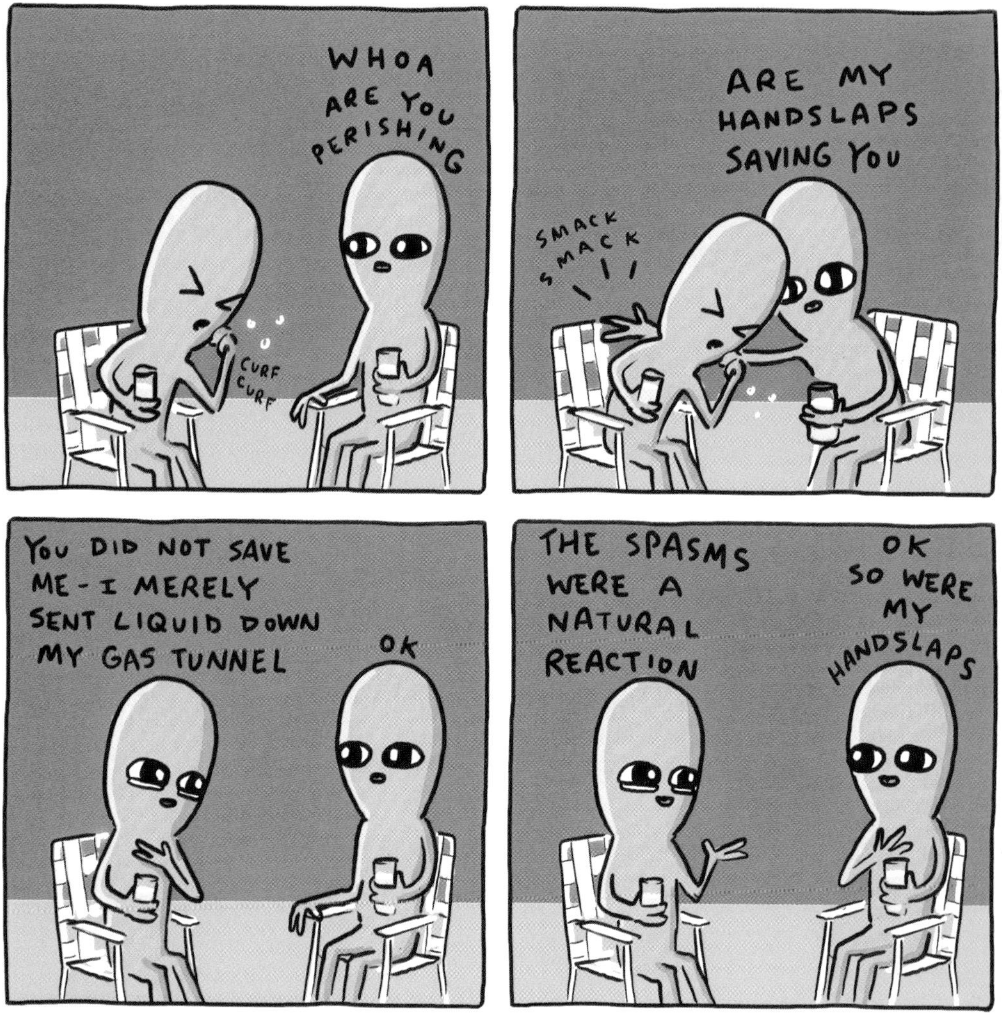
WHOA
ARE YOU PERISHING
CURF CURF
ARE MY HANDSLAPS SAVING YOU
SMACK SMACK
YOU DID NOT SAVE ME - I MERELY SENT LIQUID DOWN MY GAS TUNNEL
OK
THE SPASMS WERE A NATURAL REACTION
OK SO WERE MY HANDSLAPS

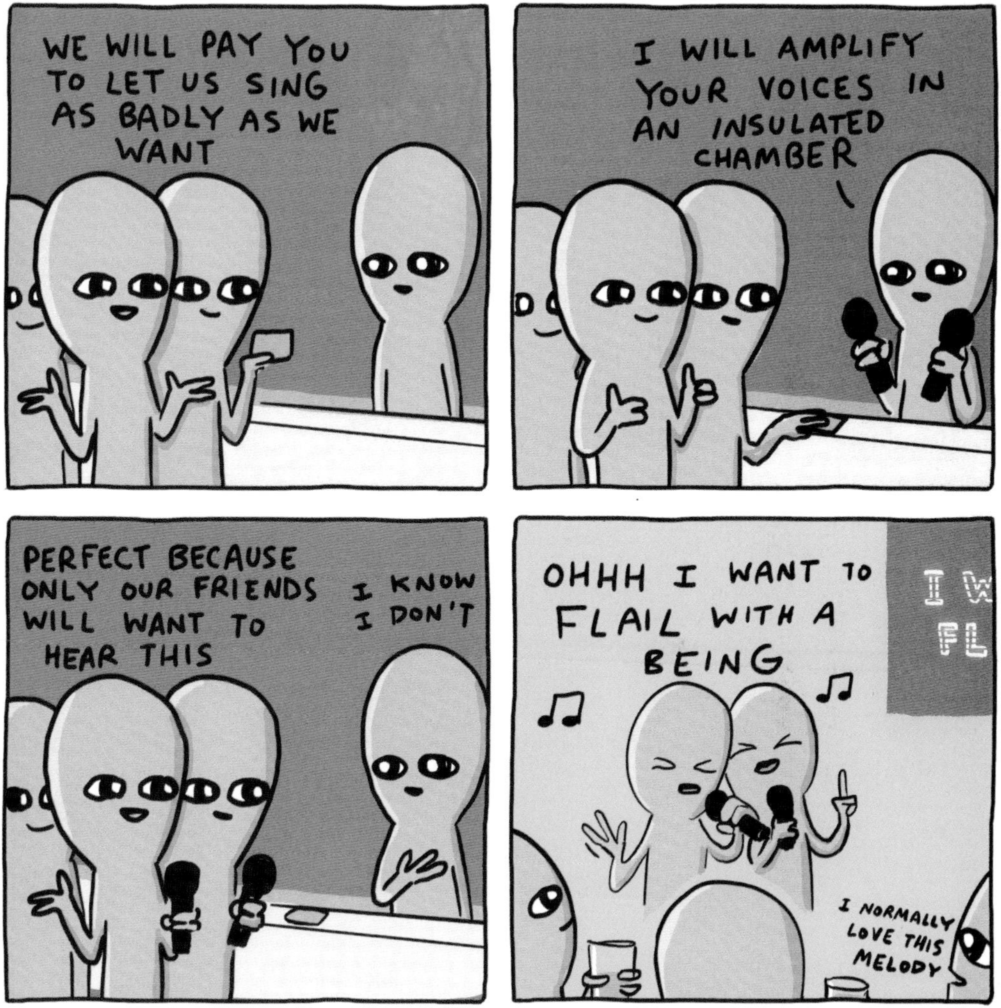
WE WILL PAY YOU TO LET US SING AS BADLY AS WE WANT
I WILL AMPLIFY YOUR VOICES IN AN INSULATED CHAMBER
PERFECT BECAUSE ONLY OUR FRIENDS WILL WANT TO HEAR THIS
I KNOW I DON'T
OHHH I WANT TO FLAIL WITH A BEING
I NORMALLY LOVE THIS MELODY

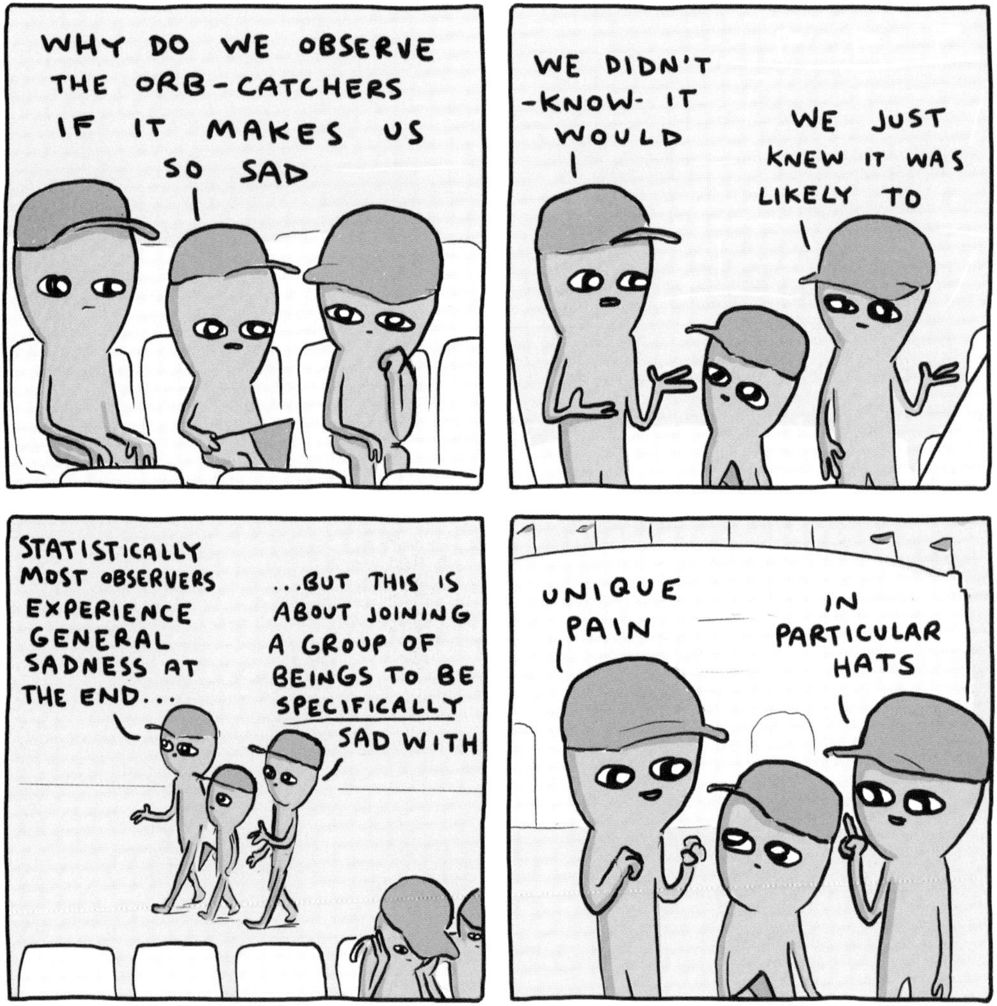
WHY DO WE OBSERVE THE ORB-CATCHERS IF IT MAKES US SO SAD
WE DIDN'T -KNOW- IT WOULD
WE JUST KNEW IT WAS LIKELY TO
STATISTICALLY MOST OBSERVERS EXPERIENCE GENERAL SADNESS AT THE END...
...BUT THIS IS ABOUT JOINING A GROUP OF BEINGS TO BE SPECIFICALLY SAD WITH
UNIQUE PAIN
IN PARTICULAR HATS

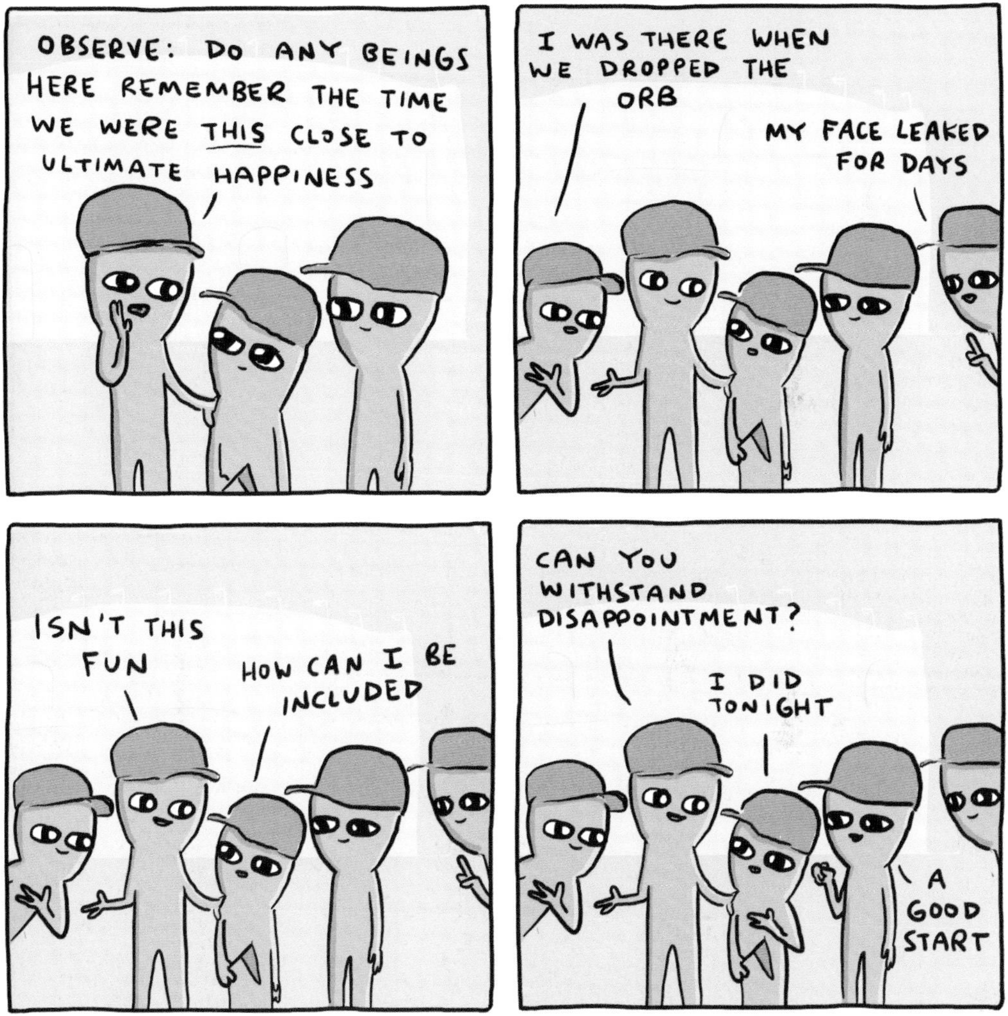
OBSERVE: DO ANY BEINGS HERE REMEMBER THE TIME WE WERE THIS CLOSE TO ULTIMATE HAPPINESS
I WAS THERE WHEN WE DROPPED THE ORB
MY FACE LEAKED FOR DAYS
ISN'T THIS FUN
HOW CAN I BE INCLUDED
CAN YOU WITHSTAND DISAPPOINTMENT?
I DID TONIGHT
A GOOD START

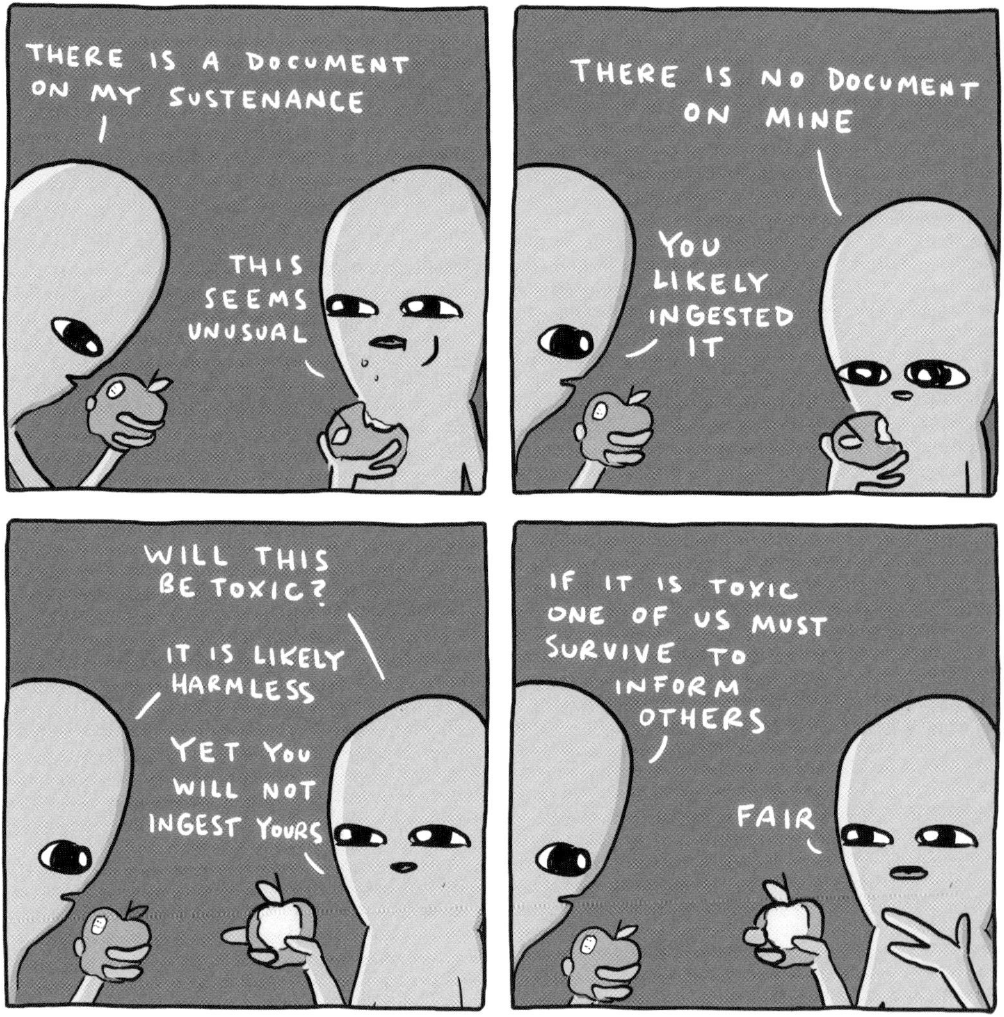
THERE IS A DOCUMENT ON MY SUSTENANCE
THIS SEEMS UNUSUAL
THERE IS NO DOCUMENT ON MINE
YOU LIKELY INGESTED IT
WILL THIS BE TOXIC?
IT IS LIKELY HARMLESS
YET YOU WILL NOT INGEST YOURS
IF IT IS TOXIC ONE OF US MUST SURVIVE TO INFORM OTHERS
FAIR

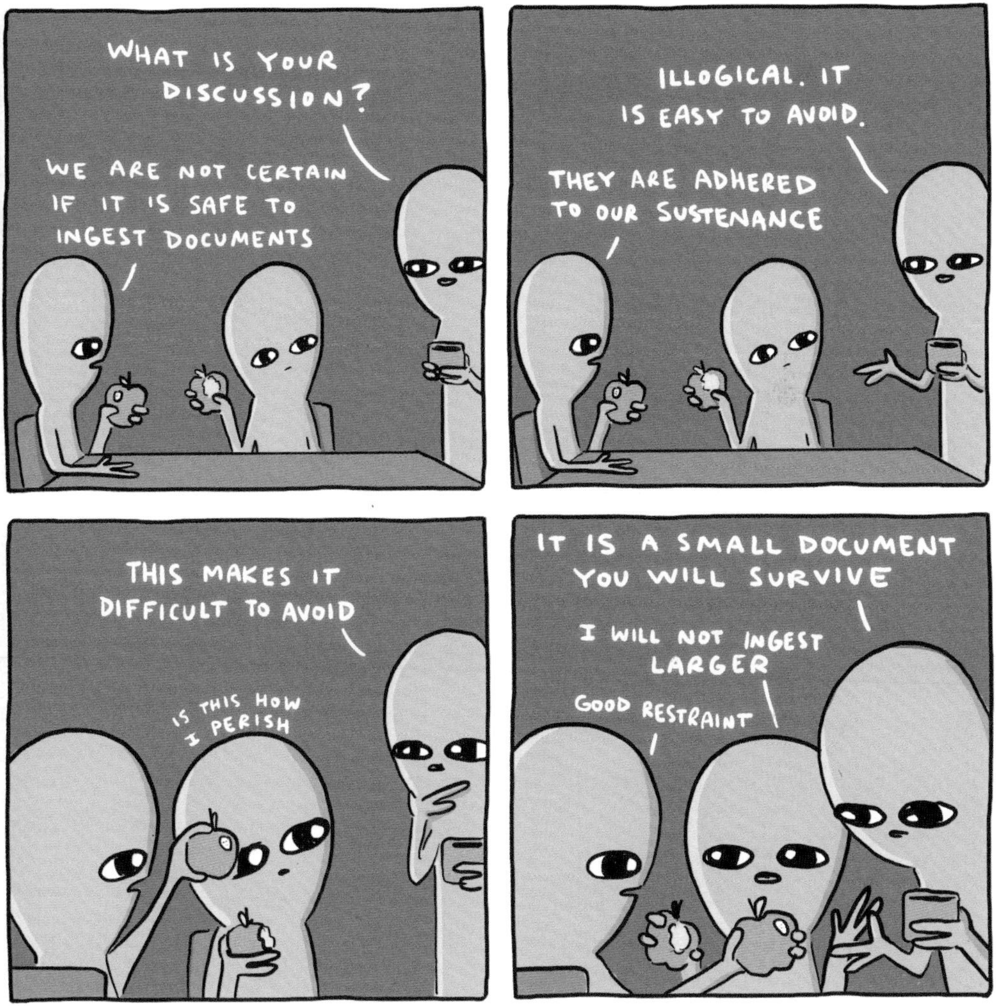
WHAT IS YOUR DISCUSSION?
WE ARE NOT CERTAIN IF IT IS SAFE TO INGEST DOCUMENTS
ILLOGICAL. IT IS EASY TO AVOID.
THEY ARE ADHERED TO OUR SUSTENANCE
THIS MAKES IT DIFFICULT TO AVOID
IS THIS HOW I PERISH
IT IS A SMALL DOCUMENT YOU WILL SURVIVE
I WILL NOT INGEST LARGER
GOOD RESTRAINT

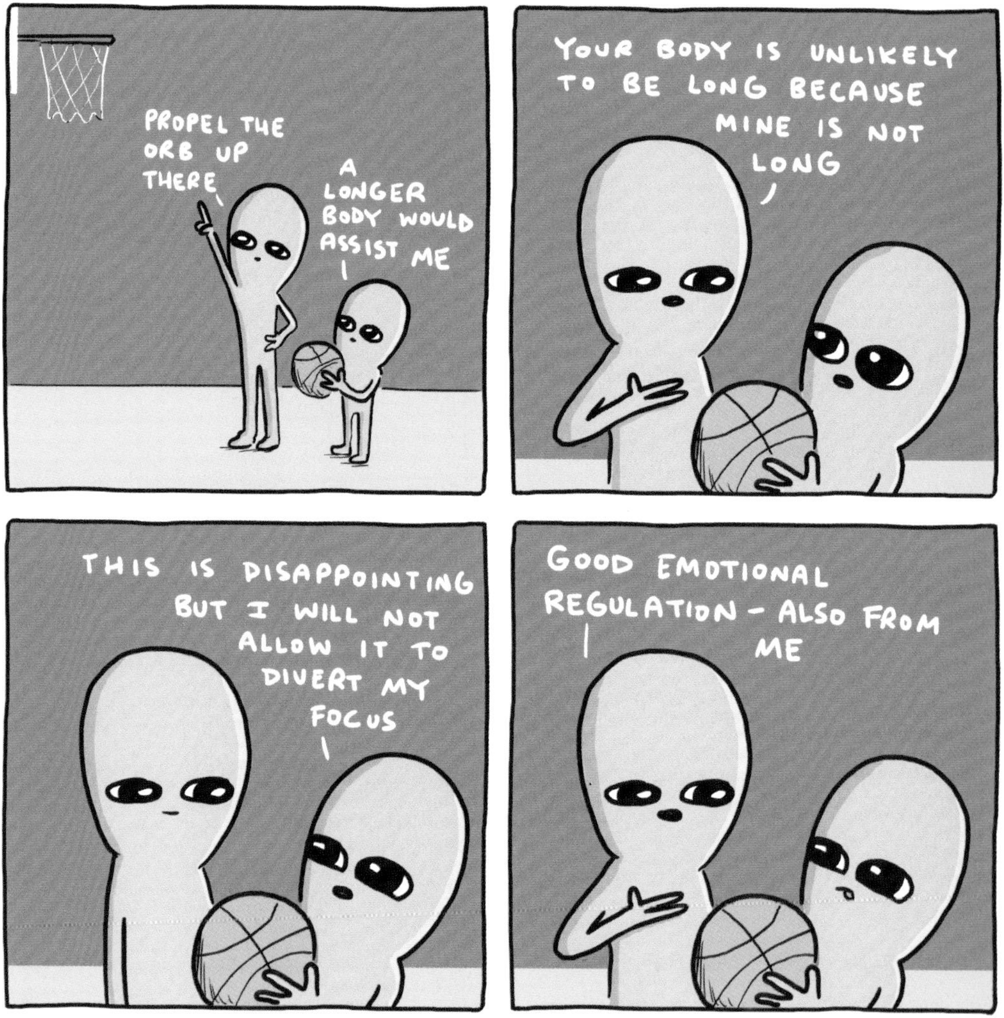
PROPEL THE ORB UP THERE
A LONGER BODY WOULD ASSIST ME
YOUR BODY IS UNLIKELY TO BE LONG BECAUSE MINE IS NOT LONG
THIS IS DISAPPOINTING BUT I WILL NOT ALLOW IT TO DIVERT MY FOCUS
GOOD EMOTIONAL REGULATION - ALSO FROM ME

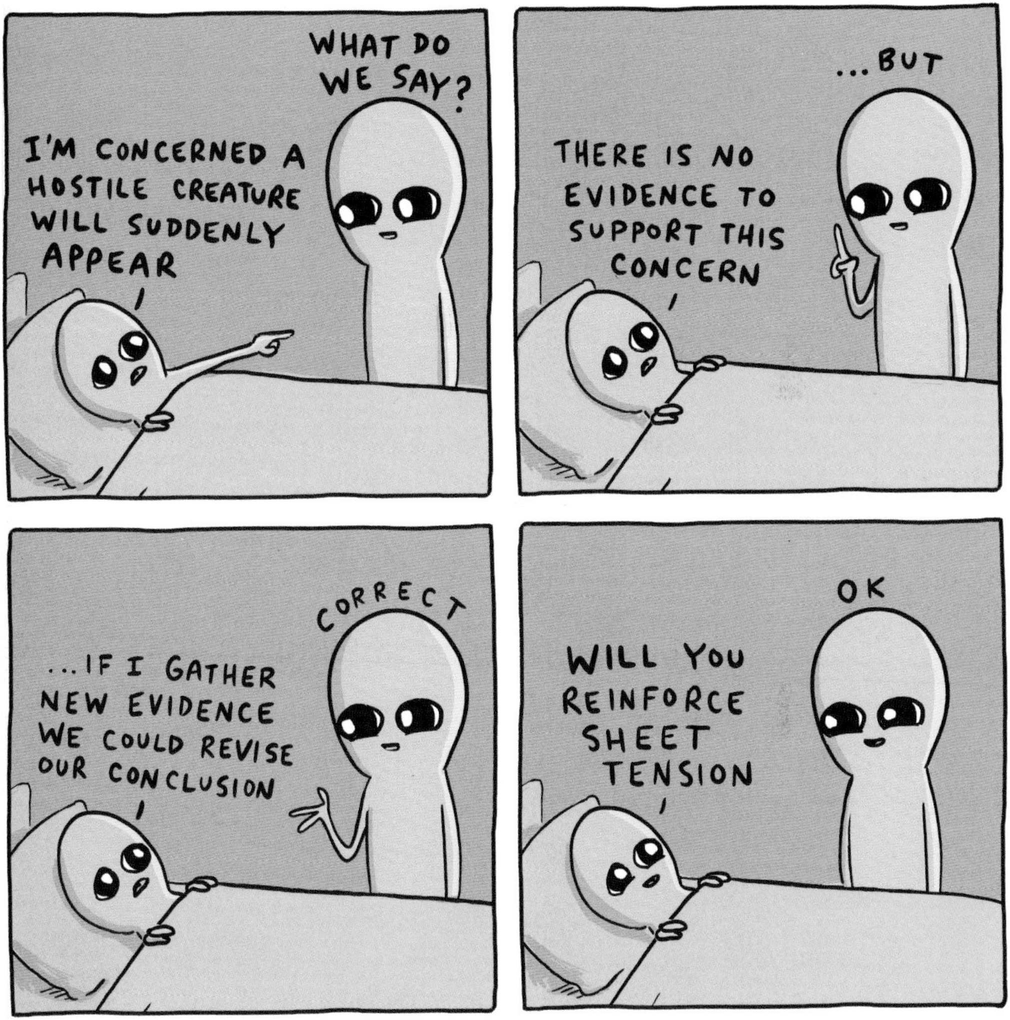
I'M CONCERNED A HOSTILE CREATURE WILL SUDDENLY APPEAR
WHAT DO WE SAY?
THERE IS NO EVIDENCE TO SUPPORT THIS CONCERN
...BUT
...IF I GATHER NEW EVIDENCE WE COULD REVISE OUR CONCLUSION
CORRECT
WILL YOU REINFORCE SHEET TENSION
OK

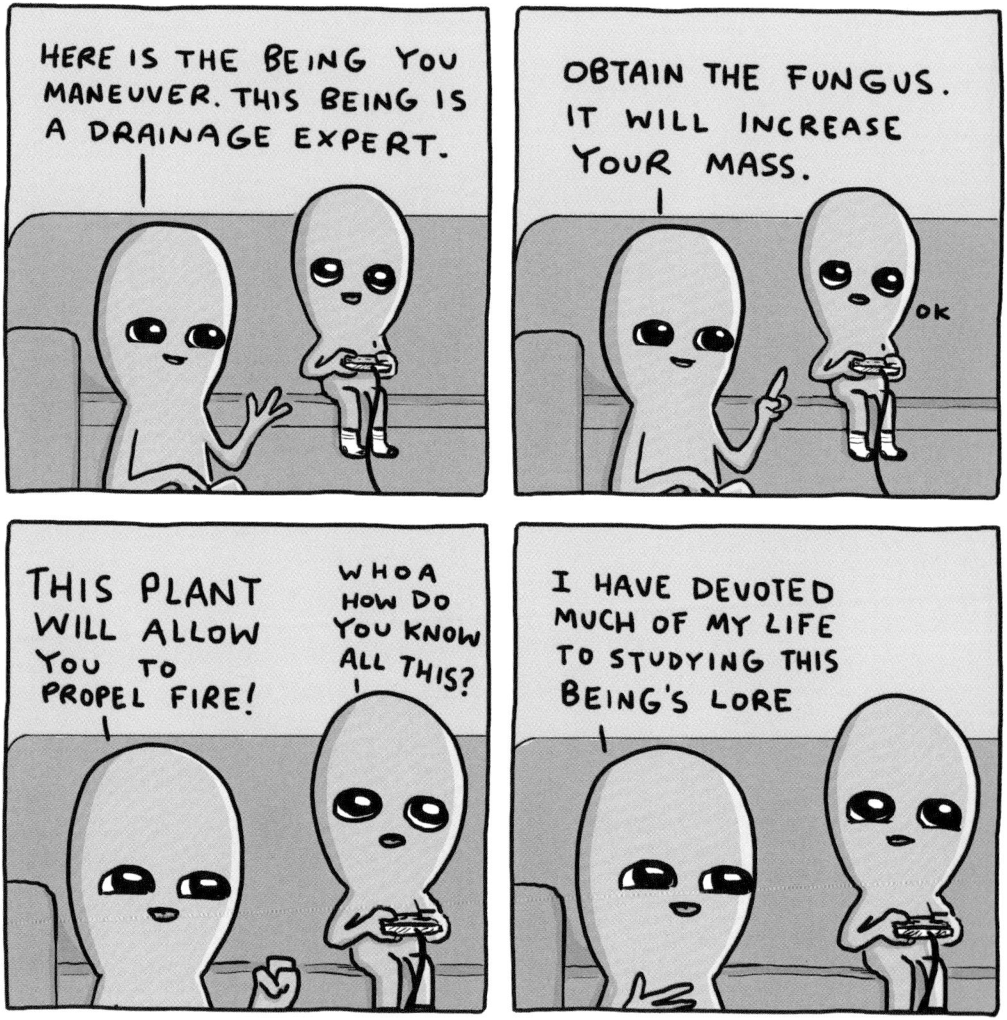
HERE IS THE BEING YOU MANEUVER. THIS BEING IS A DRAINAGE EXPERT.
OBTAIN THE FUNGUS. IT WILL INCREASE YOUR MASS.
OK
THIS PLANT WILL ALLOW YOU TO PROPEL FIRE!
WHOA HOW DO YOU KNOW ALL THIS?
I HAVE DEVOTED MUCH OF MY LIFE TO STUDYING THIS BEING'S LORE

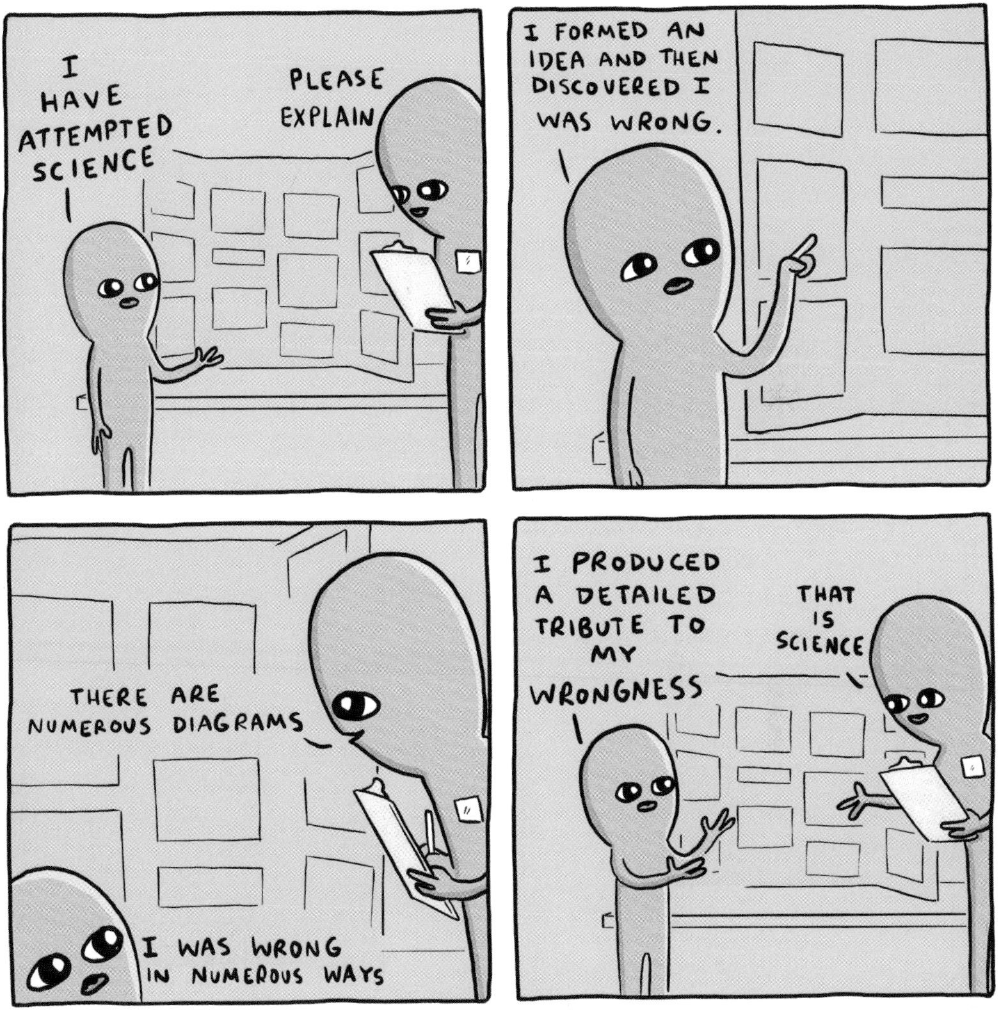
I HAVE ATTEMPTED SCIENCE
PLEASE EXPLAIN
I FORMED AN IDEA AND THEN DISCOVERED I WAS WRONG.
THERE ARE NUMEROUS DIAGRAMS
I WAS WRONG IN NUMEROUS WAYS
I PRODUCED A DETAILED TRIBUTE TO MY WRONGNESS
THAT IS SCIENCE

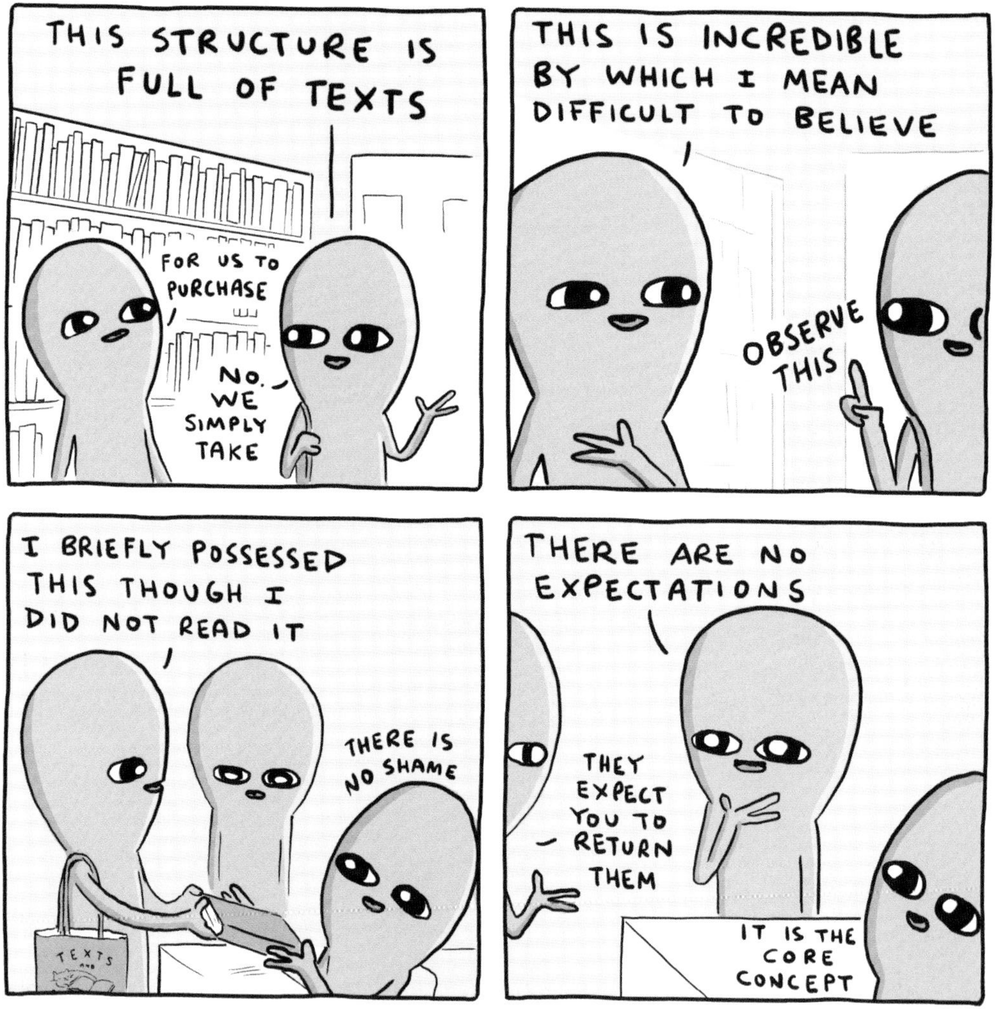
THIS STRUCTURE IS FULL OF TEXTS
FOR US TO PURCHASE
NO. WE SIMPLY TAKE
THIS IS INCREDIBLE BY WHICH I MEAN DIFFICULT TO BELIEVE
OBSERVE THIS
I BRIEFLY POSSESSED THIS THOUGH I DID NOT READ IT
THERE IS NO SHAME
TEXTS
THERE ARE NO EXPECTATIONS
THEY EXPECT YOU TO RETURN THEM
IT IS THE CORE CONCEPT

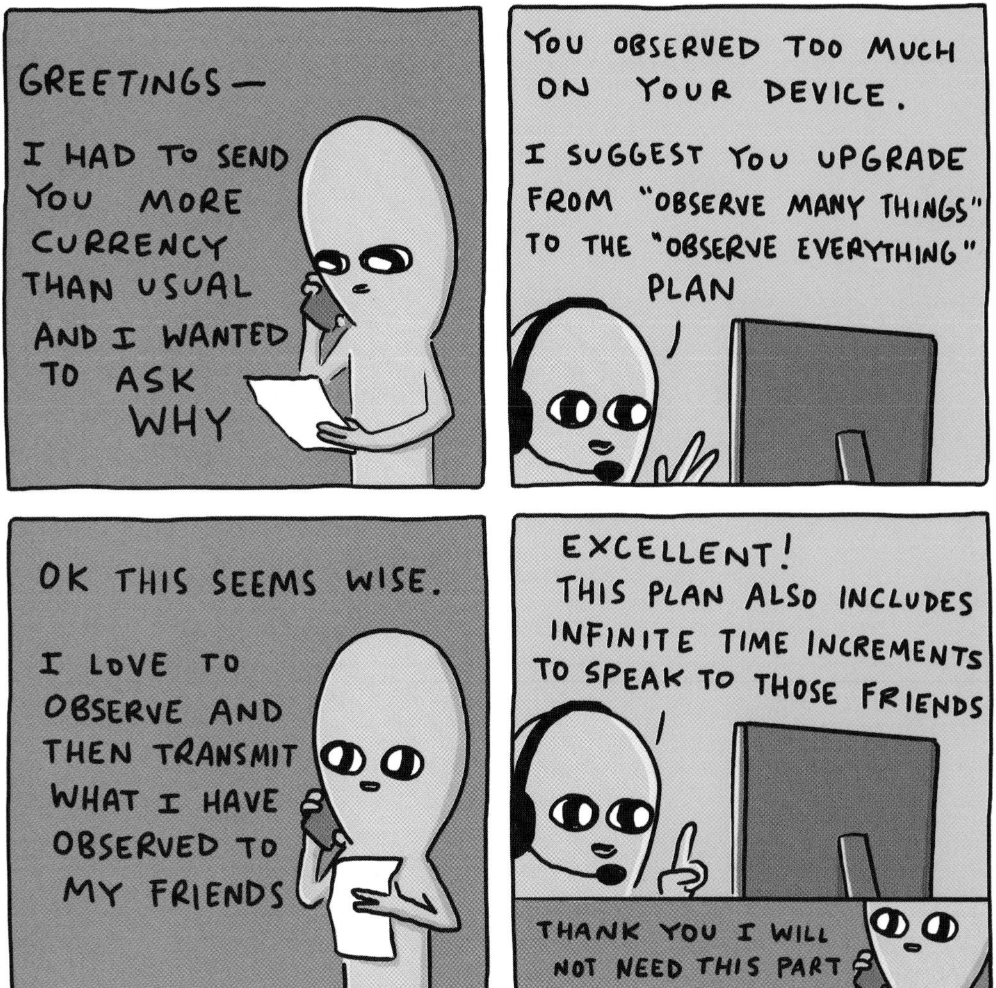
GREETINGS—
I HAD TO SEND YOU MORE CURRENCY THAN USUAL
AND I WANTED TO ASK WHY
YOU OBSERVED TOO MUCH ON YOUR DEVICE.
I SUGGEST YOU UPGRADE FROM "OBSERVE MANY THINGS" TO THE "OBSERVE EVERYTHING" PLAN
OK THIS SEEMS WISE.
I LOVE TO OBSERVE AND THEN TRANSMIT WHAT I HAVE OBSERVED TO MY FRIENDS
EXCELLENT!
THIS PLAN ALSO INCLUDES INFINITE TIME INCREMENTS TO SPEAK TO THOSE FRIENDS
THANK YOU I WILL NOT NEED THIS PART

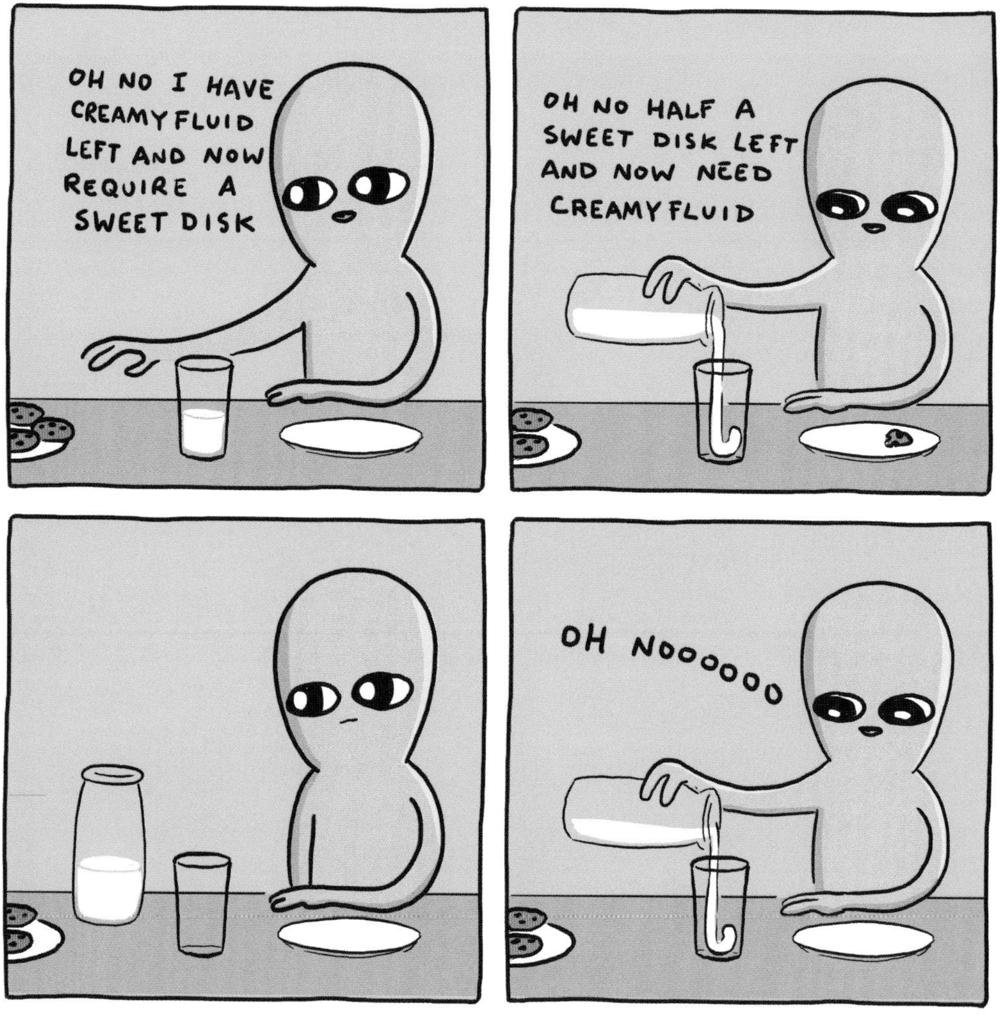
OH NO I HAVE CREAMY FLUID LEFT AND NOW REQUIRE A SWEET DISK
OH NO HALF A SWEET DISK LEFT AND NOW NEED CREAMY FLUID
OH NOOOOOOO

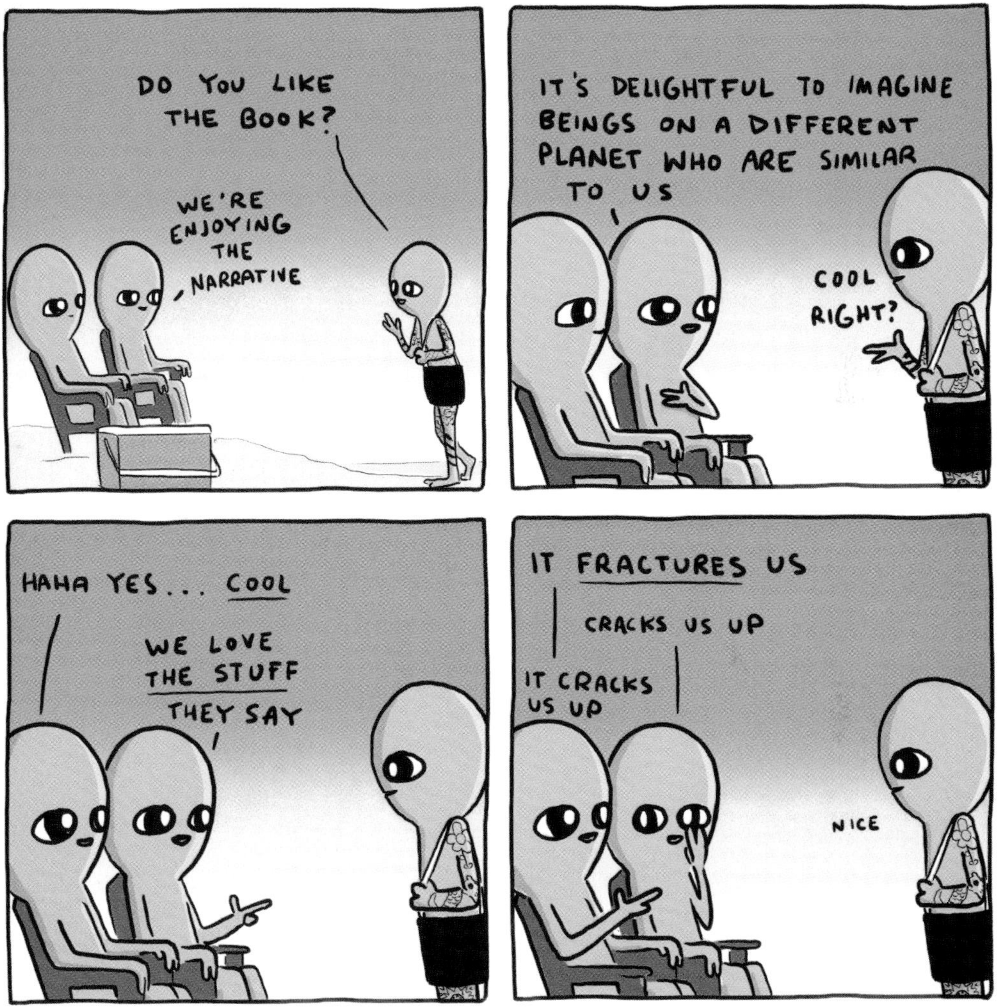
DO YOU LIKE THE BOOK?
WE'RE ENJOYING THE NARRATIVE
IT'S DELIGHTFUL TO IMAGINE BEINGS ON A DIFFERENT PLANET WHO ARE SIMILAR TO US
COOL RIGHT?
HAHA YES... COOL
WE LOVE THE STUFF THEY SAY
IT FRACTURES US
CRACKS US UP
IT CRACKS US UP
NICE

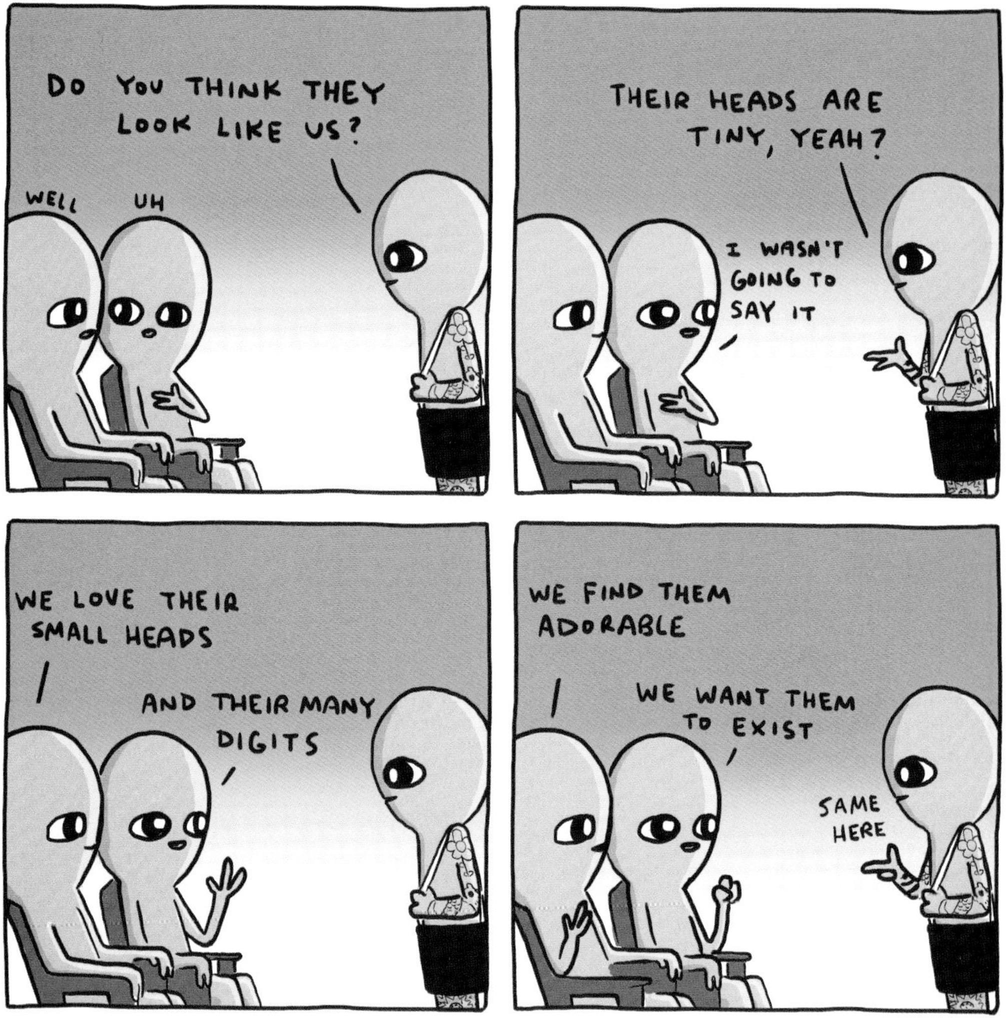
DO YOU THINK THEY LOOK LIKE US?
WELL
UH
THEIR HEADS ARE TINY, YEAH?
I WASN'T GOING TO SAY IT
WE LOVE THEIR SMALL HEADS
AND THEIR MANY DIGITS
WE FIND THEM ADORABLE
WE WANT THEM TO EXIST
SAME HERE

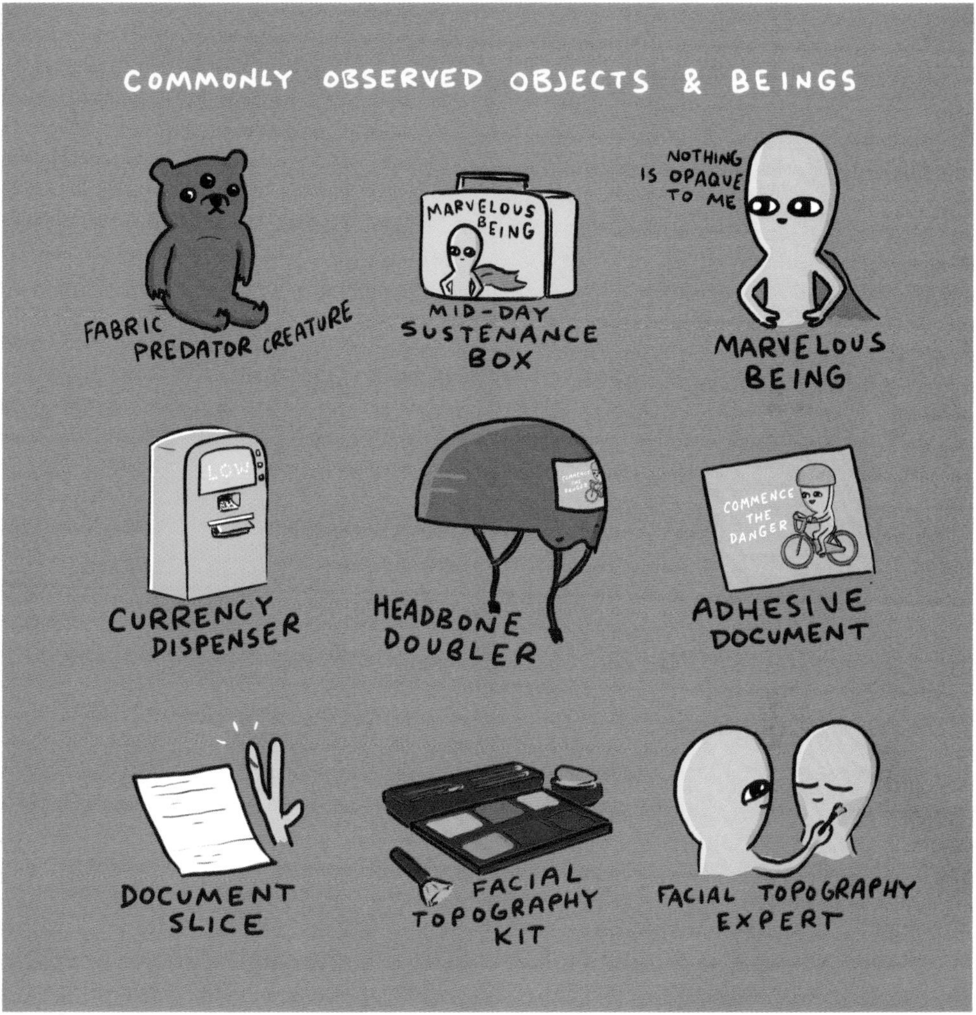
COMMONLY OBSERVED OBJECTS & BEINGS
FABRIC PREDATOR CREATURE
MARVELOUS BEING
MID-DAY SUSTENANCE BOX
NOTHING IS OPAQUE TO ME
MARVELOUS BEING
LOW
CURRENCY DISPENSER
HEADBONE DOUBLER
COMMENCE THE DANGER
ADHESIVE DOCUMENT
DOCUMENT SLICE
FACIAL TOPOGRAPHY KIT
FACIAL TOPOGRAPHY EXPERT

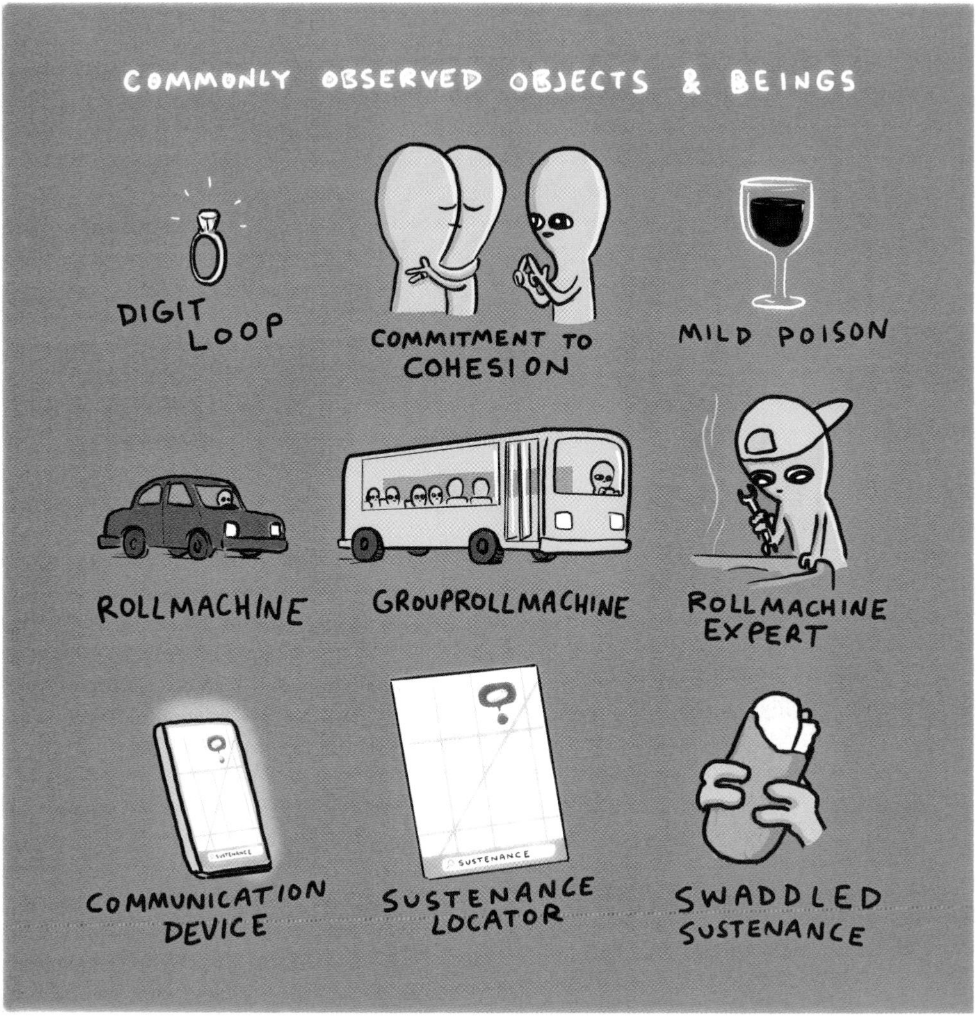
COMMONLY OBSERVED OBJECTS & BEINGS
DIGIT LOOP
COMMITMENT TO COHESION
MILD POISON
ROLLMACHINE
GROUPROLLMACHINE
ROLLMACHINE EXPERT
SUSTENANCE
COMMUNICATION DEVICE
SUSTENANCE
SUSTENANCE LOCATOR
SWADDLED SUSTENANCE

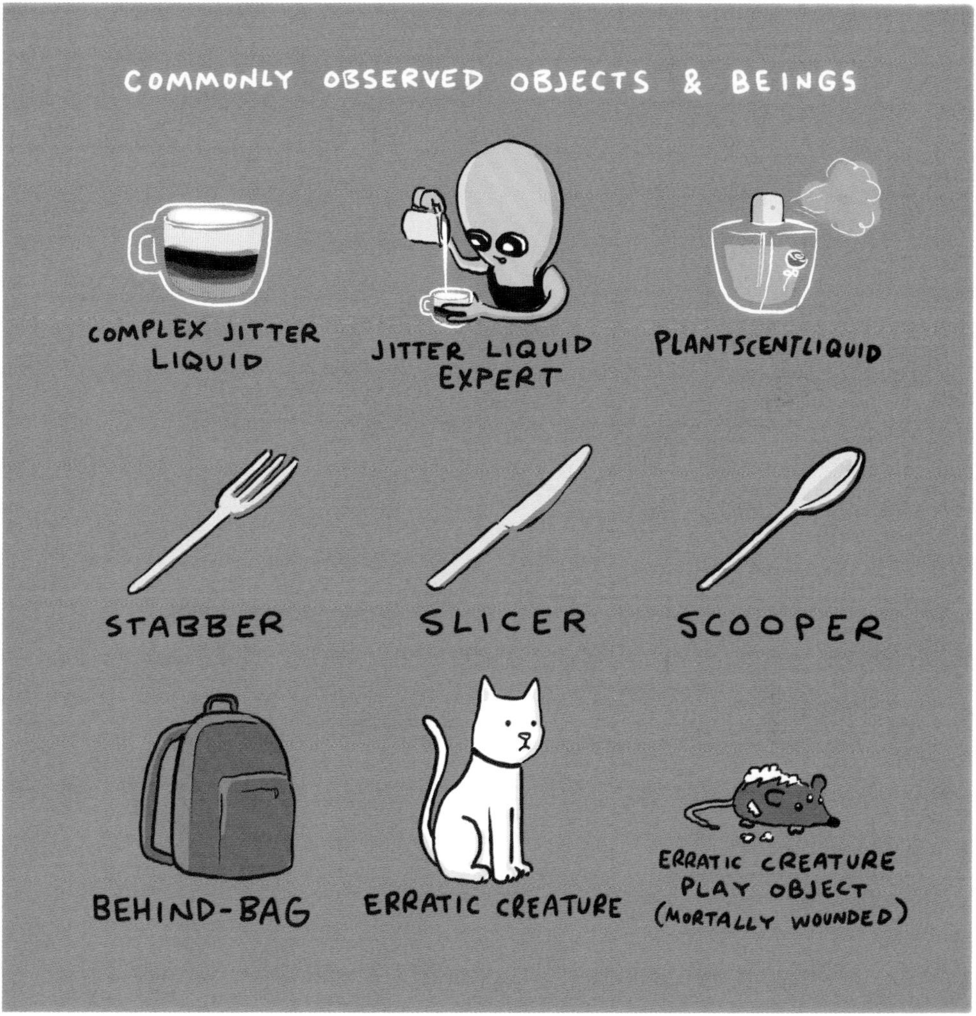
COMMONLY OBSERVED OBJECTS & BEINGS
COMPLEX JITTER LIQUID
JITTER LIQUID EXPERT
PLANTSCENTLIQUID
STABBER
SLICER
SCOOPER
BEHIND-BAG
ERRATIC CREATURE
ERRATIC CREATURE PLAY OBJECT (MORTALLY WOUNDED)

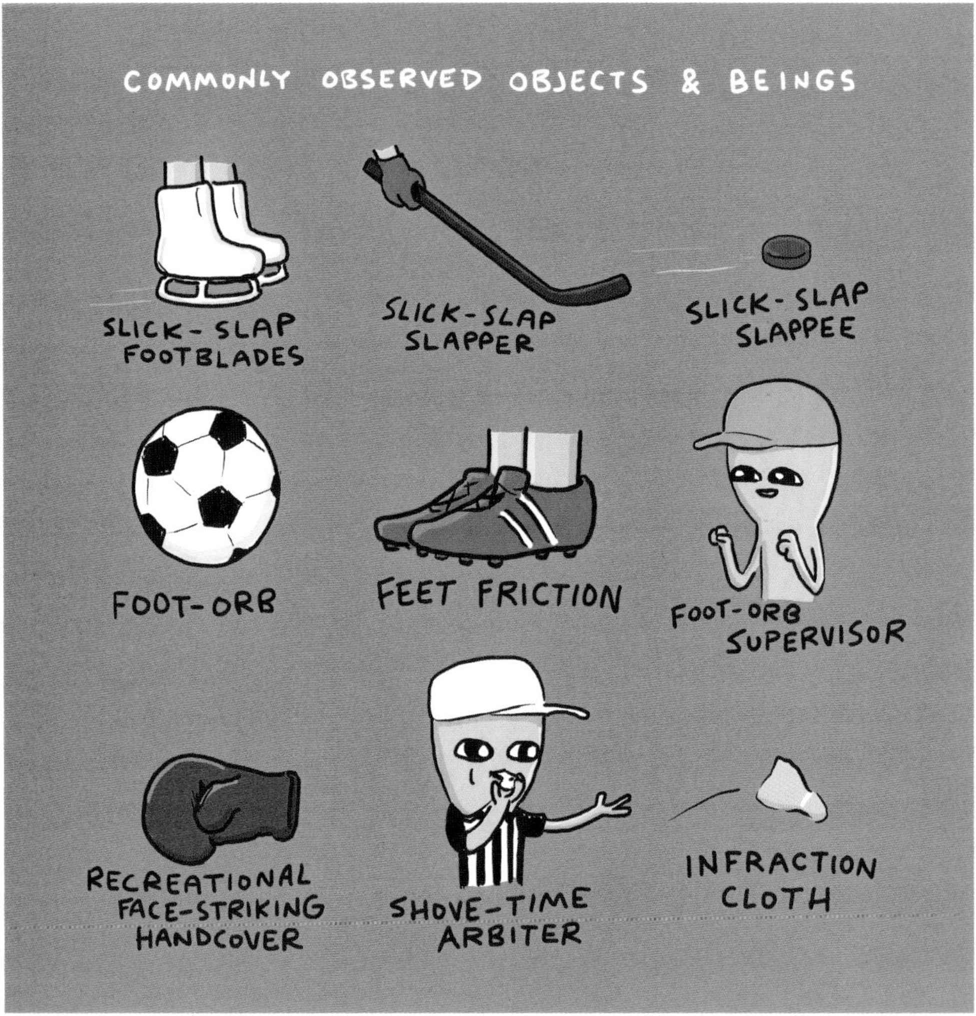
COMMONLY OBSERVED OBJECTS & BEINGS
SLICK-SLAP FOOTBLADES
SLICK-SLAP SLAPPER
SLICK-SLAP SLAPPEE
FOOT-ORB
FEET FRICTION
FOOT-ORB SUPERVISOR
RECREATIONAL FACE-STRIKING HANDCOVER
SHOVE-TIME ARBITER
INFRACTION CLOTH

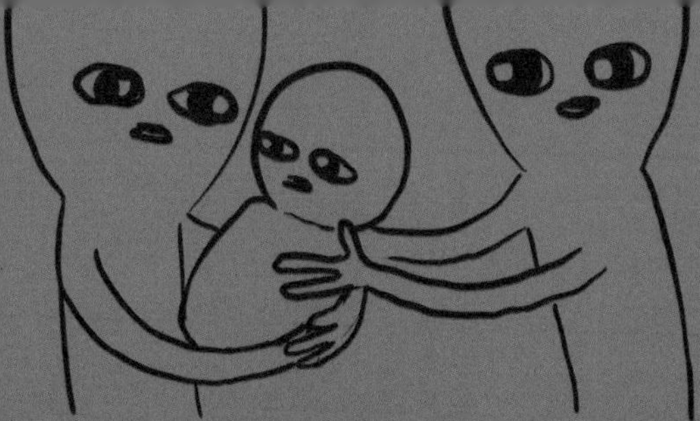

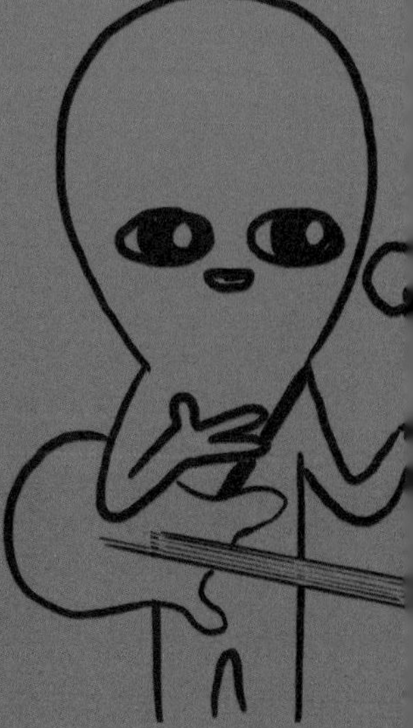

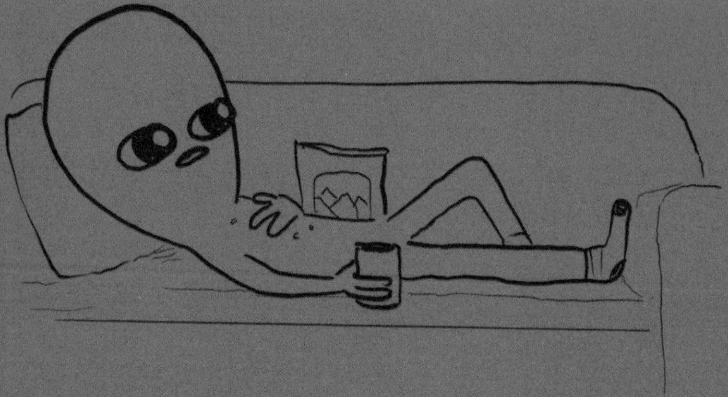

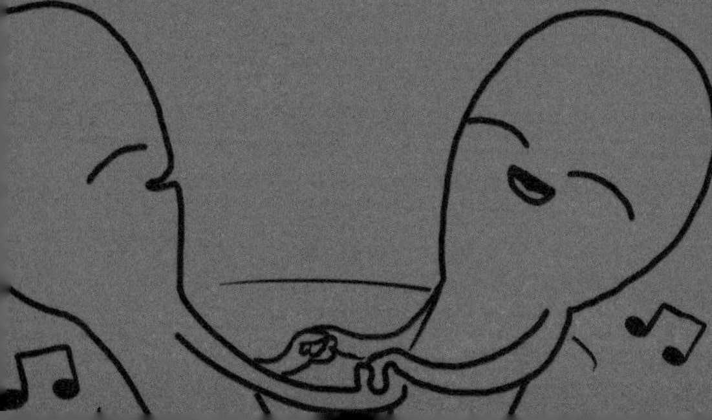

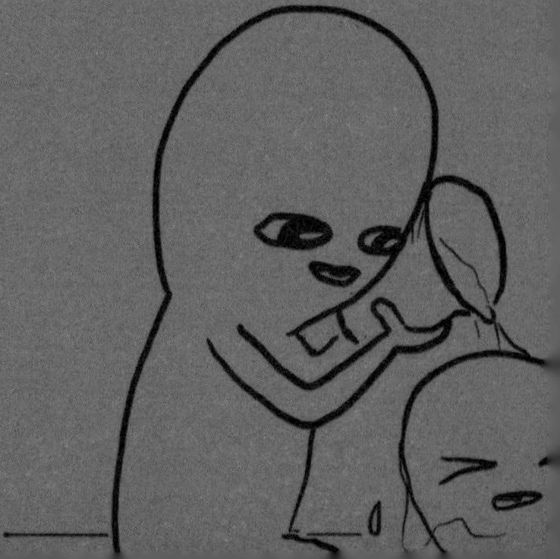

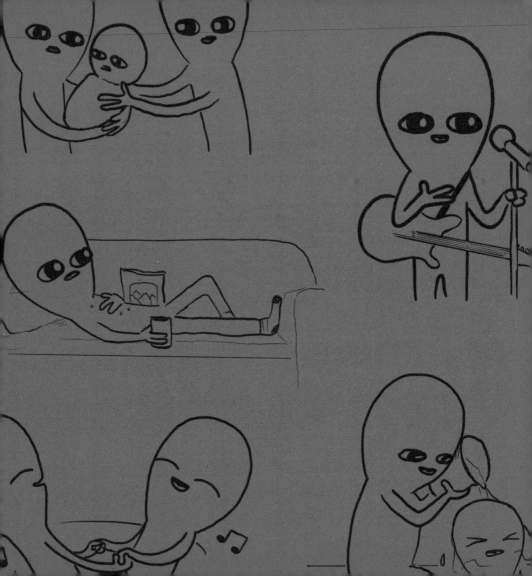